Chapman 74–75: Autu

THE WOMEN'S FORUM: Wom

CW00664607

Cover: The Husking by Joanne E Grant.
Illustrations: Tash MacLeod, Victorine Foot

ISBN 0 906772 51 6   ISSN 0308-2695   © *Chapman* 1993

CHAPMAN

4 Broughton Place, Edinburgh EH1 3RX, Scotland
Tel 031–557 2207 Fax 031–556 9565
Editor: Joy Hendry   **Associate Editor: Robert Calder**
Assistant Editor: Peter Cudmore   Advertising Manager: Mary Gordon
Volunteers:
Gillian Ferguson, Angela Finlayson, John Law, Stephanie Lewis, Kathy Wise

Submissions:

Chapman welcomes submissions of poetry,
fiction and critical articles provided they are
accompanied by a stamped addressed envelope
or International Reply coupons

Subscriptions:

	Personal		Institutional	
	1 year	2 years	1 year	2 years
UK	£12	£23	£15	£28
Overseas	£15/$28	£28/$54	£19/$36	£36/$65

Subsidised by the Scottish **A**rts Council

THE CITY OF EDINBURGH DISTRICT COUNCIL
EDINBURGH
IMPROVING SERVICES – CREATING JOBS

Printed by Mayfair Printers, Print House, William Street, Sunderland, Tyne & Wear

FOXED.

"MY SISTER-IN-LAW is something of a stickler," writes Mr. Holmes of Ealing. "And when I offered the assembled guests an after-dinner glass of The Macallan Malt Whisky the other night, she alone demurred, saying she only drank brandy.

Wishing to check a long-cherished hypothesis, I told her I had a fine old cognac next door.

I went to the kitchen, poured her a balloon of The Macallan, and returned.

She swirled it round, nosed it, sipped, and congratulated me upon a cognac of extraordinary smoothness and maturity.

I did not tell her the truth. You do not know my sister-in-law. But I think I may say that my hypothesis was well and truly proven."

THE MACALLAN.
THE MALT.

Editorial

Woven by Women appeared in summer 1980. It was something of a milestone, a landmark, a watershed, as the first Scottish publication to focus on women's cultural achievement across the artistic spectrum in Scotland. In those days you still had to argue that in almost every field not only *could* women contribute good work, but that they *already had*.

In the Editorial I quoted a male poet, now dead, who, when he heard that *Chapman* was devoting a double number to Scottish women declared loudly: "Scottish women poets! Do you mean there *are* any?" Now he was half trying to wind me up, but at bottom was wholly serious. Those were the dying days of domination by man of the cultural scene in Scotland. Yes, the big boys then were all boys, but the women, by 1980, were very much there and waiting in the wings. *Woven by Women* was the first tooting of the whistle to say: "Come in lads, your time is up."

The policy there was to make an across-the-boards statement, looking at many different areas of cultural activity in an attempt to give a rounded picture. And so, with gay abandon, we were able to give relatively full summaries of women's activities in poetry, the novel, the visual arts, music, politics, and draw attention to many women artists of the past by means of articles (Alasdair Gray wrote about the dramatist Joan Ure; John Purser on women composers, George N Scott on Willa Muir – it seemed extremely appropriate that these men, two of whom would become very prominent in the period that followed, should have paid such fulsome tributes to female colleagues. Ronald Stevenson immediately supplied me with his setting of Helen B Cruickshank's 'Shy Geordie'.) Marion Lochhead's article, 'Feminine Quartet' and Gillian Shepherd's 'Scottish Women Novelists' were the first to provide more extensive critical coverage of women's writing. That this seems so patently preposterous now, only 13 years later, is an indicator of how much has changed since. My thesis always was, and Catherine Kerrigan's anthology has proved, that the women were always there, flourishing in anonymity; now the process of explicating their work is well under way

I have written elsewhere on the theme of 'The Double Knot in the Peeny', essentially a metaphor for the inhibitions for women in a country with a lack of political power on the one hand combined with compensating male-chauvinist drive for dominance. That dominance is changing, and has to change into equal partnership.

The main litmus of change can be seen in the fact that to take that same approach now would seem ridiculous, naïve, probably even patronising and derisory. To do critical justice to each area would now require a feature to itself. To cover Scottish women poets, novelists, dramatists, to speak briefly only of literature, would require a critical volume each.

My solution to this dilemma, if dilemma it is, is to use this double number, in which it just so happens we reach our 75th issue, to launch the *Chapman Woman's Forum*. This issue is devoted to Women in Scottish Literature, and will be followed by an issue on Women in the Arts in

Scotland, but neither *can* attempt comprehensive coverage. The Forum will continue, as happened spontaneously with our Scottish Theatre Issue (43–44) in 1986, with more items to come in subsequent issues. Here is the start of the discussion. We offer a platform for description and discussion of women's work in the excitingly varied field which is Scottish culture today. We hope as many people as possible (women *and* men) will contribute, hence the fact that we have advertised widely over the last year to attract submissions from people unknown to us. That invitation, to contribute poetry, fiction, articles or features about any relevant matter is still very much open. Just write to The Ed... (with SAE).

To Elspeth King I would like to acknowledge use of information originating from her pamphlet *The Scottish Women's Suffrage Movement* (1978), original research which clearly provided information used in Margaret Bain (now Ewing)'s article 'Scottish Women in Politics' in *Woven by Women* and should therefore have been cited there as source material.

Woven by Women contained new work by a large number of women: Of those number five now dead: Valda Trevlyn, Janet Caird, Wendy Wood, Alice V Stuart and Marion Lochhead. Many others since have grown in reputation: Sue Glover's *Bondagers* is packing them in now at the New Traverse, Jessie Kesson and Liz Lochhead now enjoy international reputations, Tessa Ransford has founded the Scottish Poetry Library, and others, like Valerie Gillies, Marcella Evaristi, Ellie McDonald and others have more than prospered. Naomi Mitchison herself, whose wonderful long poem 'The Talking Oats' was the first creative item in *Woven by Women,* is here again with a fine, ambiguous story 'The Box'.

This issue presents a range of work from women of all ages. We do look back at work by our grandmother pioneers, such as Catherine Carswell, Nan Shepherd, but also look to the young, and forward into the future, especially through Alison Smith's article 'Four Success Stories' which begins the critical foray into the work of an already celebrated new generation: A L Kennedy, Jackie Kay, Janice Galloway and Kathleen Jamie. Others than these four, Jane Harris, Magi Gibson, Elizabeth Burns, Janet Paisley to name a few, also deserve such attention.

So this double issue takes us from literary grandmothers to the story of Stramullion, Scotland's first feminist cooperative publishing house, from Willa Muir to Margaret Fulton Cook, a formidable writer of the new generation, from Sheena Blackhall to Anne Frater, writing in Scots and Gaelic, showing women still writing strongly in our indigenous languages.

Whatever the subject, the medium, whatever the language, the confident enterprise and ambition evident in the writing represented here shows Scottish writers functioning on an international stage, or poised to do so if not already so engaged. After *Woven by Women* came a deluge of publishing by women and of women; after the Woman's Forum, I hope, will come an unstoppable drive towards genuine cultural and social parity, so that Scottish women's voices ring out as strongly and vibrantly as those of our male colleagues in the past. *Joy Hendry*

What happened to the tales of our grandmothers?

Aileen M Riddell

In a letter of 1845, Elizabeth Barrett Browning bemoaned the absence of poetic 'grandmothers' for women like herself, writing in the nineteenth century (*Letters*, 1897, i.229). Modern scholarship has established that there was no real absence of female forebears. Anthologies such as *Women Poets in English* (ed. Ann Stanford, 1972), *Salt and Bitter and Good* (ed. Cora Kaplan, 1975), *British Women Writers* (eds. Janet Todd and Dale Spender, 1989), and *Eighteenth-Century Women Poets* (ed. Roger Lonsdale; 1989), give the lie to that notion. Similarly, in the field of the novel, feminist literary history books such as Ellen Moers' *Literary Women* (1978), Jane Spencer's *The Rise of the Woman Novelist* (1986), and Janet Todd's *The Sign of Angellica* (1989), point towards a rich tapestry of women's writing through history, which, to stretch the metaphor a little, has been consistently and painstakingly stitched up, primarily by men.

The contemporary English woman writer need not, like Barrett Browning, founder for want of literary ancestors – thanks to the recent wave of feminist scholarship, many lost writers have already repossessed their spaces on library shelves; publishers such as Virago, The Women's Press and Pandora promise more to come. But what of the Scottish woman writer? While recent collections of poetry – Catherine Kerrigan's fine *Anthology of Scottish Women Poets* (1991) and Tom Leonard's *Radical Renfrew* (1990) – have helped to give women a sense of a poetic heritage, their literary 'grandmothers' in the novel are still very much in the dark. A survey of those literary histories which include material on the early nineteenth century (when there was an escalation in the number of women novelists in Scotland) proves illuminating, though more of the genre of Scottish literary history than of novels by Scottish women.

One of the fundamental premises of Scottish literary criticism is that there were no women novelists of note prior to Susan Ferrier. Even Ferrier's importance in terms of the history of Scottish literature is deemed to be fairly negligible by some of these critics. A good example of the attitude to women writers prevalent in the history books is to be found in David Craig (1961), when he posits the question, "Scott, Galt, Hogg, Lockhart, Stevenson – do they not together render a great range of the national life?" (p140). If perhaps not deserving the straight answer, "No", the question at least demands the qualification that this "great range" is from a singularly male point of view. While the inclusion of the writings of such women as Elizabeth Hamilton, Mary Brunton, Eliza Logan, Christian Johnstone, Grace Kennedy, Helen Craik, Jane Porter and Susan Ferrier does not necessarily completely transform the "great range of the national life" as depicted by the men, it does nevertheless add a different – i.e. female – dimension to that range. Although these women writers do not, in their novels at least, tend to promote the idea of a strongly separatist Scottish national identity, it is a dubious practice to dismiss their perception of "the national life" out of hand, with no consideration at all. As Janet Todd puts it in her *Feminist Literary History: A Defence* (1988), "women are, after all, in history as material entities... they form a kind of non-identical paradigm of the historical process itself" (p82).

The (predominantly) male critics are not altogether unaware of a female presence in Scottish literary history, but their analyses of the writings of these women tends to be at best superficial and at worst unashamedly prejudiced. An early example of anti-female bias is to be found in Millar's *History* (1903) in which the author, like others after him, simultaneously venerates and denigrates Susan Ferrier, with comments such as this reference to her satirical treatment of the Fairbairn household in *The Inheritance* (1824): "First rate, must be the verdict, of its kind; but perhaps a little cruel. No man could have barbed the dart so cunningly" (p544). According to Millar, then, Ferrier's description of the family is, curiously, first rate, and of questionable worth in terms of morality. Millar chooses the adjective 'cruel' to describe the writing, rather than a less disparaging term such as 'witty' or 'satirical', almost as if the Fairbairns were a real family, in need of defence from Ferrier's rapier pen. Millar also declares the writing demonstrably female, by virtue of the excessive cunning it displays. Women in literature, of course, since Milton's Eve and before, have been noted for their cunning; Millar deftly (and, arguably, cunningly) slips from an analysis of the passage he quotes from *The Inheritance* to an analysis of the character (practically a character assassination) of its author. Warming to his theme, he is soon inviting the reader to sample another passage which "will help to show how formidable a person Miss Ferrier must have been to those she happened not to like" (p545). This is a useful demonstration of a well-attested fact of literary history, that women writers to a far greater extent than men, tend to have not only their published works examined by critical eyes and written up for the press, but also their personalities. Mary Brunton, another of the Scottish women novelists of the early nineteenth century, expresses her anxieties about this in a letter to her friend, Mrs Izett (later published in *Emmeline with some other pieces*, 1819) as follows: "To be pointed at – to be noticed and commented upon – to be suspected of literary airs – to be shunned as literary women are, by the more unpretending of my own sex; and abhorred as literary women are, by the pretending of the other! – My dear, I would sooner exhibit as a rope dancer" (p xxxvi).

The anti-female bias in Scottish literary history, particularly the early nineteenth century, when the women do not easily fall into the categories of the male tradition as created by the male critics, is, sad to say, not only of interest historically but clearly discernible in more recent works. David Craig has already been mentioned. Elsewhere in his history, Susan Ferrier and Elizabeth Hamilton each pass fleetingly across the horizon, dismissed disparagingly within a sentence or two. Ferrier's *Marriage*, he writes, is "Scotland's nearest to a 'society novel'"(p200), implying that the novel fails somehow to live up to the appropriate standard for that category of literature. It is not necessarily the case that a 'society novel' was what Ferrier intended when she wrote *Marriage*, so her failure in achieving this aim is debatable, to say the least, and some would argue that she did not fail at all (for instance Nelson S Bushnell in his essay 'Susan Ferrier's *Marriage* as Novel of Manners' in *Studies in Scottish Literature* 5 (1968), pp 216–228). When commenting on Hamilton's *Cottagers of Glenburnie*, Craig wavers between a strong dislike of the book and the same of its author, stating that it "takes up a typically Victorian soup-and-sanitation attitude to the working classes" (p 214).

Craig however does at least know the proper title of the book about which he writes: Lindsay (1977) somewhat tellingly refers to *The Cottagers of Glenbervie* [sic] (p 323), suggesting an indifference to her work, if not a positive distaste. On the other hand, he is aware of, if not too enamoured by, the works of Mary Brunton, a writer who often escapes the notice of Scottish literary historians. His knowledge of Brunton however, on closer inspection, also seems wanting. His reference to *Emmeline* as her "best novel" (p 324) suggests he may not be aware that this novel (which was published posthumously) is not merely unfinished, but was barely started: at one hundred pages long (including unrevised notes which were appended to the text by her husband) it is little more than a fragment.

While Kurt Wittig (1958) dispenses with Ferrier's achievement in less than one sentence ("in the three novels of Susan Ferrier... an occasional secondary character is all that 'gets across' to a modern reader"), Francis Hart (1978) examines her work more fully, making special note of her similarities to John Galt. As Hart notes, Galt's first publication, *The Ayrshire Legatees* in 1820, postdates Ferrier's *Marriage* by two years, which throws out any idea that Galt was an early influence on Ferrier. As he also concedes, the connection drawn between these writers by modern critics is not one of which Ferrier would have approved.

Watson (1984) in *The Literature of Scotland* succeeds in disposing of the three early Scottish women novelists he mentions – Susan Ferrier, Mary Brunton and Elizabeth Hamilton – in a paragraph, commenting, "these writers intended to instruct and 'improve' their readers". He again singles Ferrier out for a little extra comment, a few lines of mildly favourable criticism, concluding, "she writes with more humour and penetration than her predecessors" (p 269). An interesting notion, this, Ferrier's "penetration" and her predecessors' lack of same: this is the sort of comment that screams out for feminist deconstruction! In Drescher and Schwend's (1985) *Studies in Scottish Fiction: Nineteenth Century*, again there is no mention of any of the women writers of the early nineteenth century, except for Susan Ferrier, on whom there is an essay by Herbert Foltinek (entitled, 'Susan Ferrier Reconsidered', pp 131–145). Foltinek, like so many of the other Scottish literature critics, takes the opportunity of writing about Ferrier to belittle her achievements. He writes:

> Why is it that even in her first novel lively scenes are never sustained for long, that epigrammatic reflections are always superseded by prolonged sections

of insubstantial and rambling moralising? ...Seen in its entirety, each of the three novels shows basically the same weaknesses. Vivid descriptions, telling incidents, and superb dialogues are embedded in drifts of inferior writing... Even *Marriage*, which carries greater conviction than its successors, comprises long passages where mere penmanship has to make up for the absence of original design. (p140)

In the light of such sweeping, hostile criticism, it is perhaps difficult to believe that in her own age, Susan Ferrier was often compared favourably to Jane Austen. Scott famously referred to Ferrier as the Scottish member of "that feminine trio to which England supplied Jane Austen, and Ireland Maria Edgeworth". Blackwood wrote that he was reminded of "Miss Austen's very best things" in *Marriage*. Foltinek, in his Introduction to the OUP edition of *Marriage* (1986) sourly comments that "Today few would still subscribe to Blackwood's claim...", but that "references to the author as the 'Scottish Jane Austen' are far from obsolete". Susan Ferrier herself blatantly invites comparison with Jane Austen, by opening her second novel, *The Inheritance* (1824) with the sentence, "It is a truth, universally acknowledged, that there is no passion so deeply rooted in human nature as that of pride" which both in syntactical structure and content closely parallels the opening sentence of Jane Austen's *Pride and Prejudice*, published over a decade earlier in 1813. More recently still, in his Introduction to *The History of Scottish Literature, Volume 2, 1660–1800* (1987), Andrew Hook notes that only "in the early nineteenth century does writing become for Scottish women a possible source of supplementary income" (p8), providing this as an ingenious if questionable excuse for the exclusion of women (with the exception of those "remembered for occasional poems or songs in Scots" (p7)) from his volume of the *History*. To judge writers by their earnings lacks vision, to say the least; and only in the case of women does Hook find it necessary to rely upon the writers' earnings as an indicator of their worth.

Furthermore, contrary to Hook's implication, there were, in addition to the song-writers, quite a few Scottish women novelists publishing work in the late 1700s. Lady Mary Hamilton wrote several novels, the first of which – *Letters from the Duchess de Crui* – was published in 1776; Anne Eden's novel, *Confidential Letter of Albert; from his first attachment to Charlotte to her death* was published in 1790; Elizabeth Hamilton's first novel – *Letters of a Hindoo Rajah* – dates from 1795; and Helen Craik's first, *Julia de Saint Pierre*, was published a year later, in 1796. However, Hook's essay entitled 'Scotland and Romanticism: The International Scene' in the same volume, is exceptional for containing a reference to Jane Porter, whose name rarely turns up in the Scottish literary history books. Jane Porter's *The Scottish Chiefs*, was phenomenally successful upon its publication in 1810 and reprinted several times thereafter. Hook credits this novel with having played a part (if not, in his opinion, a particularly significant one) in "producing the situation through which in the nineteenth century Scotland gained its mythopoetic identity throughout Europe and America" (p310): all the more mysterious then, that Porter is so consistently absent from almost all of the Scottish literary histories.

In the third volume of *The History of Scottish Literature* (1988), which deals with the nineteenth century, Douglas Gifford, in his essay 'Myth, Parody and Dissociation: Scottish Fiction 1814–1914' concludes a less than enthusiastic discussion of Ferrier, Brunton and Hamilton, the "improver-satirists" as he pigeonholes them, with the comment, "These women may be detached; but they lack a consistent point of view, so that their work is no real and coherent social critique, and all that remains is the nostalgic love of old Scots songs and old-fashioned couthiness" (p238). Such dismissive generalisations are just as harmful to the standing of these writers as the condescending attitude of early critics like Millar. To lump the three writers together in this fashion (as so many critics before Gifford have also done), is to deny their real differences from one another. They do all write novels with morals, and thereby might with justification be termed "improvers" – but then so could many other novelists of their era: Ann Radcliffe, Jane Austen, Fanny Burney and Walter Scott for instance. Similarly, this latter grouping of novelists could also be said to lack "a consistent point of view".

It seems fair to say that in the Scottish literary histories, women writers of the early nineteenth century have been subject to a restricted number of fates: (1) total exclusion, (2) cursory mention, or (3) more adverse criticism than seems justified by the calibre of their work and the success/critical acclaim they earned in their own day. This is not to suggest that popularity necessarily equals true merit. However, the contemporary reviews seem to suggest the writers are deserving of more notice than they have been accorded in the present century. For example, the *Quarterly Review* (No. 11, July 1814, p355) in a review of *Waverley*, ranked Elizabeth Hamilton with Maria Edgeworth; the *New Monthly Magazine* (No. 13, March 1820, p273) considered her superior to the Irish writer. Mary Brunton's *Self Control* caused a stir upon its publication: in the words of one critic "...parties have been formed respecting it; some extolling it to the skies, and others depressing it below its real merits" (in the *British Critic* No.38, September 1811, p213). The reviewer in the *Glasgow Magazine* of September 1810 ranked Porter's *The Scottish Chiefs* "with the first of the modern race of novels". Many other enthusiastic praises may be found in the journals of the day: belittling the writings of women such as these seems to be a more recent pastime.

In her essay 'Flying Pigs and Double Standards' Germaine Greer poignantly comments on what she calls the "phenomenon of the transience of female literary fame" as follows: "almost uninterruptedly since the Interregnum, a small group of women have enjoyed dazzling literary prestige during their own lifetimes, only to vanish without trace from the records of posterity" (*Times Literary Supplement*, July 26, 1974). Contemporary critical success does not necessarily confer lasting literary status upon any writing: literature, like all aspects of culture, is subject to trends, to new ways of thinking. So-called 'improving' literature, looked down upon by twentieth century critics (as by Craig and Gifford above) was not so very long ago considered in a much less censorious light. The main point here however, is that while male writers go in and out of fashion, they do tend to retain their place in literary history (Richardson and Fielding serve as good examples of this: rarely read in the twentieth century, they are nevertheless unfailingly accorded considerable status in the history of the novel) while women writers, once out of fashion, are not only excluded from the canon, but also dropped from literary history.

Canonicity is an issue hotly debated on both sides of the Atlantic in recent years, particularly by feminist and Marxist academics. Literary critics of these schools of thought tend to base a part of their studies upon the recovery of 'lost' writers, whose omission from the canon is believed to be a direct result of gender or class. In Scottish literature, Tom Leonard, in the Introduction to his anthology, *Radical Renfrew* (1990) argues:

> A person must feel free to go back into the past that is Literature, go where they like and meet equally with whom they will. If a model of Literature has been created that prevents this, that model should be removed, and with it the metaphors that restrict the open nature of people's access. (pxxvi)

Such a preventative "model of Literature" as Leonard critically outlines above is much in evidence in the histories of Scottish literature. The authors of these, by their disparaging tones, strenuously caution the reader against sampling the writings of early nineteenth century women since these are beneath notice. Thus writers as varied and interesting as Elizabeth Hamilton, Mary Brunton, Eliza Logan, Christian Johnstone, Grace Kennedy, Helen Craik, Jane Porter and Susan Ferrier lose what has been, since their deaths, a rather shaky foothold on the bookshelves and, barring a rescue mission, are consigned to oblivion for good.

It is up to today's Scottish women – readers and writers alike – to root around in the archives and rediscover their foremothers. Virginia Woolf outlines the rewards awaiting those who undertake such exploratory research in *The Common Reader* (first published 1925, reprinted 1938):

> ...one likes romantically to feel oneself a deliverer advancing with lights across the waste of years to the rescue of some stranded ghost ...waiting, appealing, forgotten, in the growing gloom. Possibly they hear one coming. They shuffle, they preen, they bridle. Old secrets well up to their lips. The divine relief of communication will soon again be theirs. (p116)

Scottish women novelists of the early nineteenth century have been hidden from sight for far too long; they await delivery from the gloom in which they are constrained outside the Scottish literary histories. Their suppression is now nearing its end: the publication of an anthology of women's prose writing, *The Other Voice: Scottish Women's Writing since 1808* (ed Moira Burgess, Polygon, 1987), was a major step forward in restoring a voice to some lost women writers. Similarly, women-centred editions of journals, such as this one promise a brighter future for the dimmed female literary lights of the early nineteenth century.

It is well worth the effort, though. Recovering the tales of our grandmothers will as a matter of course bring about a revision of Scottish literary history, an exercise from which today's women writers in Scotland undoubtedly have much to gain.   *Aileen M Riddell*

SCOTLAND
A L B A

SALTIRE SOCIETY

Walter Scott and Scotland

Paul Henderson Scott

Sir Walter Scott was acutely aware of the historical position he found himself in *vis-à-vis* Scotland, making it the theme of all his best work. Paul Scott examines in detail how Scott's historical context influenced his writing and, in turn, how this affected Scotland.

Paul Scott is a prolific author, and received the Andrew Fletcher Award for Services to Scotland in 1993. Mr Scott has published a large number of books and articles including *The Thinking Nation* (1989), *Andrew Fletcher and the Treaty of Union* (1992), and *In Bed with an Elephant* (1985).

To be published in April or May 1994. ISBN 0 85411 056 9; £8.95

The Saltire Society, 9 Fountain Close, 22 High Street, Edinburgh EH1 1TE

The Box

Naomi Mitchison

When the net came in there was nothing in it of the kind we had hoped for and spoken about so quietly with no-one else about, so quietly that you would never guess at it, even if you were watching us a bit, as those not our friends might be doing. No, there was not the whiff of a salmon, not even the big grey mullets that are as good for eating though not for selling. Still and all, they would have been something and we wanted the money, yes, right down to our guts we wanted it. It was this wanted money that was at the back of all our thinking for us four men, five if you count in the boy Colin and you should do just that if you ask what happened; he had only been out once before and that too had not been one of the best, but he was still happy, as we older ones were not, just because it was new to him and the moon rising above a bright-edged cloud.

So, there it was, nothing in the net but a few wee flatties that Red Sandy threw back, but one was a big fellow and the hotel likely to take it, though they would only give drink for it. Young Colin had not yet got a taste for whisky, maybe did not yet need it before he could be happy. The rest of us would be glad of the whisky, but there would be nothing at all for giving to the hotel girls. There was this one I wanted badly and she was for ever putting me off, sweedling me with sweet words, good enough in themselves but not what that other, angry, pressing part of me wanted. One day though, it came to me in my deep fancy, I would say to myself *now*. Now, and it would come true even if she screeched a little. And maybe, I thought, it was something that she wanted as well, but how could I ask because that would be putting it into words and the only words for it that I knew were dirty words, not for a sweet girl. No, those would never do.

All this flipped through my mind as we hauled in the net and saw there was nothing in it of the kind we had hoped for, the kind that would make a man feel warm with hope. Likely enough it was the same for all of us, as we pulled at the wet, dark tangle that was the secret net, shaking hard at the weeds from the sea bed, tough and slippery as sin itself. We were angry at the net that had done so little for us and now must be shaken and cleaned and put away quickly and safely. We could not risk another go with it because of who might be around and jumping on us. But we were trying, all the same, to laugh it off a bit – mostly for Colin so he would not be put off the net for a lifetime. I had promised him something different. At least the tide would come up and strew the bunches of seaweed and flatten out our own footsteps, heavy along the cold sand.

And then we saw it. It was, you might say, a little box, bigger than a money box but not big enough for tools. There could be plenty of small things in it. Kenny was the one who spotted it first as it fell at his feet where he was shooking out his end of the line. But we all came quick and quiet to look. The net had picked up a thick sclather of weeds which had tangled over it, but we had the thing out of that in a moment, only what was it? For there was young Alan pulling something out. It was a box, right enough, and the first thing was us all trying to open it. But it was locked, and locked tight so that you could not put even a knife edge into it. Indeed she was such a well-made box that she might have kept the salt water out. But where did it come from? How did she get swept in to our beaches? And most of all, what was in it? In her? Could we, for once, have had a spot of luck? It was time, surely.

That was what each one of us might surely be thinking, for we needed the luck hardly enough. We could see in one another's faces the wondering what could be inside and was it something which could change our luck and make the world different towards us? Then we shone the big torch onto it; the battery was still good enough. That wet box, yes, she had a smart look. And there along the edge were the white letters – and I said to myself could that be ivory or an inset of some kind of metal or china or perhaps something I had no name for. What the letters said was Do Not Open, along one side across where there was a key hole. But none of us heeded that. It happened that I had brought a bunch of keys, for I liked the rattle of them, fun like, and who could know what might turn up. We tried them. Surely we had some luck at last?

Two or three of the small keys seemed to fit, but yet the box stayed shut tight, and we found ourselves wondering could it be some way dangerous to go on. But we were mad to get her open. Surely we could get into her by force, even if we broke a bit of her wood. Red Sandy tried to get the blade of a knife in under the lid, but Jonkie and Kenny and I said no, better not, wait for the morning light. We might spoil it, going on now. If we could find out whose it was, maybe we would get a big reward, and the light of that notion jiggled in front of us for a while. Alan's cousin had read about someone who found a bag full of foreign papers and took it to the police and ended with a big reward.

We could do a clever thing and find out about a reward. There might be something in the papers. We could even ask the police and that indeed would be something new for us. Or maybe some words in the papers? But no, we would need to keep it to ourselves unless, that is, we were to force the lid; but that might be a new kind of danger that none of us knew about yet. It might be an enemy from Germany or Russia or more likely The East which was full of horror stories that this could fit into. We began to think of all manner of dangers, there on the sand under the high moon, which had got itself clear of the clouds and reaching down to us. What was best then? Should we defy the writing on the box or could this be totally dangerous and something might escape from this box which should never have been let loose?

We passed the box round; all of us took a guess at it, but none seemed to get the right answer. If it was not to be opened, what was it doing on the beach or just off? How, why, getting itself into our net? We hated it a little. But we could not bring ourselves to saying we should go to the police. If the thought came to one or the other, we put it away quickly.

I tried to weigh the box a little in my hands, slowly, thinking what might be in it. Nothing very heavy, not gold coins. And somehow paper money seemed the wrong thing. We shook it and listened. Just in case. Was there a noise of anything moved or moving? Not really. Not in any truth. We passed it round again. Young Colin was mad to force it open. We older ones were less sure. At last I said that I would take it, the message it had and all, but I would put it into a safe place until we had it well thought over, bottom and top. And so the thing was passed to me and around midnight I was back with it under my arm, and me trying all the jokes I could think of – and some of them dirty enough. But I needed to warm myself up with other men's laughter.

So, good and well. And I could see that Colin thought I was brave and some way noble and that was good enough for me to hold onto, at least until I was standing again in my dark little room, which was at the back of one of the better houses that was used mostly for summer visitors. I waited there for something to happen. But what in all the world would it be? I half knew it could come in some way that was not in the Good Book, nor yet in the motor advertisements or the lies about the good life for tourists and that. And it did not come from inside the books about history and how things looked long ago for folk like you and me, for I had read enough to know about the great horror beasts that ranged about long before men and women, and later on, far towards now, came Scotland and the Picts and that even before the Scots themselves, and all stuck with work and hunger, except the ones away up top. It was clear enough that we common ones had the dirty side of whatever was going. But I had thought little and never deeply on all that, until this very night. But then I began to turn over all that I had heard and it seemed that most of it was lies and rotten promises and here we were stuck in a lump of living land and sea just the way it always is and no twisting to get us out of it.

Most of all, I thought, that things are bad enough and full of the lies that we got from men, aye, and women, on whom we had put trust and belief. Aye, from our baby days on. Inside me there was a kind of boiling on all I had ever thought and angered myself with.

So there was this anger swirling around in the back of my head and me waking in the cold, black time that hangs around after midnight, and saying to myself that everything was against me, even more than it was against all of us. I pointed my own torch at the box, but the light was bad, it needed a new battery but that meant money to spend. As I looked, the box seemed to have grown thicker as though it had something to spew out, but then again it seemed flat as a dead leaf. Most likely, I said to myself, there is nothing at all inside it and the sooner we see that, the better for us all and I searched around for something to hit it with, something that would make an end of stupid hopes. All I needed was a thin, strong knife to get under the lid.

It was then I began to have a kind of singing in my ears, and the like of a voice, but a sweet one, a voice of promising, and it said not yet, not yet. And suddenly I fell asleep and of all things I dreamed I was still a wee boy and I could smell the cake my mother was making for me and I knew there would be a present in it and it would be somewhere in the ben-room, wrapped up in pink paper. So, even after I woke there was a shadow of happiness. By then it was the cold edge of morning, but I had been that happy in my dream; some of it was still about. I asked myself, how had it been with the rest. Had they dreamed? Had young Colin dreamed or was he awake and still stirred up by the goings-on he had seen, been part of? Would it be something for him to remember for always? If only that box would speak, would it tell me?

And then, yes, then, the thing that was not possible was there under my nose. The lid shifted all on its lone the tiniest wee trifle which yet and yet was beyond anything in the world. And this had come to pass in my presence, under my very eyes. Something for me myself and only me.

I knelt beside the box and there was still a smell of the salt, weedy sea that it had come out from. But now it was as if it had invited me to touch it, just as a woman might do, a young lassie just out of school and not knowing the cruel things this world was offering to her. Yet that too was a lie, since most of them, I thought, know the way the world wags, aye, better than the boys. At least this box is old enough surely to know what it is doing. And I stretched out my hand to grab it in case it went shut again.

What at all was I expecting? I did not know anything, only that there could be no more desire for the common things of this world. This was the necessary tie-up between me and the box. Queer things have happened long ago, that is if we believe the Good Book or, for that matter, gypsies' and old folks' stories. So now I found myself picturing back into my childhood as I put out my hand towards the box and felt so happily that now there was no problem, not any longer.

So the lid lifted lightly, as though it had never refused the strong hands of five men tugging at it. And as it lifted, straight in front of me, I looked above and away, so as not to see, for I had a sharp thought that I must call the others, at least Kenny and Red and young Colin. But what at all would they be thinking if they did come? Surely, that I had done it somehow, perhaps had used force by metal and, following that, the thought that maybe I had taken for myself this or that out of the box.

How, then, was I to tell them truly what had happened? To the box and me. We are all used by now to ask hard questions, even of ourselves sometimes, and there would be plenty for me and no easy answer. How to tell them the truth and have it believed? Or would some kind of lie, if I could find the right one, fit better with what I had seen happening? And while I was in a kind of whirlpool of what to do and say, the lid lifted a little more. But suppose it took against me, against all my lot of folk, suppose it hated us, as well it might, what then? Would it shut again?

No, I said to it, no, stay there the way you are, speaking hard but lovingly as to a child running too near the edge of the corry, stay there, I'll not look. And I was sure I would be listened to and there would be no answer back. Oddly I did not think to look carefully at what was inside the box. It seemed that this no longer mattered, we did not even need to know. And yet, remembering it now, it seems that there were pieces of brightness which perhaps were things of great value, though that mattered little. And the inside of the lid which had seemed so impossible to move, with strong hands and knife blades, now seemed to rustle with colour like a butterfly in flight, almost asking to be lifted. Wait, I said, stay where you are, speaking hard as if to a child or a woman that belonged to me, the way there could be no answer back. And I hurried into boots and trousers, always keeping the edge of a glance on it, and I turned the key in my door and ran for it.

So now, would the others come, my old mates, would they believe, for then would we all change into a different kind of person, as I was myself feeling at that moment? Changed, happy, changed, but into what? I had to find them, to get an answer, to find who they were now. So I went first to young Colin, who was in the ben-room of his mother's house, with bright-coloured advertisements of foreign places stuck on the walls, and told him in great seriousness to go straight over to where I lived, for I had the box waiting, but not to ask questions yet, just to wait outside my locked door. Then on I went to get hold of Kenny and Red Sandy at least. Kenny came quick enough, but I could see he only half-believed me, but wanted to be in on it.

But Red Sandy was away drinking; someone had passed on the end of a bottle that had enough in it to knock the sense out of him. Kenny I found and after not believing a word of it, he changed all of a sudden and said yes, he would come. But it was Sandy who had been the most angry about the box not opening and when I spoke to him softly, for I did not want everyone's ears stuck onto what had happened, he had nothing but bad words about the box and me. As though I had found it alone and he was backing away.

The other one of us who had been on the net, Alan, was sober enough, but he swore at me too, thinking that I was playing a bad joke on him. I tried to make it sound as the straight truth that it truly was, but that did not work, not at all. After that I told myself we must wait. This would need strong thinking and perhaps action. Who of us would be strong enough? Would it have to be me again? It was the last thing I wanted.

Yet in the end I had to face it, that it must be myself and Kenny and young Colin. Also I knew that I must not make things too hard for a boy with little knowledge of people in the big world and the lies which could hurt everyone in it. Because, in this thing we had got ourselves into, something had happened which would break our whole pattern of truth and not-truth. Anyone who reads the newspapers reads of things he cannot understand or believe, but then it is forgotten by the next day. This would be different. This would stay.

So that was that. There was only Kenny and young Colin, and how strong would they be? I took my key out of my pocket into the door lock, turned it very quietly and opened sharply, as though to catch whatever was behind. There was the box on the floor where I had left it and suddenly I felt it had always been here, not just for the end of a night. I think I stood there staring at it, for now it was shut again. Shut. But nobody had been. Nobody could have got in. And the box was shut again. I found myself whispering at it, why did you do it? Why? I shone my bad old torch at it and the light seemed to tremble, but that was only my hand stickily trembling. There was no answer from the box, and young Colin looked at me as if I was drunk. Or mad.

I said, stupidly, and after noticing that both my hands shook a little: "It was open – before."

"What was in it, then?" asked young Colin. But all I could say was that it was beautiful, better than anything on telly, better than all the girls in all the Sunday newspapers in all the whole world. And young Colin only giggled – if a boy can do that. Kenny was angry. He said little except that this had come of trusting it with me, but never again. And I began to ask myself, what do I really remember? Could it have happened? Truly, like something real? To me?

"Let's forget it", I said. "That's best."

"But did you get it open?" Colin asked.

"Not me", I said. "No. It opened itself." And I saw it at the back of my mind, flowering.

Colin shook his head: "It cannie have. You were dreaming, just. Or something. Aye, drunk you were. Where's the bottle, then?" And he kicked at the shut box.

"Drunk", said Kenny and spat on my bed. And I knew that he would never believe me and we could never go on being friends. Never any more.

"Think what you like", I said. "I'd rather have it be that. The way you said. More easy." And now I was wondering, just, was I sure in my mind of what had happened? What I'd seen? What I'd think now I'd seen then?

"Ach", young Colin grunted at me. "Throw the dirty wee box back in the sea. Better than teasing us stupid. And setting yourself mad. Aye, a wee bit off, aren't you? Dreaming and that?" He looked at me kindly and I was thinking it was not the best thing to have a young boy as he surely was, holding out a hand to a grown man like myself.

I pulled myself together. "Aye well," I said, "it must be that." I picked up the box. Was it, I asked myself, a wee bit lighter? Or heavier? What did it say to my fingers? "We'll throw it back in", I said. "That'll be the end and good riddance."

Kenny said: "Aye, you want to get rid of us, keep it all to your fucking self."

I tried not to hear him, for if I had I might try to kill him. I turned back to Colin. He was not so angry, but worrying away

"I'm throwing the thing back in", I said. "Deep."

It was young Colin who answered: "But still and all it might have something…"

I jumped on that. I told him I had opened it, though indeed it had opened itself. But there was nothing, that was what I told him. Nothing.

"Maybe someone's bad joke on us. Or most likely some kind of toy, but we fools had taken it seriously." And I ended speaking hard, as a man grown.

But by that time Colin had picked it up himself. "No", he said. "I'll take it." I saw he was trying to open it, but of course nothing could come of that. Nothing at all. And when he was broken by it, maybe he would pass it on to Red Sandy. And the same again. But would it open for any of them as it had for me? As I remembered?

"Go your own way, Colin," I said, "but mind you do the right thing by it." And I pushed the door open. But, some way, and for all his talk, he had left it lying. The box. He was not back till the next day and that was with a friend of his, a gawky young lad who picked it up but had no notion what it was. They took it away with them. I turned my back.

That was last week. I happened to get a small job. Nothing to do with the box. It kept me busy. I have not looked carefully at any one of us. It is as if a string has snapped. I think I can always guess who has the box back in his room, who is asking and begging it, who is angriest. Some way, we are not doing things together, not any more. The net is put away, I think I know where. Maybe not for this season. Maybe for ever not. Will we ever be ourselves again and do we for all that want to be? One thing is certain. The box has not opened again. I think perhaps one of us will throw it back into the sea. *Naomi Mitchison*

Summer School 1994 Writing workshops on the West Coast

June 26 - July 2 **Dilys Rose**
The Whole Story
*An in-depth look
at short story writing*

July 2 - July 9 **Brian McCabe**
The First Book
*Working towards the first
publication of your poetry or fiction*

CREATIVE

S P A C E

For a brochure write or phone:
Lunga Mill
Ardfern
Argyll PA31 8QR
(08525) 526

Margaret Fulton Cook

The day the rot set in

clear water once flowed
under these bridges
that now stagnate
with human remains
of twelve year old mothers
feeding their pimp
who fixes their lives
nicely
through
the bend of their arm
as the kind man hotly
takes their picture
while God
pushing heaven
for a penny's worth of faith
is immune to the smell
of sympathy
that scuffles and troubles
the eyes
of the men
who question the path
they already walk

(and i think)
(when i remember to)

of these streets
of litter
these pavements of
cracks
and crap
and crack
that drags the sight seers
through gutterish dead oceans
of
youth
going
nowhere
drifting
through national front ranks
bursting
their special smiles
into clouds of
hate
as the holocaust spreads
and we
sleep on

Linda

Linda is in the dining room
she is thirty two
and has a hard plastic bib
round her neck

around her mouth
she has bits
of the butchered meat
she refused to eat
at lunchtime

Linda is vegetarian

from her hair drops
the mince
she threw at the nurse
who crunched the spoon
against her teeth
squeezed her nose
till she
couldn't breathe
packed her mouth
when she
gasped for air
held
it shut
rubbed her throat
made her choke

it was then she threw the mince

Linda is in the geriatric chair
staff nurse said
leave her there
till
tea time

The Dark

the dark
wasn't the problem

it was when
he shone the torch
on my knickerless thighs
    I wanted to cry

as my brother
collected sixpences
from his mates
    and I
    got
    nothing

Curses

rose up
from beneath
our bed room
window
    we creaked
    over the boards
    from
our iron ended bed
and
    wide eyed
    shivered
    in the darkness

as Grampa
and Uncle Sam
sickled and scythed
in the moon light

After Sunday School

    in our best
frocks
and socks
    we would
    slink out
from kissing visitors
    skip down
the twisting lane
    to sit on the dyke
lady like
and wave
to passing motorists

but
if they didn't
wave back at us
    we whispered
    "bugger"

and laughed
out loud
    all the way
    home

Four Pioneering Novels

Margaret Elphinstone

The Scottish Renaissance of the 1920s and 1930s is usually seen primarily as a poetic revolution, dominated by the work of MacDiarmid and Edwin Muir. A neglected aspect of the impact of Modernism on Scotland is its effect on the writing of fiction by Scottish women. The impetus of the Scottish Modernist movement combined with developments in women's writing in English outside Scotland, opened up new possibilities of expression for Scottish women writers. With this in mind I want to examine common themes in four first novels of this period: *Open the Door!*, Catherine Carswell, Virago, 1986 (first published in 1920); *The Conquered*, Naomi Mitchison, Jonathan Cape, 1923; *The Quarry Wood*, Nan Shepherd, Canongate Classics, 1987 (1928); and *Imagined Corners*, Willa Muir, Canongate Classics, 1987 (1931)

A characteristic of all these novels is the juxtaposition of opposites, which has itself been a major theme in Scottish literature, first identified by Gregory Smith in *Scottish Literature: Character and Influence* (Macmillan, 1919), and reiterated in the 1920s by MacDiarmid. Each of these women novelists uses juxtaposition of contraries, in terms of wilderness/imprisonment, the social world/the inner self, using images of houses, prisons, enclosed spaces, as opposed to the physical wilderness outside the social, human world. They also use the contraries most discussed by Smith: the ordinary as opposed to the marvellous, the prosaic outer world and the inner dream world. It is the use of these oppositions in relation to constructs of gender which is a radical innovation into the Scottish tradition.

The idea of the divided female self is also expressed by contemporary English feminist writers, for example in Virginia Woolf's description of "a splitting off of consciousness" in *A Room of One's Own* (Penguin, 1945). The perception of the social construct of 'woman' as a restricted, imprisoning role which cannot contain or express the whole self is essential to the critique of gender that we find in feminist writers of the early Modernist period.

It is the conjunction of the Scottish and the feminist contexts within which these Scottish women writers situate their exploration of identity, that allows them to develop a voice which had not been heard before in Scotland, as they examine the old Scottish themes of marginalisation and divided identity in terms of gender. A consideration of the four novels shows how this is achieved through the images I have described.

Open the Door!

Catherine Carswell's *Open the Door!* chronicles the long search of Joanna, the central character, for fulfilment and identity as a woman. Joanna grows up in Glasgow, as Carswell herself did, surrounded by women enacting the partial roles available to middle-class women in the 1890s. One thing

Joanna's mother, Juley, does provide for her children, is a close and loving family life. But this in itself is a kind of prison. Joanna needs the affection and emotional nourishment her mother offers, but she also recognises the limitations and compromises of her mother's life. Not until she achieves an inner reconciliation with all that her mother represents, including the part of herself which is Juley's daughter, can she in any way be free.

The novel opens with the family travelling from Glasgow to Edinburgh, the first of many journeys throughout the novel. When the reader first encounters Joanna she is merely a part of the family. The first focus is on the mother: "For Juley Bannerman to leave home was in any case a heavy undertaking." (p5) Closeted in the railway carriage, the children at once make the confined space their own, repelling all would-be sharers of their compartment. They even talk in a private language, double-dutch. Joanna is first introduced struggling to free herself from this corporate identity. Moved by the view of the river from the railway bridge, she finds her family's reaction to her private dream an intrusion:

> The familiar, absurd thought came to her that she was perhaps a changeling or foster-child to the Bannerman family, no real relation to any of them (p10)

Joanna's struggle throughout the novel is to separate herself from her family, most of all from her mother. The domestic social life of women is represented by the recurring symbol of the cage. The longing for freedom, for a wildness that is both an external place and an inner state, is represented in the recurring symbol of birds flying free. The main problem with these symbols in the novel is that they are explained in far too much detail. Carswell's close working friendship with DH Lawrence may have something to do with this, as he tends to use portentous images in much the same way. Perhaps it also suggests a lack of confidence that the novel would be read with understanding. Willa Muir does the same thing in the moralising passages in *Imagined Corners*, as if neither author quite dared to let women's experience speak for itself.

Juley's struggle for freedom was fought and lost before the book begins. Her own family had no mother, and lacked cohesion and emotional warmth. Juley, lacking a family, finds meaning in her own highly emotional form of religion, which seemed to offer her the emotional fulfilment she sought, but she gave up the possibilities of this for marriage. Sholto persuades her that "As his wife she would be fulfilling her true destiny." But Juley is never sure of her decision. When her marriage fails to fulfil her, "She would ask forgiveness of God for having married."

She is never satisfied sexually. Sholto praises her for loving him in a sisterly fashion, and is pleased that she shows no passion. In this he is totally deceived, but Juley cannot articulate her need:

> When she felt the stirrings of passion in herself she was dimly ashamed, and had to reason that after all this world was peopled by God's own ordinances. Only the yielding up of oneself to mere delight was sinful. (p25)

Having failed to fly free in her own life, Juley centres all her ambitions on her children, and these are, naturally, religious ambitions. But all her children reject this imposition, Joanna most of all. To begin with it is

Georgie who openly rebels, but she is the first to succumb. When she too is a mother, she abnegates any active part in the world, settling all her hopes and ambitions on her child. When she and Joanna go to buy baby clothes for young Sholto, Georgie has taken over the role her mother:

> Georgie herself might be a stupid failure – she laughed happily – in everything she had tried save motherhood. But what did that matter? All that mattered was the new generation, which was so wonderfully to profit by our mistakes. THEY would do, and do far better all that we had left undone. (p336)

Joanna refuses this kind of self-abnegation, but remains ambivalent about her family throughout her adult life. She knows she needs the emotional nourishment they provide. This is Joanna at a family reunion, just before Sholto emigrates to Australia:

> Breakfast was happy and noisy, and Joanna, taking part, but always a little outside, thought that surely there had never been such a pleasant family party. She longed only for Sholto to join them! How entirely different from any other family they were! Was there not an atmosphere, a charm, impossible to explain! (p195)

Joanna needs love, she needs people to whom she belongs, and yet they are dangerous to her, as they limit the possibilities open to her. To fit in, she too must become a caged bird. Family life is centred upon interiors – rooms, houses, closets. The Bannermans belong in the city, and in their city life Joanna must always be contained in a restrictive social role, shut up in one house or another.

Joanna's inner world reflects this restriction. As a child her mind is likened to a room: "the dark lumber-room of the child's mind" (p25), and later, "the dark chamber of her mind" (p51). She tries to make an interior of her own, building a temple out of boxes and candles: "The result was a conflagration which left a large hole in the nursery carpet" (p40).

All Joanna's attempts to construct enclosures have a similar result. In her series of relationships with men she tries again and again to make a temple, a safe enclosed space in which the relationship can be contained, and every time this ends in a symbolic conflagration and collapse, a re-enactment of her childish nightmare, when her father, seen through the glass door as a devil figure, tries to break into the house, and Joanna frantically tries to close the door upon him (p27). Sexual passion has been identified with imprisonment and sadism ever since Joanna's encounter, aged seven, with her cousin Gerald at Duntarvie, whose hobby was shooting birds:

> Smiling, [Gerald] pointed his penknife that was still blood-stained against the child's breast…and he threatened to skin her like a little wild bird. To his surprise – for he expected her to wriggle or protest – Joanna stood dumb and quite still and strange in his grip. So he soon stopped teasing her. But he had provided her with a theme which she afterwards embroidered out of all recognition in many an erotic rhapsody (p35)

Joanna learns to expect imprisonment as an essential part of emotional fulfilment, and she finds it with her first husband, Mario, who says to her:

> 'How would you like to live in a cage, a cage full of sunshine and beauty and delight, a cage of which the man you loved kept the key?' (p98)

Joanna refuses to be warned, and does indeed find herself immured in the house in Italy. Joanna escapes this particular cage by Mario's fortuitous death, but she still cannot escape the mental imprisonment she learned in childhood, that in order to have love there must also be a cage of some kind. In her relationship with Louis, she creates another interior, furnishing a room in the new house where sexual fulfilment with Louis at last becomes possible: "This innermost chamber, the very kernel of fire, was their safe hiding-place" (p 249).

The irony of this particular temple is that it is literally created out of Juley's belongings. During the flitting, Joanna has been going through the mysterious wardrobe that contains Juley's private things. Joanna herself is well aware of the meaning of her encroachment

...in the sacrilege of the wardrobe she would allow no one else to share.
As the great, curving mirrored door swung heavily back upon its hinges Joanna was a child again; and the enclosure with its trays and drawers, and its middle place lined with faded blue box-pleating appeared to her as the very ark of romance. But at the quick of her excitement was something which had nothing to do with memory or with childhood except in so far as signi- fied the departure from both. This, not the hour of her marriage with Mario, was the time of severance, the final breaking of the umbilical cord. (p 242)

And in London too, Joanna makes her rooms in Mayfair a sanctuary for Louis, a place where their relationship can happen behind closed doors.

Joanna tries to find a sense of self through relationships with men, a dubious undertaking perhaps, and possibly the most unsatisfactory aspect of the book is its ending, when we are asked to believe that marriage to Lawrence will solve all Joanna's internal conflicts. Lawrence may seem an inadequate solution, but the background to Joanna's emotional rebirth at the end of the book is crucial to the concept of escape and freedom.

Elaine Showalter uses the term 'the wild zone' to refer to the part of woman's experience that exists outside the paradigm of patriarchy[1]. It represents the part that cannot be enclosed within the overt framework of language or social structure. In *Open the Door!* Carswell's images of flying birds reflect something similar. There is infinite possibility outside the cage, but it can only be read subversively, against the overt social script provided for women. For Joanna to open the doors that enclose her, and fly out, she has to return to an inner self that she had forgotten, which is also allied to an actual, outer untamed area which had once been the most important thing to her.

Ironically, Joanna owes this wild zone to her mother, who rented a house for them at Duntarvie every summer of Joanna's childhood. Duntarvie is the only place where the child Joanna is free to run wild physically, the only place where she has the solitude and freedom to express outwardly what goes on within her. Joanna the child vows to Duntarvie "If I forget thee, may my right hand forget its cunning." (p 33) This is the forgotten world, where there are no doors, no prisons, to which Joanna finally returns at the end of the book. In childhood, it is the place where she first encounters sexuality. Alec Peddie's offer to the twelve-year-

---

1. 'Feminist Criticism in the Wilderness', *The New Feminist Criticism*, ed Showalter, Virago

old Joanna to "...come up yonder on the moor wi' me, Joanna. I'll show ye what lads is for", is finally fulfilled by Lawrence, the man who shows Joanna, up on the moor, what a man can be for, outside any constructed prisons. Their meeting is positively Laurentian, but not altogether convincing. Carswell's novel shows how closure is not possible; there is no neat resolution of all the conflicts in Joanna's life, and it is hard to accept a final rescue from all the paradoxes of her time, society and gender:

> Never before had their primary flames of being leapt up so nakedly. And they were full of recognition, each for the other. There on the moor that vibrated with noonday, he was Adam to her Eve. There among the broom bushes whereon the dark seed pods went crack cracking in the strong sunshine, the past was shed from them both like a garment. (p397)

Wonderful, if you can believe it.

The Conquered

Naomi Mitchison's first novel, *The Conquered* is outwardly quite a different type of novel from the other three first novels we are considering. It is a historical novel, set in the first century BC, dealing with the subjugation of Gaul by Julius Caesar's Roman army. It seems to be nothing to do with Scotland, and little to do with women. However, there are implicit connections with the other books.

Mitchison in her non-fiction writing concentrates on class issues in her analysis of social division. In *The Conquered* she takes the question out of a capitalist society and into a slave economy. The Roman Empire is full of the dispossessed. The Roman élite survive on the labour and service of their slaves, recruited from the conquered peoples of the expanding Empire. Titus Barrus the centurion (later tribune) has three slaves, Lerrys, Dith, and the hero of the novel, Meromic. Meromic the Gaul suffers an agonising division of loyalty and identity. He owes loyalty to Titus his Roman master who saves his life. He also owes loyalty to his own people, among whom he was once a king's son. Punished with mutilation for his part in a rebellion, he returns to his Roman master, and at the end of the story he is a servant in Titus' house, being polite to his master's wife, and playing games with his master's children. But just as the reader recoils from the complacency of this travesty of a happy ending, Mitchison shows that it is after all ironic. Meromic, of the Wolf tribe, slips out of the Roman world into a supernatural Celtic twilight which overturns the apparent historical reality of Rome:

> Meromic's room stood empty; his knife lay on the windowsill, rust beginning to gather in the dew spots; on the paths and under the bushes there were tracks of wolves, and one wolf that went lame of the right fore-foot; the tracks went north... (p318)

The slaves in this novel are men, who were once free men in a tribal society, and are now slaves in an Empire. The novel is about imprisonment and its effects. The slaves have lost all rights and are in captivity, and yet they have access to an inner world which is denied to their masters, an inner world that correlates to the physical wilderness beyond Rome's boundaries. Virginia Woolf described the situation of

women in patriarchy in almost identical terms in *A Room of One's Own*.
Part of Meromic is untouched by Rome. He is still the wolf, although
outwardly beaten and destroyed. His inner world can never be contained
within the confines of a Roman reality. Like the other slaves he takes on
qualities that in a different society, dealing with a different oppression, we
are used to assigning to the so-called feminine. The three slaves are
anxiously deferential to Titus, although they give him love and loyalty.
They belong in the domestic interior of his tent, rather like wives:

> Titus Barrus was late that evening; there was a cold wind blowing, with a whirl
> of leaves over the ground; he pulled his cloak tightly round him, wondered
> how the new slave's education was getting on, and also whether he'd find
> a decent meal ready, and wished the Gaul were back, temper or not. At any
> rate, the fire was burning well outside his tent, and he could smell the roasting
> meat. Lerrys, with his back to him, was unhooking the joint from the crossed
> sticks over the glow... (p147)

This little group become Meromic's family. The part of him that is Celtic
warrior is always at odds with the part of him that runs Titus' domestic life.
He has sworn an oath of loyalty to Titus, but the morality of his
faithfulness is always ambiguous. Mitchison treats the division with an
irony that is sometimes hard to bear, showing how close to the bone
Meromic's dilemma is for the woman reader. And Meromic pays the price
of deciding to submit – he takes on the mentality of a slave:

> [Titus Barrus] understood that after this glimpse of the old life, the contrast
> in [Meromic's] slave's mind was no longer between now and the Roman house
> of fear and pain, but between now and the open woods... (p156)

Within Roman houses, Meromic takes on the identity of a slave, but the
'open woods' reflect the untamed part of him, the part that finds its image
in the wilderness of unsubdued Gaul. When Meromic, out foraging for his
master, finds Molhir the Druid dying, he is reminded of the compromise
he has made. Molhir, thinking Meromic is a free warrior, charges him with
a message to his chief: "Tell him I died, and that I know – I hope – oh,
freedom's not a dream!" (p164) and Meromic, in response, "had never felt
the shame of his slavery like this before."

Meromic, in stating his own dilemma, gives the image of a domestic role
to describe the tie he feels to his Roman master:

> 'Can't you see, Lerrys? There's half of me aching to get off, to be fighting on
> my own side, the side I ought to be on; and there's the other half – oh God,
> Lerrys, I'd give my life for him, I would truly; he's all I've got, he's wife and
> child and home and everything. I don't care what he does to me, not really.'

Gilbert and Gubar[2] explain how an overtly patriarchal text by a woman
may contain a palimpsest, a way of reading between the lines, of making
subversive connections, which express a reality that cannot be explicitly
stated. Mitchison, in this first novel, avoids making women her central
characters. Instead, she shows what it is to be a particular kind of slave
– the kind that has known freedom, who has belonged to a world outside
the imperialist authority of Rome, who knows his own people and where

---

2. Sandra M Gilbert & Susan Gubar, *The Madwoman in the Attic: The Woman Writer and
the Nineteenth Century Literary Imagination*, Yale University Press, 1979

his allegiance lies, but who is bound by ties of love and domestic closeness to *one* of his oppressors. Once the connection is made between the containment of women and the situation of the slaves, this ceases to be a novel about a remote time and long-ago events, but becomes a pertinent, political fiction. When we read with this meaning in mind, the novel becomes radically explicit.

This is a first novel, and it seems Mitchison could handle the parallel between women in patriarchy and slaves under imperialism, but she could not yet bring the two together. In her later historical novels she synthesises the two to great effect. In her 1939 novel *The Blood of the Martyrs*, for example, the Christian slaves are mostly women, and Mitchison deals with the implications. The slave Lalage "...did not own her own body. She did not know if she had been born slave or free. She did not remember exactly when she had been a virgin." In *The Conquered* Mitchison avoids this synthesis of subjection, as if she were not yet quite ready to deal with it. In doing so, she perhaps perpetuates the divided image of women, the angel or monster, that Gilbert and Gubar criticise in literature. There are no whole women like Lalage in *The Conquered*, only fragmented aspects of women, peripheral to the male characters. They are not drawn into the conflict. We meet no women slaves at all.

The novel begins with a heroine, whom we meet just two pages after Meromic. Meromic has been lying in bed thinking about pretty girls, when "Suddenly the curtain over the doorway was swept aside, and Fiommar, his sister, stood over him, a fishing-line in one hand." (p13) The first four chapters centre on the conflicts in Fiommar's life. She is as active and brave as her brother, but the only role open to her is to make a disastrous strategic marriage with the Briton Gandoc, who shames her by failing to bring help to her father and brother when they are fighting the Romans. Fiommar is quite clear about what this marriage means: "'Oh think, this is the last day I shall be really free: after this evening he can send for me when he likes!'" Her brother doesn't know what she means until he too finds himself another man's chattel.

But Fiommar is never properly married and she is never enslaved either. Instead she chooses suicide, returning to the islet where she and Meromic used to fish, in order to kill herself. There is no place for Fiommar in a world which is all Roman, so she leaves it for an island to the west, an island like the Celtic land of the dead, choosing death rather than submission to what Rome represents.

Her suicide feels like an escape for Mitchison as well as for Fiommar – she doesn't now have to deal with Fiommar's likely fate as a Roman slave, facing up to the reality of a Lalage. She pushes the girl off the edge of the world, to an ironically Roman form of death. Certainly her suicide is too seemly to be credible. She dies tidily, with no unpleasantness. Nothing that happens on the island seems quite real, and the simile used when Meromic buries her, adds to the remoteness: "at last he got her lying along with her arms at her sides and her hair over her shoulders like a princess in a fairytale." (p86) The episode is disturbing. Mitchison is usually historically meticulous, and yet here is a Celtic girl dying a Roman death, looking like a fairytale princess. In short, the author is guilty of rescuing her character from the meaning and consequences of her time, place and gender, thus depriving us of the real story.

The other women in the novel are minor characters, but their very insignificance points to what is not being said. Coisha, the wife of Lerrys, avoids the consequences of defeat, and instead marries Lerrys and has a house in Italy and some babies. Titus Barrus' wife Aemilia is a typical child bride. She is presented as an object, seen entirely through male eyes. One is reminded of Schweickart's criticism of Joyce's presentation of the young woman who represents Stephen's epiphany, in *A Portrait of the Artist as a Young Man*.[3] Schweickart says Joyce's text invites a woman reader to what she calls 'immasculisation', that is, to read as a man. But here we have a woman writer doing the same thing:

> She was young and shy and slender with black hair, coiled and pinned, and drooping eyes; she would hardly speak to him at first. Sometimes he could not help comparing her with the strong, full-breasted Gallic women; this girl, in her straight, clinging silks, could never run beside a horse, nor swim against a foaming current, nor stand in her doorway with a spear, threatening the soldiers. Nor could this little shoulder pillow a tired man's head, these unskilled fingers and mouth and body set him at rest and make him fit to work again.

If this were juxtaposed to another way of seeing, if we ever saw Aemilia as subject as well as object, we could read this ironically. But we don't. This is the real price writer and reader pay for Fiommar's death. Once she is eliminated from the story, there is no further place for women as subject. Fiommar's banishment from the world of the novel necessarily makes that world a masculine one. Aemilia is object, little girl and angel, not woman. The drift into immasculisation shows itself elsewhere, for example in the account of the atrocities that follow the final defeat of the Gauls: "however much people ran from (the soldiers), now and then one would be caught, an old, sick man perhaps, or some half-crazy woman."

The horrors of reprisals are there, but they lack impact. The woman here is not an individual, she is 'some woman'; she is not even possessed of a mind of her own, she is 'half-crazy'. We are, in fact, encouraged, as the soldiers are, to distance ourselves from her as a human subject. It is a long way from here to the women characters in *The Blood of the Martyrs*.

The Quarry Wood

Martha, in Nan Shepherd's *The Quarry Wood* is also caught in a web of paradox through which she has to find some identity of her own. Martha too is surrounded by dualities, of gender, class, self and family, emotion and intellect, and also a linguistic duality between the Scots of her background and the English of her education. Perhaps there could not have been a satisfactory ending; certainly the ending we have leaves the reader frustrated, as Martha never does reconcile the elements which

3. Petrocinio P Schweickhart: 'Reading Ourselves: Towards a Feminist Theory of Reading', *Feminisms*, ed Robyn Warhol & Diane Herndl, Rutgers University Press 1981

make her who she is. To choose, for example, education over her own social background is to lose too much, but at the same time, to turn her back on the University and all it means to her is also to lose too much. Either way, Martha is forced to sacrifice a part of herself. This is shown in the division between Scots and English which gives linguistic form to the division within Martha herself.

It is Emmeline, Martha's mother, who is the strongest Scots voice in the book. Her language has an ironic turn of phrase and an imaginative power which makes other people's speech comparatively pale and wan.

> "Latin," said Emmeline again. "Fat sorra div ye need wi' Latin for a teacher? Ye're nae to larn the geets Latin, I'm hopfu', an' them disna ken ae year's en' fae the t'ither." (p 28)

> "Ach," cried Emmeline impatiently, "you had aye a saft side to Madge. Onybody wi' their twa een in their heid cud a' seen the road she was like to tak. Wi' her palaverin' an' her pooderin' an' her this an' her that. She had a' her orders, had Madge. An a stink o' scent 'at wad knock ye doon. Foozlin' her face an' bamboozlin' her face wi' her pastes and her pooders. Eneuch to pit faces ooten fashion." (pp 170–171)

Aunt Josephine's language is also lively, although her pithy sayings tend to be aphorisms, expressing a shared common sense rather than the rich individuality of Emmeline.

The Scots speakers continually demonstrate to Martha one side of her heritage, which she rejects. Martha as a child speaks Scots like the rest of her family. She changes to English in Chapter Four, where we find her trying to do her Latin exercise, without success, in the bustle of the family kitchen. Her thoughts are in English, in sharp contrast to her mother speaking to her in Scots:

> "Ye micht dicht it up," she said to Martha.
> Martha...suddenly wanted to scream, to cry out at the pitch of her voice, 'I haven't time, I haven't time, I haven't time! What's a kitchen table in comparison with my Latin, with knowing things, with catching up on the interminable past! There isn't TIME!'

The language echoes the thought expressed, Scots against English, a kitchen table against a Latin exercise.

In dialogue, the two voices speak for themselves in ironic juxtaposition. The narrative voice distances herself from Scots. Her habit of putting Scots phrases in the narrative (as opposed to dialogue) in italics emphasises her own distance from them. She seems to be treating them as quaint, as something she, being educated, only uses with self-consciousness; the italics signal distance, a hint of explanation (see pp 10, 18, 78, 95 etc). Moreover, the Scots words come in groups, several italicised words together, and then none for several pages. Sometimes the narrator uses Scots words without the italics to signal them, as if they came naturally to her. She seems to be as unsure of her relation to Scots as Martha.

This ambiguous use of Scots extends to an ambiguous presentation of the country characters. The treatment of Geordie in particular is paradoxical. The narrator shows him to be stupid, slow, and inarticulate, but at the same time he represents truth, a widening of meaning and possibility, which Martha is only gradually able to learn from him. Martha, in her search for wisdom through a University education, takes a long time to discover, as we hear "that man does not learn from books alone." By the time she is twenty-four she is able to acknowledge that Aunt Josephine "had taught her wisdom". She never acknowledges her debt to her father. The narrator shows what Geordie has to offer, but at the same time she ironically reveals Martha's partial vision of him.

On p16 Geordie is described as elemental, and, it is Geordie who first offers Martha the possibility of wider horizons. He takes Martha and Dussie out to look at the Northern Lights. Up until then they have never looked at the night sky:

> They were jammed together in the huddled kitchen, under the smoky and flaring lamp. But one evening Geordie, from the open house-door, whence a guff of caller air flapped through the stifling kitchen, called the girls out to the night. (p18)

It is Martha's first sense of wider horizons:

> Something inside her grew and grew till she felt as enormous as the sky. She gulped the night air; and at the same time made a convulsive little movement against her father. She was not afraid; but she felt so out of size and knowledge of herself that she wanted to touch something ordinary.
> 'Some feart kind, are ye?' said the ploughman, taking her hand tight in his own. (p18-19)

It is Geordie too, who says that Martha shall go to the University. He listens to Emmeline saying that such a thing is impossible:

> He ruminated soberly. In the cramped kitchen prodigious horizons lengthened out. There were vast unenclosed tracts within him where his thoughts lost themselves and disappeared. He pursued them deep within himself, past his landmarks.
> ...'We'll nae be nane waur off wi' Matty at the college than we are e'noo whan she's at the school, will we?' (p34)

Martha, at the University, finds her own world expand in almost similar terms to Geordie's 'prodigious horizons'. Such images subvert the duality of education as possibility, home as confinement, because they make an explicit connection between the elemental world that Geordie represents, from which Martha came, and all that she later learns. Martha's horizons could never have widened if she had not learned the nature of possibility from her father.

The world of education and the world of nature conflict, but they also connect. They are set in juxtaposition to a world of containment, the domestic world inhabited by women in houses. The contrast between expansion and containment is made clear at the beginning. Martha, as a child, dances to her Aunt Josephine:

> ...[Josephine] had never heard of cosmic measures, but she knew quite well that the force that urged the child to dance was the same that moved the sun in heaven and all the stars. (p9)

Two paragraphs later we find Jean and Leebie obeying a different law:

> To rise on Tuesdays for any other reason than to turn out the bedrooms, or on Fridays for a purpose beyond baking, would have seemed to both sisters an idle attempt to tamper with an immutable law of life.

Emmeline, Martha's mother, has no such control over domestic life; she has become the victim of it. Her house imprisons her, and she tries to bring life into it by fostering every illegitimate child she can get her hands on. Martha, as she grows up, rejects her mother's attempt at spiritual survival. In aligning herself with the university, she tries to shake off her whole domestic and social background.

But Martha is as much Emmeline's daughter as Geordie's, and the ambivalent mother/daughter relationship is one of the most subtle aspects of the book. There are obvious comparisons with Carswell's depiction of the relationship between Juley and Joanna: the same determination on the part of the daughter to become a separate individual, and the same rejection of what her mother represents, but also the same indubitable connection, a daughter who inherits from her mother whether she likes it or not, who cannot be completely herself until she has resolved her relationship with her mother.

Emmeline, like Juley with Joanna, has hopes that Martha will heal her own disappointment, and become what she could not be. Emmeline, by marrying Geordie, has forfeited middle class respectability, and her dream is that Martha will regain her lost status. But Martha can no more alter who she is than Emmeline, and at the University it is the remembrance of her mother that makes her realise she does not fully belong.

Emmeline, growing fatter and fatter, reminds Martha not only of her origins, but her own physicality. Martha's love for Luke gradually teaches her that she is physically a woman, not pure spirit, and passion is physical as well as spiritual. It's as if Martha's attempt to escape her mother is an attempt to escape her own physical nature, and in the end she has to realise that this is not possible.

Dussie, once Emmeline's fosterling, and now married to Luke, is aware of this lack in Martha, while Luke rejoices in Martha being, as he thinks, pure spirit rather than real woman. Dussie is the one who really has Luke; she is married to him and they have a physical relationship resulting in children. When Martha begins having lunch with them, Dussie complains:

'You are not a rapturous eater, Marty. Now Luke is. He really pays attention to what I make for him.

To which Luke made answer: 'Well of course you know, flame is fairly indiscriminate as to what it takes for fuel.'

'Oh!' she cried, exasperated, 'you are crazed with your flame. Marty has a stomach like the rest of us, I suppose, and she should be made to know about it.' (p63)

Dussie's physical liberation is two-edged. She has no status outside her marriage to Luke. She has no learning, is not a student, but is part of University life because she is his wife. She cooks and entertains for his friends. The narrator shows far more approval of her role than she does of the unfortunate Lucy Warrender. Poor Miss Warrender "was noted for an ardent feminist" (p105), although "there was something lascivious in her eyes and posture" (p106). Clearly Miss Warrender is not a suitable role model. The liberation which the narrator suggests for Martha is different. Martha is not to be a feminist, but nor does she seem ever to come to terms with her physical self as Dussie has done. There are suggestions in the narrative that she should learn to regard herself as object, to become Muse rather than author. When she does try to finish Luke's poem (not her own, incidentally) we hear:

> to tell the truth her verses were by no means as beautiful as her eyes had been when she tramped the Quarry Wood beating out the metre (p89)

Luke betrays Martha by thinking of her as pure spirit: "I have learned through you to worship flame," he tells her, "the flame of life. Like Beatrice." (p76). The narrator too compares Martha to Beatrice and to Artemis, and to liken her to stars, flames, crystals and candles. She ironically exposes Luke's inability to reconcile the spiritual and the physical – he never finishes his epic poem, leaving the Archangel Gabriel "in a parlous state between heaven and earth, and Luke was unable to extricate him from his plight." (p88)

Finally, after confronting the animality of Roy Foubister, Martha realises how Luke has betrayed her, and her anger is expressed in an image of physical violation:

> Luke had no right to all he had had of her. He had wiled her on, taking all she could give: as he had taken the contents of Lucy Warrender's brain; raped her of what he wanted in her and flung the rest aside; deflowered her, using colour and contour and perfume, and refusing to see that he had plucked the blossom whole to have them. (pp159–160)

Martha's final statement of identity is dubious. The ending seems to be an invitation back into the domestic cage, a closing down of every horizon. Certainly Martha shows herself to be her mother's daughter, and is reconciled to the part of herself that is Emmeline, but it is hard to see this as in any way a liberation. Martha has set her face against the endless stream of fosterlings, but finally she decides to adopt the last of these, the baby Robin. Martha has indignantly refuted all the rumours that the child is hers. Physically, of course, he is not, but in another way rumour proves true. The boy does become hers, emotionally and spiritually. Even the fact that he is not her own is a kind of failure, the result of her denial of the physical in her love for Luke.

She adopts the child, she is reconciled with Luke and Dussie, and the final image of the book is Martha playing the woman's role in a domestic interior, serving tea. Quite explicitly, the possibility of wider horizons, the theme that has led her forward throughout the book, is denied:

> Of the two Martha was the happier. She had acquiesced in her destiny and so was delivered from the insecurity of the adventurer. *Sail not beyond the Pillars of Hercules.*

But Shepherd cannot deny what she has already shown us. The 'prodigious horizons' are there, whether Martha turns her back on them or not.

Imagined Corners

Calderwick, in *Imagined Corners*, is another kind of prison. It consists of interiors: rooms, houses, indoor worlds shut away behind doors which are often portrayed in the act of being fastened. We see characters immured inside, or locked out. This town of interiors adds up to a symbolic interior itself. It is the enclosed human world, shut away from the wilderness outside, both sea and moor, and equally shut down upon the wilderness within. But nature cannot be safely bolted out; it forces its way in, to the destruction of the carefully-constructed world of appearances that Calderwick represents. It's worth examining some of these interiors, some of these lockings in and lockings out.

In the Murray household it is Ned who is confined to the house, just as when he first had his breakdown he barricaded himself into his room at college. Sarah describes how at the Manse too he will "never set a foot across the outside door." Ned, in his self-chosen imprisonment, turns out to be writing a story, which he describes as being "About the world as it should be. Every house in all the towns empty... No WOMEN." But the manse is not empty; there is no safe retreat for Ned. His imprisonment becomes real when he defies Sarah and finally tries to escape. When Sarah takes the key and locks him in, he tries to escape by the window, but he is too late, and Elizabeth's impassioned plea for his freedom reads more like a cry of help for herself. She is far too late to help Ned, when she says "How is he to know the world isn't cruel if he's kept under restraint?"

The restraint imposed on Ned seems ironically to reflect a female rather than a male destiny, as if, by receiving the label of madness, Ned has also taken on the attributes of femininity. For Ned, Elizabeth's image of the separate waves (individual lives) being parts of one vast ocean is all too true. Ned reflects back to all the other characters the dangers of non-conformity. When he is finally shut up in the lunatic asylum he has become the scapegoat. The partial freedom of those who escape is bought at the price of his incarceration. Other characters feel guilty because of Ned. Elizabeth, for example, feels "she ought to have done something, and could have done something, to prevent it." (p220)

Apart from Ned, it is the women characters in this novel who are imprisoned by and identify themselves with houses. Two years later, in *Mrs. Ritchie* (Secker, 1933), Muir gives us a terrifying study of a woman who shuts herself off so completely that in the end she becomes her house. She physically identifies with it; its boundaries are her boundaries, and her whole identity is at risk if an unauthorised person – her own son, John Samuel – holds the key. There are incipient examples of that separateness in *Imagined Corners*. In the attempt to become Mrs. Hector Shand, Elizabeth too is under pressure to identify with her domestic space, her house. The house is introduced before Elizabeth, as an empty space waiting for her occupation, which is described in detail (p13). Later we find Hector feeling let down because she is not in her right place:

> As he fitted his latchkey in the door he was excited because he was to see his wife immediately, and his disappointment was all the more overwhelming when he found the drawing room empty. (p45)

So Elizabeth's induction into wifehood is to learn that her place is in the house, literally. There are reflections of this state of affairs in the women who surround her. Mary and Ann Watson come to blows over entry into their house. The house belongs to Ann; it has always been her territory, while Mary had to take the boy's part and work in the shop with her father. Ann, now bedridden, responds to Mary's bullying by locking her out.

Then, when Mary brings the minister along, Ann taunts her sister through the window, and throws out her treasured possessions into the dirt.

The house has become Ann's last defence; by locking herself in she gathers together the last shreds of her identity. And yet she has already told the minister what that same house meant to her when she was first immured in its domestic life:

> "...I aye had to keep the house, you see... [mother] couldna bear to see Mary flinging the things aboot, so I bude to bide, and Mary gaed to help father in the shop. And she just stayed on there. I never got a chance to do anything else. I've just been buried alive here – buried alive." (p20)

The house begins as a prison, into which the young girl does not easily fit and then becomes an identity, which appears to fit her so well she can not leave. To break its bounds is to become mad, like Ned. The imprisonment of women in the houses may seem an external, social phenomenon but we come to see it as a threat to their fundamental sense of self. A house is truly a prison when it becomes an image of the self, because then the very desire for an identity precludes escape. Mabel is another prisoner, isolated in a house. With nothing else to distract her, she becomes absorbed in the image of herself. She sees herself not as subject but object, framed in her mirror, contained in the four walls of her house. She stands at the window playing with the blind cord, thoroughly bored. Having shut herself as far in as she can, she amuses herself trying on all her dresses: "She was no longer bored... she was pleased by her own prettiness." (p82) But the room has become an extension of her, and when she goes, it retains her state of mind: "The acorn bob hung listlessly at the window of the empty drawing room".

But there is no privacy in enclosed isolation. "Thou God seest Me", the text which is to become the horrific motto of Mrs. Ritchie's house, is already here in William Murray's study (p17). In Calderwick everyone is always seen. As Hector says, it is impossible even to walk down the High Street anonymously. For women, the only way to see themselves is through others' eyes. Elizabeth struggles with this demand, and almost succumbs. Early in her marriage she has a nightmare, in which she is in the wrong house:

> She had been dreaming that she was at home, but now the window, faintly perceptible, was in the wrong place, and she knew without seeing it that she would collide with unfamiliar furniture were she to get out of bed...The world stretched out on all sides into dark impersonal nothingness and she herself was a terrifying anonymity. "...I'm me," she thought; "me, me; here behind my eyes..." But the clue she was striving to grasp still eluded her, and if she could not seize it she would be lost forever. (p64)

She finally escapes the nightmare by remembering her maiden name.

The reading of Elizabeth's escape suggested by her sharing a name with Lizzie Shand, now Elise, implies that it is her encounter with another, liberated Elizabeth that offers her escape from prison. Certainly Elizabeth herself is prepared to see an alter ego in Elise: "another Elizabeth Shand! ...it gives me the queerest feeling. It's like seeing yourself in a mirror for the first time."

Freedom in the end is very unlike Elizabeth's initial conception of it. Her expectations were based on a notion of freedom through emotion, love as the basis of all. Muir's clinical examination of a relationship falsely based on sentimental excess is ruthless and unrelenting. Her moral tone looks back to George Eliot, her stern rejection of emotion rather than thought as an arbiter of morals looks ahead to Muriel Spark. She exposes sentimentality, and shows that sexuality, and nature which reflects it in a familiar pathetic fallacy, are dangerous and disruptive. Passion, like storms and blizzards, cannot be locked in or out, but must be faced. Elizabeth is living in a world of romantic assumptions that are demonstrably false. She also appears to have been reading *Wuthering Heights*, and her author is quite aware of the irony: "'the real ME,' she struck her bosom, 'is made of the same stuff as Hector'" (p.50), and later: "'You're a part of myself. I simply couldn't fall in love with anybody else.'" (p61).

Elizabeth thinks that marriage has liberated her. She fails to notice that it means an imprisoning house, and a man who looks to her to be a mother figure within that interior. She also ignores the proofs of her own and Hector's separateness, until confronted by her own isolation in sleep:

...her thoughts came back to the question of her own identity. Elizabeth Ramsay she was, but also Elizabeth Shand, and she herself, that essential self that woke from sleep, had felt lost because she had forgotten that fact. (p65)

Accepting the whole self also demands acceptance of the physical. The minister William Murray's symbolic drowning has in the end to become physical, because the physical is the aspect of existence which he has assiduously repressed. Elizabeth cannot name her physical self. She doesn't even notice when her foot touches William Murray's, although everyone else in the town is all too aware of the fact. She calls lust love, and that is the mistake that leads her into a foolish marriage in the first place. In the novel, symbolic struggles are continually being enacted on the physical level.

Elise takes Elizabeth away at the end, to a new and liberated life, we are to assume. But how much proof of that liberation so we actually have? Elise returns to Calderwick in answer to her brother John's invitation, but also because she needs to come to terms with her Scottish past. But she leaves us with the notion that a woman can never heal the divisions within herself and remain in Scotland (Sarah Murray and Mabel, it seems, are doomed because Elise cannot rescue them from Calderwick too):

Elise's own escape is ironically ambiguous. Muir makes clear that until she has returned to Calderwick it is not complete, although we are shown how she has avoided the possible roles mapped out for her. She is, in Gilbert and Gubar's terms, neither angel nor monster, neither wife nor fallen woman. And yet she is not a whole person without Elizabeth, as she points out, between the two of them they would make one whole woman. Elise has rejected Elizabeth's notions of underlying unity of being, just as she rejects Elizabeth's empathy with nature. Elizabeth Shand, in fact, is similar in many ways to Hector, as her author makes clear. Hector, like

Elise, took refuge from Calderwick in flight, and Elise herself says, on first meeting Hector, "What a curious experience it is to meet someone so like oneself." (p166)

Both Hector and Elise escape in the first place by running off with a lover, and betraying a wife. In leaving in the wake of Elise, meeting Elise's need, and still not making a life for herself, is the younger Elizabeth not re-enacting the same role again, using a second Shand as a peg on which to hang her illusions? Perhaps Sarah Murray and Mabel Shand, left behind in Calderwick, have an opportunity to achieve a female identity in Scotland, a possibility from which Elizabeth and Elise have excluded themselves. Sarah Murray leads the social life of a dogsbody, but she always has access to a world beyond the interiors of Calderwick. After all the agony is over, we still hear that "A mere fall of snow could not keep Sarah Murray indoors" (p270).

Elizabeth's redemption lies not in her apparent rescue by Elise, but in her own access to a life beyond social relationships and boundaries, which is aligned to the vibrant but ruthless life to be found in nature. At the very end we find that Elise's Europe is another Calderwick below the surface; Elise and Ilya's conversation may be more direct, more racy, than anything heard in the drawing rooms of Calderwick, but it is not in their words but in the new landscape that presents itself that Elizabeth finds an image that reflects her inner state:

> she had imagined something more lush... not this dry, bright landscape with those gnarled little trees, that looked as if they had been maimed and tortured... crippled, like herself. (p281)

The vines have been twisted and tamed, but Elizabeth has already found in her native Scotland a wilderness beyond the imprisonment off social boundaries. It is significant that Elise always finds Scotland too cold. Elizabeth Shand, on the other hand, like Shepherd's Martha and Carswell's Joanna, finds in the Scottish wilderness a unity with outer nature that opens the way for reconciliation with her own inner nature. Even in Calderwick she has access to a private, inner wholeness that can exist alongside the appearance of the domestic, social role demanded of her.

This implicit source of freedom is there throughout the novel. Calderwick is a town under siege from the elements. The town does its best to protect itself from the sea on the one hand and the moor on the other, and the wind that blows from both. Nature continually forces its way in, as far as the High Street, as far as the doorways and windows of the houses which do their best to resist the pressure from the wild world outside. When the sea forces its way in, men are drowned, and so William Murray is overwhelmed by the sea, just as Ned Murray is swept out of the social world by the tide of his own unruly consciousness.

Elizabeth herself is fully conscious of this constant struggle between untamed elements and organised society. At times of stress she takes herself to the interface between the two worlds, and rejoices in the struggle on the boundaries. Early on we find her gazing out of one world and into the other:

Mrs. Hector Shand was standing at her drawing room window gazing at the low clouds racing behind the few leafless trees of her garden. The prospect was bleak, but Elizabeth, being accustomed to unkind weather, was not depressed. She was planning to take a run on the links, for when a strong wind blew she could not help taking to her heels and following it. (p46)

After Elizabeth has lost her social role, she and Elise climb up to the moors. Elizabeth

...gradually surrendered to the impersonal peace and beauty of the scene...But neither speculation nor reverie could long outface the wind that blew upon them as cold and pure as if it came straight from the Pole. (p244)

Elizabeth knows where to find a reflection of her own inner world, but neither nature nor unconscious life are kind, and she has to seize her kind of reality in bearable doses. Nevertheless, the door is open to her, and the possibility is there.

In this survey of the four novels I have tried to show how each one uses fictional narrative to present the paradox of human experience. Each one shows an inner world of freedom and natural expression, closely allied to the wilderness of the non-human natural world, that exists within a social reality of constriction and enclosure, represented by the literal constructs of society: cupboards, rooms, houses, communities, institutions.

On one level these are novels of social realism. Three of them deal with contemporary Scotland, one presents a fictional historical world that has all the trappings of social realism within the terms of the historical novel. But fictional narrative is never a simple reflection of reality; there may be the illusion of mimesis, but reading does not stop there. It leads us on to grasp the concepts behind the appearance of actuality.

The narratives within these novels invite us as readers to construct an image of ambiguous relation to society and culture, in terms of Woolfs 'splitting off of consciousness.' I have tried to show that each, in its particular manner, indicates an unexplored world that lies within the gaps that social communication cannot cover. Each suggests obliquely that within and behind the authoritative narrative there is another kind of consciousness. When Mitchison's Meromic finally escapes through a gap in the Roman version of the world into his secret, unarticulated Gaul of the imagination, it is the storyteller who leads him:

"What are you doing?" Meromic asked, "so far from Gaul?" "It is not so far as you would think," said the storyteller.

Margaret Elphinstone

Pat Buik

Rondeau to Lake Baikal

The lake's an icy hostess: from this hill
Her glitter knifes my eyes. Not Chekhov's 'pearl',
    but steel, hiding beneath her winter gloss
    ducks that nest in ice, omul, promise
of sturgeons' eggs, transparent fish, and seal.

Some lorries cross. In war, they laid down rail
to Stalingrad – trains trundled on until
        her gases warmed, than plunged. What cracks, what hiss,
            Baikal!

I walk her stoic crust. Climatic pull
has upreared paving stones of ice, which fell
        and crazed dark window panes. I slip on glass,
        peer down the criss-cross strata, grey abyss,
and chilled, relate to her, unknowable
            Baikal.

Lulach, Macbeth's Stepson, Speaks

To be a merlin's better than a king.
Skies hold no treason. I was Gruach's son,
and much afraid. I witnessed everything.
I wanted life. They called me Simpleton.

Duncan's father had my father burned.
To be a merlin's better than a king:
such lessons as a child are quickly learned.
When much afraid, I witnessed everything.

Macbeth killed Duncan not at home, but war.
(Duncan's father had my father burned.)
I was the weak, the feather-wetting heir.
Such lessons as a child are quickly learned.

I lived in mountains, flying peregrines.
Macbeth killed Duncan not at home, but war,
then ruled, crusaded, crushed rebellions,
for I was weak, the feather-wetting heir.

When Malcolm murdered peace round Aberdeen,
I lived in mountains, flying peregrines,
and rued the death of him who wore my crown,
had ruled, crusaded, crushed rebellions.

In Moray, they proclaimed me King of Scots,
when Malcolm murdered peace round Aberdeen
and slew Macbeth. Unhooded were their plots.
I rued the death of him who wore my crown.

The jesses dangled from my destiny.
In Moray, they proclaimed me King of Scots.
I was their partridge, knew that I would die
like slain Macbeth. Unhooded were their plots.

I was their partridge, knew that I would die,
for, much afraid, I witnessed everything.
My eyes were keen. I loved this earth and sky.
To be a merlin's better than a king.

Watching Tomorrow's World on TV

I've missed the information how to move
ten tons of scaffolding with just one man,
and how cervical cancer can be screened
a more efficient way, but Judith Hann
is now switched on in thigh boots in a sewer,
testing fluid heights with cabbage dye –
but no! it's gone! leapt like a startled frog –
we're looking at our ozone layer supply,
which has a hole that deepens every year.
A planet like a pink blancmange is on,
a rosy haze, which must be meaningful,
and leading to some kind of Rubicon.
Now sympathies are roused by shivering mice,
who die, afflicted by defective genes,
so new ones are the order of the day,
with scientists supplying them. How humans
benefit I'm not quite sure, but look!
we're back to drains. Can alligators dwell
in sewers? Yes, as Mr Tanner proves,
making his alligator mating call
beneath New York, he captures one, and lets
it go into a nearby river. Someone
will be surprised. We're now in Scotland, where
anthrax was experimental fun,
except for sheep. It's taken forty years
for Porton Down to get the island clean.
And finally they spray, on acid squares,
a 'chequered' paint. How useful for latrines

The Western woman wears a Chadri

The Afghan women wear them in the street,
floating cotton tents, steely-blue or black,
with flash of lace-filled pantaloons, and feet
in gum-shoes sliced from tyres. The pleated sack
reminds her of a Templar, fighting Turk,
made vulnerable, comic, by his casque,
but here the faces, hilled and hollowed, lurk,
their eyes corralled behind a gauzy mask.

When in Herat, she tries a chadri on,
is unprepared for panic creeping in
beneath the musty folds, the woman gone,
become a nyctophobic child. Her skin
protests. She asks why womanhood's a sin
for daily punishment, cloth Holloway,
protecting men from their indiscipline,
keeping those lovers, wind and sun, at bay?

Before Visiting a Dying Friend

Slit my scarf, thorn,
I'll clothe you in its rags – though
propitiation's too late.

(She must have cut a lone thorn:
occupied, it screamed and bled.
Little people take revenge.)

The muddy lane's thick with spattered blood –
ruby haws –
Diogenes' lantern dropped.

Over hedges swirl
devil's guts in wedding veils,
and bramble wreaths – unplaited – shine.

A travelling man was here:
ashes are warm.
He's left his tortured jacket in the ditch.

Irish fairies were reputed to live in or under lone thorns; if you disturbed
   them, you'd become ill or die.
Devil's guts is a Dorset name for old man's beard.
Bramble wreaths were plaited over graves to keep the dead from walking.

Irene Evans

For the anonymous made famous by the Magnum Studios Photographers

Here's a whore in Essen, 1947.
Tight-eyed, bold, brave and sad.
Masculine. Feminine. Shades of both.

There's a suspect in a police car.
New York, 1978. Rear view.
Arms crossed behind his back.
Handcuffed. The veins stand out
conveying his worried blood.

Over there on East Side 100th Street
a Mother and Child.
No visible possessions
but their own dark-skinned bodies.
Tender. Calm.

And that girl. Europe 1948.
Standing beside her drawing of tangled wire.
Barbed. Angry-eyed. All
unforgettable.
Lending themselves
to the lens.

Ruaridh

Your fine hands are gentle with the ewes
at lambing. Careful
with the blade at shearing.
Fine and strong would I spin
their wool for you. At my door
in the sunlight of summer.
In winter by the firelight of the hearth.
Deep, fast and full
would be the colours of the cloth
I would weave for you.
Soft to touch.

Would that your life were not
threaded elsewhere.
Woven already with others.
I can spin for you only these words.
From my heart.

Charles Rennie Mackintosh
London 1928

Life's been a school of art far harder
than the one I left behind in Glasgow.
That was built to my own design.
                              And yet,
since then we've wandered well together,
Margaret. You and I. On nothing but
ourselves.
                    Walberswick. Chelsea. France.
Hampstead. (Another Willow Road.) To die.
You took our lodging here. By the willow
in the garden. Silent now. Your hand. Mine.
Cancer has stolen my tongue. Beauty
lies in the bones of things. The eye
survives.

For a Change

No more periods. Full stop. Dried out
from what has been essential
to my sense of self since I was twelve.
This reverse
adolescence takes me by surprise.
My body has started to panic. Turns hot
cold. Not in dangerous situations.
Stranger. At my own table. Sink. Fireside.
Sleepless, in my bed.

I find myself drawn
to mirrors. Try on
grey hair and glasses. New lines.
Tell myself
they might suit me quite well now
my tide is cut off from her moon.
Still waters. Old girl.

Closet

Listen. Whispering. From the wardrobe.
I think it is my empty clothes
gossiping among themselves. Telling
how I felt
the last time they wore me.

Dave Morgan's Funeral

At the graveside some one says
a few words about you
who loved and lived by them.
Sealed in print. Spilling out
into argument. Live.

Now we hold for a minute
your silence. Then return.
It to you. Us to our lives.
Walking back we begin
gently. Talking again.

In touch

I loved to feel
your skin on mine.
Unguarded. Unforeseen.
At the frontier of ourselves
we used to meet.

That day

coming home from the park with our children,
one in the pushchair, one holding on and
you walking apart at a rope's length
as if to show you'd been captured and
should not be here but with some one some
where else.
            Once dearest now you are my saddest
image. The gypsy with the dancing bear.
Each at the end of the other's tether.
Am I my husband's keeper?
                        Hard to know.
Yet by the time we reach the house
My fingers have spoken. Unclenched. Let
go.

Women and Love
some thoughts on women's love poetry

Margery Palmer McCulloch

She walks in beauty, like the night
of cloudless climes and starry skies…

O my luve is like a red, red rose
That's newly sprung in June:
O my luve is like the melodie
That's sweetly play'd in tune…

Although different formally and in tone, what these poems by Byron and Burns have in common is that in each, woman, the loved one, is presented as an object, not as an individual self. The object of Byron's love would appear to be unreachable, unattainable, and this is confirmed by the closing lines which tell of "a heart whose love is innocent" and "days in goodness spent" – a lifestyle much at odds with that of the poem's author. Yet, although we have these generalised comments about her goodness and her dark, night-like beauty, the woman herself is absent from the text. She does not speak; there is no sense of communication or interaction between admirer and admired. The reader is encouraged to wonder from afar, as if viewing an idealised but lifeless portrait in a silver frame.

Burns poem is more passionate and intimate, with declarations of everlasting love, but the warm, emotional tone is deceptive, achieved through the vernacular "my bonnie lass" and the repeated "my dear, "my luve". There is no doubt about the impassioned role given to the speaker, but here too the woman is objectified and nullified. No less than in the Byron we are led by the imagery away from a living woman to the beauty of a summer rose, to a melody well played. The woman is projected on to natural elements so that she becomes 'other'. The very extravagance of the protestations – "Till a' the seas gang dry … and the rocks melt wi' the sun"; "ten thousand miles" – undermines the possibility of genuine interaction and sustains the rhetoric of self-reflexion. Thinking about the changing position of women throughout this century, I began to wonder about love poetry in general: whether it is still possible to write the kind of traditional male love poem found in anthologies; about the kind of love poems previously written and being written now by women themselves.

A leafing-through some contemporary collections suggests that the male love poem, although suffering a decline, is still self-reflexive, with the woman/love object still projected away from its centre as silent beauty or source of male pleasure, a creation of the male poet who is in the poem's real subject. Tom Leonard in 'Words, for E' (we notice that she has no name), finds that "your words are hands, stroking me, stroking the sky … It's marvellous. I'm king". Or, "You are beautiful, sometimes. Now./ I feel for words for you… I like to think of you as giving/ Structure". Giles Gordon sees a former love "stepping, streaming along the pavement,/ head tossed high". Then, "she saw me,/ swooped head to breast,/ rushed past". At this sight, the girl with the spring in her step becomes a drooping, frightened bird; she attempts to make herself invisible and the role positions are kept secure. Alexander Scott's "Continent o' Venus" is a fine poem. Yet here too, in spite of the warmth and intimacy of its Scots vernacular, woman and the love between man and woman are presented from the male perspective only. Woman as depicted is made for man's pleasure: "she's at aince thon Tir-nan-og I've dreamed ... she's the uncharted sea whaur I maun fare/ To find anither undiscovered land,/ To find it fremd, and yet to find it dear,/ To seek it aye, and aye be bydan there". This is a moving love poem which communicates a sense of deep, genuine emotion as opposed to the rhetoric of Byron and Burns; yet, it also consents to woman's absence from the poem in her own selfhood. The relationship is depicted without her voice being heard.

What, then, of love poems by women? The editor of *The Virago Book of Love Poetry*, Wendy Mulford, comments that "traditionally love poetry has been written by men", and asks: "Are love poems by women notably different from those written by men?" She finds that women do not appear "to exploit the love-object as muse" and that while "there is little veneration in these poems [there is] markedly more rage, and sometimes sheer bad temper. Quite a lot of these poems determinedly and ruthlessly cut the Don Juans down to size. They also celebrate the joys of independence, of celibacy, of women and sisterhood." This Virago selection is international and centuries-wide, but many of the qualities isolated by its editor appear in the anthologies of Scottish poetry I have been looking at. There are, however, few Scottish poems which exhibit rage or "sheer bad temper", and I have found nothing to compare with this anonymous 'Lament for a Husband' from the Buin Tribe!

> O my hornbill husband, you have a bad smell,
> and when Kaaeko comes and smells you
> he will take you to Panirai, and your spirit
> will enter a pig.

In women's love poetry, the dominant tendency is for the definition of love to be extended away from a concentration on the praise or blame of a love-object towards contextualisation and interactive experience.

This wider concept of love can be clearly seen in Catherine Kerrigan's *Anthology of Scottish Women Poets* which ranges in time from the medieval to the contemporary world. While Virago's editor found that "good erotic poems are rare", in Kerrigan's anthology poems with the strongest erotic element come from the Gaelic tradition, as in the following translation by Meg Bateman of Isabel, Countess of Argyll's sixteenth-century poem 'There's a young man in pursuit of me':

> There's a young man in pursuit of me,
> Oh King of Kings, may he have success!
> Would he were stretched out by my side
> with his body pressing against my breast!

The passion here is not rhetorical but set in a context of consequence and cultural separation. The girl wishes to be with her lover for ever, yet there is a hint of possible pregnancy and an accompanying awareness that this, no less than distance and social separation, may change their relationship:

> If everything were as I would wish,
> no distance would ever cause us separation,
> though that is all too little to say
> with him not yet knowing the situation.

> But it isn't easy if his ship doesn't come,
> for the two of us it's a wretched matter:
> he is East and I am West,
> so what we desire can never again happen.

This preoccupation with reality is a recurring element in the anthology. The ballads may feature enigmatic, elliptical narrative and supernatural – even, as in 'The Twa Sisters' surrealistic – resonances, yet their essential tales are of everyday passions and their consequences: jealousy, death in childbirth, separation by betrayal and unequal birth. If, as Kerrigan says, the ballads were originally written by women as well as preserved and orally transmitted by them, then their contents are witness to what the word 'love' really meant for women in a patriarchal society without female representation, financial independence, status and access to contraception. One of the most chilling 'love' poems is 'Fair Mary of Wallington', where the female speaker has watched her five sisters courted for love and dead in childbirth, until only she and Maisry are left: "There is nane but you and I, Maisry,/ And we'll go maidens mild." Maisry's turn for courting comes, however, and in no time at all "the gaggs they were in Maisry's mouth,/ And the sharp sheers in her side." Nor is there solidarity between generations. Whether out of a fatalism born of helplessness, or out of a perverted determination that her remaining daughter will risk and endure the fate she and her other daughters have had to endure, the mother does not support the girl's fearful determination to remain single:

> O hold your tongue, my ae daughter
> Let a' your folly be,
> For ye shall be married ere this day week
> Tho the same death you should die.

This rejection of the rhetoric of love and concern with its realities is to be found throughout Kerrigan's collection, although in the Victorian and post-Victorian period one is more aware of the pressures of religion and the Victorian notion of woman as 'angel in the house'. This internalising by women writers of the dominant ideology about their position in society and the moral virtues of which they were supposed to be guardians, is different in its consequences from the stark dramatisation of the social situation of women found in the earlier poetry, and is perhaps the reason for the fewer poems of quality in this Victorian section. Its effects are present still in early twentieth-century writers such as Violet Jacob and Marion Angus, who, despite the vigorous quality of their Scots language and imagery, are hampered by unwillingness to depart publicly from woman's traditional role in poetry as love-object, the silent 'other'. In 'Tam i' the Kirk', Violet Jacob adopts a male persona and tells the story of the love between Tam and his Jean from Tam's perspective. The Kirk and congregation are present, as are the pu'd reid rose and the lad's passionate memories of what "my lassie gied him", but Jean herself is absent and has no voice to tell her side of the story. The girl speaker in Marion Angus's 'Mary's Song' uses imagery from nature and the sacraments to tell of her unrequited love and her willingness to sacrifice herself to her beloved despite her awareness that "he be nae mine, as I am his".

A more recognisably modern attitude in early twentieth-century poetry is to be found in the love poetry of Muriel Stuart, an English writer of Scottish ancestry who, for some still-undiscovered reason, was claimed by MacDiarmid as a leader in his 'Scottish Renaissance' movement. Context, overt or implied, is a hallmark of Stuart's poetry. 'In the Orchard' is a dramatic exchange between two young lovers, a girl who unwisely has taken her lover's protestations too seriously, and a young man for whom love is play. In a poem which demands reading aloud, it is the silences which speak to us – the pauses, hesitations, the unsaid. Although nothing is stated explicitly, we have no doubt that this girl came to tell her lover of her pregnancy, but, like her sisters in countless ballads and poems of all time, his manner communicated to her before a word was spoken that she had been mistaken and that there was no future for them together. Stuart is unusual also in that she is able to dramatise the sexual dilemma 'in the round'. Despite her feminist approach, it is never a one-sided affair. Thus, in 'The Father', it is the woman who exploits her biological power in a bitter domestic quarrel, taunting her husband/partner with the challenge: "'*Your* child?' you said. '*Your* child?'..." And if in 'The Father', the love which produced the child has turned to hatred, then in 'Mrs Effingham's Swan Song' it is age which devastates. The speaker here has willingly spent her youth as love object, has disguised oncoming age and taken new young lovers until she can no longer play the love game. Alone, ignored, abandoned among the elderly and distraught at her physical *un*loveliness, she for the first time questions her past lifestyle and the social system which encouraged her and others to behave as she has behaved.

As with Catherine Carswell in fiction, Muriel Stuart's voice anticipated the mature questioning of accepted ideology in regard to women's place and experience that we find in contemporary women's poetry, and especially in the poetry from the 1970s onwards. Liz Lochhead has been a seminal influence in this movement, in many ways a direct heiress to Muriel Stuart, since she combines the same elements of challenge, vulnerability and awareness of that vulnerability in her work. These were among the most striking qualities of Lochhead's first collection, *Memo for Spring* (1972). She has said of that early work that her "country was womankind", and her women speakers are recognisably of that 1960s/70s world: educated, independent, freed by contraception to have sexual liaisons; free, apparently, to determine the direction of their lives. Yet Lochhead's insight – and it was an insight which struck a chord with her female readers – was that these young women were not truly free. In a society still structured for and dominated by men, they had in the end to conform to male mores and rules. In 'The Box Room', the girl who comes to visit in order to "state my permanence", recognises the impermanence of the relationship as she lies among previous discarded hobbies and love-objects in a bed similarly occupied by previous female companions. In 'The Choosing', the student speaker, laden with books, sees on the bus her old schoolfriend and rival for top place in class, now heavily pregnant and involved with the young man accompanying her. Unlike the speaker, this girl's family could not or would not encourage her to go to university where her talents so clearly pointed. The speaker ponders on choice and value and wonders "when the choices got made/ we don't remember making." And it is not only social ideology which determines the course of Lochhead's girls' lives. The subtext is biological – the girls themselves are often driven by forces they do not fully comprehend towards mating and reproduction just as their earlier 'less free' sisters had been. 'Getting Back', 'Song for Coming Home', 'Morning After', 'Inventory', tell of a repeated surge towards relationships which turn out to be ephemeral, and it is usually the man who lays down the parameters of the relationship and "flicks too casually through the pages". In 'Poem for my Sister', the speaker watches her little sister play grown-ups in her own high-heeled shoes and wishes she could somehow stay "sure-footed, sensibly shod" within the bounds of her childhood competence, not strain towards her adult sister's loss of balance. What makes this poetry so vital is its element of knowingness in the midst of vulnerability. Although waylaid by biology and misled by external forces, these girls are not helpless victims. There is irony and wit in their examination of their misfortunes. We sense this is a generation in transition who have been dealt a better hand of cards than their predecessors.

Lochhead has described the beheading of Mary Queen of Scots as a metaphor for the suppression of the feminine principle by the imposition of Calvinism on Scottish society and culture and, in specific relation to our purposes here, on Scottish literature. The decades since World War II have seen an amazing resurgence of that feminine principle within and outwith Scotland with the recovery of 'lost' women writers of the past and a consequent revaluation of women's writing and of the literary canon generally. Lochhead herself has extended the country of womankind into economic, social, historical and political areas, dramatising sexual relationships and the forces that shape them with wit, humour and satire. *Mary Queen of Scots Got Her Head Chopped Off* deconstructs the myths of Scottish history, religion and gender, recreating a relevance to contemporary life. The new perspectives, subject-matter and forms of expression brought by women into a previously male-dominated area are especially noticeable in the domain of the traditional love poem, which women have transformed to accommodate in an overt way the female voice which was either silenced or communicated elliptically and within constrained parameters as in the poetry of the ballads.

The focus on interactive relationships and the quality of inclusion which I believe characteristic of women's love poetry generally, are to be seen in Scottish contemporary women poets who explore identity and selfhood, friendship, family relationships and non-sexual love as well as the more conventional sexual subject-matter. Meg Bateman's 'Picture of my Mother' brings together images of nature and the loved one – a characteristic of Scottish traditional love poetry. Yet, instead of the loved one being distanced by projection into the natural environment as in Burns' 'Red Rose' poem, Bateman brings the elements together so that the individuality of the mother and the love between mother and daughter are foregrounded, while alongside this the instinctive care of animal for its young and human joy in the natural world. In 'You called me poet' from the anthology *Fresh Oceans*, Margaret Elphinstone's speaker recognises belatedly that true love is not necessarily sexual and between man and woman, but can involve the gift of recognised identity bestowed by one woman artist on another: "You called me a poet/ and took me in your arms, laughing/ with the terror of it... You kissed me – you –/ but no man ever said I was a poet". In another variation of the love-poem theme, Sue Gutteridge in the Kerrigan anthology depicts the joy of female friendship, yet the distrust of society to such 'out of character' relationships, even more than to extra-marital heterosexual liaisons:

> For the most par it was a married female relationship
> Conducted Monday to Friday, nine to five.
> No all nighters.
> No no-holds-barred drunken confidences.
> No weekends.
> Married female friendship –
> An art form, freed of constrictions
> Which are the stuff of it.
> Fitted in the spaces between the children.

Yet, for all its difficulties, this was a relationship "rich with significance./ Mutual, pleasurable self-analysis when you said, 'I like the shape of our friendship'" – a relationship which reminds one of the comment in Lochhead's *Mary Queen of Scots* that the basis for Mary's love and friendship with Riccio was "because he is the only man wha has ever touched her *withoot* he wants tae tummle her."

Virginia Woolf and critics such as Cora Kaplan in our own time have drawn attention to the problems posed for women by the attempt to enter into poetry. Poetry (apart from folk poetry) has traditionally been a high-art form and lyric poetry has been associated particularly with the male voice. As women have traditionally played a private role within society, with the public speaking voice given to men, how can they then find a public poetic form for the subject-matter which preoccupies them and inspires or drives them to write? This was an even more pressing problem in previous centuries when girls were largely excluded from higher education and classical and literary education. Little wonder that Emily Dickinson complained of being "shut up in prose" or that her poetry was ridiculed for its idiosyncratic nature and departure from traditional forms. In the post-1945 period, on the other hand, Sylvia Plath demonstrated that she could use classical imagery and mythical registers as well as any male poet, although this imagery was used to communicate a subject-matter which was peculiarly female and deeply disturbing. In the contemporary world where the education of boys and girls is similarly patterned (at least in theory) and where the register of poetry itself has become increasingly informal, it is perhaps subject-matter rather than form which offers the greater challenge to the acceptance of women poets. In reviews of the anthology *Fresh Oceans*, for example, both Robin Bell and Iain Crichton Smith singled out a 'sameness' in subject-matter. For Bell this was the negative effect of an unnecessarily gendered anthology. For Crichton Smith the gender grouping was justified by is concentration on "women's matters: children, birth, marriage, anorexia, care for the old, rape (in a classical setting)" etc. Yet these aspects of life concern us all, male or female, and have been long present in dramatic and epic poetry, though often disguised as a result of imagistic language, elaborate verse-forms or mythical metaphor. The difference may be that the plainer language and forms used by today's women poets throw subject-matter into higher relief, thus making its everyday applicability more apparent.

Nevertheless, a writer such as Naomi Mitchison demonstrates that 'women's matters' topics need be no barrier to epic-scale poetry. In 'Clemency Ealasaid', the poem prefaced to her 1947 novel *The Bull Calves*, the baby clothes in the drawer and empty cot by the bedside, the breasts painful and running with milk, provide the starting-point for a movement into the grief of all bereaved mothers and into the grief and devastation of a Europe at war. The disappointed love of mother for dead baby is turned into a love and grieving for all humanity.

This capacity to 'write woman', to use the material of women's everyday lives in a vital, meaningful way is one of the attributes I find so refreshing about poetry written by women. This will keep the love poem alive in an age when it is no longer possible to write convincingly about a relationship from a position in which one member of that relationship is presented as object only, silent and excluded from account. In *Tradition and the Individual Talent*, TS Eliot remarked that each new work of art changes the way we perceive the work of the past and necessitates an alteration of the existing order. Eliot did not, I think, envisage his words being directed towards a new wave of innovative women writers. Yet they are no less applicable to the recovery and development of women's writing than they were to the innovative male modernist work of the early twentieth century which was his primary concern. Byron's comment, patronising but unfortunately often only too true, that "man's love is of man's life a thing apart,/ 'Tis woman's whole existence" is no longer apposite in the negative connotation intended. Although there is still a long way to go – and women's poetry provides much evidence for that also – women's horizons and opportunities are continually expanding. The transformation women writers have effected in the traditional, hegemonic love poem provides some of the best evidence there is for a new-found selfhood and changing sexual relationships.

Margery Palmer McCulloch

She & He In Mid-Life Crisis

Eva Fleg Lambert

"You keep the goldfish in a DRAWER?" he asked, eyes bulging in disbelief. "The top drawer of your DESK?"

She nodded. "Top *left*-hand drawer", she amended, wanting him to understand, perfectly.

She opened the drawer to show him, but he had turned away from her and was stalking out of the room in long angry strides. "Look!" she called, wanting him to see, wanting him, wanting… "Please", she added in a voice gone smaller, tighter. But he refused to turn towards her, reaching the door in a mighty stride more like a leap, so anxious was he to get away. He slammed the door behind him with such force that the goldfish, alarmed perhaps, jumped out of the drawer and landed on the carpet by her feet.

The carpet was a 19th century Chinese rug with a central medallion of golds, rusts and pale blue. The goldfish had landed on a pale blue circle and was flopping in its centre, as if desperately trying to get out of the circle, out of the water. She thought of dolphins, hadn't they, so a story goes, crawled out of the sea and then, at disgust at what was happening on the earth, disappeared back into the sea? Something like that. Doesn't matter. She prodded the goldfish with her toe. She was not wearing shoes and the nail varnish, a dark red of almost maroon depth, complemented the gold of the fish. She liked the colour combination and nudged her toe closer. The fish gave one flop, away from her toe, out of the blue circle and onto a curlicue of leaf in a russet red where it lay, as if waiting to be born. Like the baby under the cabbage leaf she almost thought except her attention was still on her toe. She had moved it close to the fish again but now the nail varnish clashed disturbingly with the goldfish, and with the russet leaf also. She sat down at her desk unaware of the water dripping from the still open desk drawer, or the cat, Mingle, tail held high in a curve of question, walking soft-padded with dainty measured movements towards her. Somewhere a telephone gave three short rings. Somewhere a murmur of voices. Somewhere a light clicked on inside her head as Mingle jumped, purring, onto her lap. Absently she stroked him as he settled between her thighs and the light searched an image: cat, fish, toe…

Luckily Mingle, blind in one eye, his left one, had not noticed the fish still lying on the russet leaf, or he would have pounced and eaten it. Fish was a favourite. With more deftness than anyone would have given her credit for, she bent, picked up the fish and replaced it in the drawer, all in one graceful motion. The cat never even blinked its good eye, and she sighed. The light in her head had gone out.

It was autumn, hence the maroon nail varnish. For winter she changed to a bright cherry red, to give herself a lift. Summer meant a pearly silvery pink to go with the tan she always hoped she'd get but never did, and spring was a dusty pink, a girlish colour unsuited for her now middling years perhaps, but she still believed that a renewal would come.

Married twenty-two years, the two children children no longer but living independent lives, and she still believed in renewal. She raised her eyebrows at her own, stupidity? stamina? naïvité? Spirit perhaps, yes, that's what she would like to believe, spirit.

But now she was bored. When she had been little and complained of boredom, her mother would recite in a singsong, *Boredom bumboredom tee-alika toredom, tee-legged tow-legged bow-legged boredom,* and she would laugh. But she'd still be bored.

"You need an interest, something outside of the home", he had said to her last week. She had thought about that and yes, it was true, she needed an interest, something beyond romantic novels, her three afternoons at the Save the Children charity shop and the odd night out with her mate Susan, whom *he* disapproved of. Mightily. Susan was vulgar he had said.

Was vulgarity another word for spirit she thought suddenly? She sat up straight, causing Mingle to spread his claws and arch his back. What she wanted was a good fuck. Mingle settled back between her thighs. A night out with Susan. Into a pub and pick up a man and, yes, a good fuck. Like a dose of bicarb or something. *Fuck bumbuck tee allika tuck, tee-legged toe-legged bow-legged fuck.* He never used words like that. Nor had she until recently. What had brought about the change?

"It's the menopause", he had said, ruckling his forehead in concern for her. "Have you considered hormone treatment?" he asked, seriously, terribly seriously and solicitously so that she had answered in the same manner, no, she had not considered hormone treatment, but her voice suggested she now might.

Like hell she would.

But she remained quiet, demure almost. Withdrawn really while he fussed with his model of the QE2 made entirely of Swan Vestas. She watched him deftly cut off the matchheads with his red plastic-handled Happy Hobby Knife which she had given him last Christmas. He had never asked her whether she had been to the doctor.

The doorbell rang. Footsteps, his, to the front door which opened quietly, closed quietly and whoever had come talked quietly. A soft murmuring was all she heard. She was tempted to go to the door and open it to see who had come but no, it would be someone for him, of no interest to her. More murmurings, the front door opening and closing again, her curiosity tweaked but not enough to go to the door, to call out to him, to do anything but to sit, stroking the cat, remembering that renewal was possible. Worms cut in half become two worms, a lizard which has its tail cut off grows another one. There were lessons in nature.

She got up abruptly, spilling Mingle from her lap, and walked to the window. It was a grey nondescript day; there was nothing in that suburban landscape that called her attention, nothing on which to focus, nothing on which to...

The door opened behind her and she heard his steps, not determined now but cautious, as if visiting a patient in a hospital. She not turned but watched his reflection in the window as he came towards her. "That was

Dr Bliss." With a name like that he should be doling out happy pills she thought. But no such luck. An old-fashioned doctor with his shirt collar always buttoned tight so that a small but unsightly wedge of fat spilled over the collar, he lectured abstinence, control and laxatives. In that order. Hormone treatment for him would have meant something to do with planting out cuttings of his begonias. He won a prize for them last year. But why had he called?

"*Why* do you keep the gold fish in your desk?" His voice was calm, too calm. "Why? I want to know." She smiled at his reflection and he leaned towards her, as if wanting to catch every nuance of every word she would say. But she remained silent. "Shall I go to the drawer and see the fish, shall I?" He was talking to her as if she was a child, an idiot in fact.

So that was it. He thought she had gone barmy. Had called the good doctor who had advised controlled calm. "Yes, that's what I'll do", he wittered on, "I'll go and see the fish." He walked over to the desk, and, looking over his shoulder towards her back, asked, "Shall I, dear?" She gave a little snort, of derision really but he accepted it as a positive answer and opened the drawer.

But his action was clumsy and the drawer shot open, spilling the fish out. Mingle's good eye saw the fish and pounced.

"That's why I kept the goldfish in my drawer", she said, turning to him. "To protect him from the cat." She walked out.

Yes, a good fuck was what she wanted but, that failing, a drink with Susan.

   Eva Fleg Lambert

Tash '93

Maude Devine

Ukiyo-e

She is on parade in her kimono
bright as a peacock light as a fan
lady of the night of ancient Edo
He is by the stream. Moon beams on the fisherman
Hokusai peace perfect as a surimono
craft and craftsman of the courtesan.

Fragile is the beauty of his courtesan
translucent as porcelain in her kimono
Foxfire she appears to tempt the fisherman
who dreams beyond the walls of Edo
When he wakes she is gone his geisha with fan
and he smiles at the moon alone in his surimono.

As a dove in snow she is lost in the surimono
paper white face of his courtesan
body shell locked in her kimono
amuse-gueule oyster prised by the fisherman
from her ocean bed to display in Edo
shut-open-shut, Lady Fan.

She may pass as a breeze to fan
her samurai, compose haiku for his surimono
be night rain, morning dew, his courtesan.
Shutters clack. The Spring breeze ruffles her kimono
where the wild geesefly and whispers to the fisherman
through the rushes by the stream that flows from Edo.

As the geese fly North, in the gardens of Edo
trees blossom like the cherry orchard painted on her fan.
She folds spring away, puts on her kimono
discarded in the night as courtesan
for love ritual as sake or the surimono
of happiness, Hokusai's fisherman

She sees a golden carp in the net of the fisherman
grow dim, cold grey. Sun has set in Edo
and the tears which fall being her fan
turn to quicksilver minnows in the stream of the surimono.
On the black heron rock the courtesan
hears an ocean break soft as her kimono.

Butterfly lady in your kimono caught by the fisherman
the women of the fan are long gone as love and Edo.
The beauty of your surimono lives on, courtesan.

Ukiyo-e – A term in Japanese art for picture of the transitory world
Hokusai – One of the Ukiyo-e artists
Surimono – A small print of high of high quality produced for special occasions
Amuse-gueule – Appetiser

Anne Scott

Dwelling Place

No, he said. They will not translate.

The old croft where his Gaelic father sang
And mother danced
Had fallen.
Rain seeped and soaked and pooled
The boyhood hollow where he slept
With limedust on his head.

No, he said. They will not pull it down.

They built around, confined it in another stone
Until his windows darkened
In a rim of ancient house
Humble and outfaced.

Suddenly we heard
The aftersilences of women walled.

He made no sign,
But every day,
Intent upon the real construction
Of his life,
Defied the burial of his verse by eager men

For they would tongue his words,
Groove them
With a different tool,
Alter the beam and lintel
Of his line
And render it
Untrue...

Offer a daytime for a sunlit noon.

No, he said. They will not translate.

This wintertime
His house is watertight. No shift of stone
Allows a drift of night
Or comma of the starlight in.

His words are safe:
And broken in their surface
Perfectly.

Ann D Gwilt

Mourning

The old man's black hat
was swathed in white
beard as pale to his black coat, brown face.
He stood as still as a Bach pause
hands hidden in a back clasp.
He was a dark tree
among green and white birches,
a Friday man in the Sunday mosque
where bare-armed, fair-haired women
albumed him with outside eyes.
He, upright, was unseeing
in the strange place which was his home.

Uygur Girl and the Slip

She took a chance, that pretty Uygur girl,
her embroidered cap sedate over black hair,
laughing foreignly with other chambermaids,
smiling as if she knew me – and so she did –
when she saw my black underskirt –
elastic waist, slinky length, lacy edge –
hanging up to dry.
Without a word, eyes worldly sure,
stroking its silkiness with unashamed longing,
she motioned me to give it to her.
How could I refuse?

An arrangement of wild flowers –
daisy, speedwell, poppy,
in my bedroom
colour and pattern of her Uygur cap
reminds me of that missing
wicked black half slip.

Symbol

Roofs curved in smile
temple, palace and pagoda
sunrise red, gray,
aristocratic yellow
presented orientally.

But there, at the corners,
figures perch the slant,
beasts on guard,
and at the edge
the named traitor
accused wrong doer
banished
crouched on a precipice
enduring his sentence.

UNIVERSITY OF STRATHCLYDE
Faculty of Education, Jordanhill Campus

MASTER OF SCIENCE DEGREE AND
POST GRADUATE DIPLOMA
EQUALITY AND DISCRIMINATION.
Part -time and Full-time

An innovative study and developmental programme for those individuals and organisations wishing to further their understanding, knowledge and skills in this field. Sponsorship for individual employees is now offered by several Scottish Local Authorities.

The one year (part or full-time) Post Graduate Diploma provides a detailed consideration and analysis of contemporary responses to discrimination within a series of study Units . These are; Ideology and Exploitation, Research, Historical and Contemporary Patterns of Resistance to Oppression, Legal Intervention, and Policy and Provision. The opportunity exists to specialise in any single area of discrimination within these themes and apply this to practical/work situations.

Successful completion of the Diploma gives access to the MSc (one or two year routes, full or part-time) though suitable candidates may enter MSc directly (full or part-time).

Features are; flexibility of access to course, distance learning, highly qualified staff actively working in the field and progression to M.Phil. M.Lit. and Ph.D .

For further details and application forms for course comencing mid - October 1994 ring, Andrew Johnson; 041 950 3357 or Catherine McCord 950 3209. Places are limited, early application advised.

MLitt in Women's Studies

Postgraduate taught course

full-time (one year) or part-time (two years)

UNIVERSITY OF STRATHCLYDE

COURSE CONTENT: CORE COURSES IN FEMINIST THEORY, FEMINIST METHODS AND WOMEN IN SCOTLAND PLUS ONE COURSE FROM A RANGE OF OPTIONS AND A DISSERTATION

Entry requirement: a good honours degree (or equivalent) in any subject

For further details and application forms contact:

Stevi Jackson, Co-ordinator MLitt in Women's Studies, Department of Government, University of Strathclyde, McCance Building, 16 Richmond Street, Glasgow G1 1XQ Telephone: 041 552 4400 extension 2976 or 2734

Cultural Revolution

Val Warner

I

Drawn in the painting, you couldn't not flinch off that Janus eye, full-face in a caved-in profile. Lengthening via twigs and rain and meshing the picture like external nerves or the global village's skin of wires, the hair trailed into stick figures, sometimes holding hands – Lowryesque more than Dufyesque – round the border. Round the neck, a plaid like a football scarf skirled fading into blue hills, with mist that truly wreathed. At first, the eye didn't pick up the gallows that saltired the canvas, while in each corner nestled the couthy 'national symbol', thistle, rose et al among those stick people on the margin. Perspective had been tweaked to make the thistle's quarter central for the hill's execution. For all some weird insouciance beyond even stylised dying – a touch of Jessie Matthews, "over my shoulder goes *one* care." It could have been Caledonia crucified.

II

"Dead to the world, are we?"

We were in floods. Away on the hill, with a cause that – reprobate that he was – he'd never espoused, he heard the question through a *piobaireachd*.

"Maggie's really put the boot in, Jim."

All he wanted now was for his eyes like flies to crawl on over that impasto-hewn face of HUNG, DRAWN AND QUARTERED. But you couldn't not hear a name if it was – once – the only name. But he'd told nobody about Margie. Except Keir. Keir as gossip? Good old Dobbin as gossip? The dumpy little man spun round, in a mist of medium dry sherry, unsipped as he'd sucked in pigment instead.

"Margie?" Two croaks for two syllables.

"Maggie. Mrs T. I was saying, she's really done for you. I'm so sorry."

So it was only the universal vandal, not the personal one.

"All the best for the future, Jim."

Jim couldn't put a name to the face, who'd not the stomach to look long in the face of misfortune. In courtesy, he pressured his lips into the shape called smile. And slid his eyes up the barbed-wire stalk of the virile thistle ramming a pinkest dog-rose in THE FLOWERS OF THE FIELD. Or, as it might have been, CALEDONIA RESURGENS? BLACK GOLD showed oil platforms against a golden sunset like a Tay Bridge scenic view postcard, with their struts rooting down into the lower half of the canvas as mega-meaningless characters on white: the handwriting on the postcard verso, complete with address and a £1 note stuck on as stamp. Perhaps he wasn't a good enough Scot to see how the painter was extrapolating from Scotland to Apartheid (if she was? – he was aware of missing dimensions if excited enough to fall over what he had).

He was at least a good enough human being to see if not blanch at RED ROSE, WHITE NUKE, as his eyes crawled after the white missile lodged like an insect in a Richard Dadd in the musky heart or cunt of a red rose rampant over the upper canvas, above a horizon of dunes of petals by the trillion, sometimes freakishly blown into playing cards' symbols: hearts and clubs. Death was only the last card, he reminded himself again, as his eyes jumped like fleas to the next canvas to be swept up into a Mother-of-God-blue robe billowing into sky. Then it dawned on him she was being crucified. HER PASSION hadn't been painted from the kindest angle. And however lustily his eyes leapt flea-like between pictures, on the canvas they were flies trapped in treacly impasto.

CHARM OF LULLABIES was a cat and mouse piece, set in an old-fashioned pram. A fluffy black cat hanging from the pram squared up to a golden mouse – or a beat-up pig? – dangling from a charm bracelet on the wrist of the hand tending the baby. This last was a blur, left hand, behind the cat-net, whose mesh continued in the wrist's texture. At the extreme right hand, a rosy herring-boned column running the entire height of the canvas could have been the edge of a bare forearm, conceivably attached to the wrist.

Jim was glad to find himself in the pink and green lyricism of EARLY DAYS, a woodland clearing at a very early day with a naked figure, back to the viewer, on the edge of the picture and the day. He was always a sucker for a green thought in a green shade. Currently, Tracey... They would meet in front of a picture... a lyrical picture... like this... and out of their shared perception of the picture... all manner of things would be shared... Except it was unlikely she'd have been invited to this private view. (And was his mind's natural level women's magazines? Surely the *Ulysses* version?)

He mused the old musings: should he have made his feelings clearer a few months ago rather than wait for her to get her degree? He'd never felt drawn to any of his students before, overgrown schoolgirls who tried not to open their eyes too wide at *Lolita* as set text, or too fluffy and feminine and somehow pert with it. And the mature students had generally been married. With Tracey still so vulnerable after her divorce and sitting Finals so soon, it had seemed a far, far better thing to do nothing. In a couple of weeks, after the results were out, he'd write her a little note. If he didn't see her around.

Lulled by dawn's pinks and greens, he was luxuriantly cogitating or vegetating when it dawned on him that the man in the picture was not only standing gazing into the pending wide blue yonder but peeing into that wide blue yonder. So he became more vulnerable and Jim, well-versed in the ways of the world, began protectively on his behalf to peer through the salmon and greens for the snake in the garden. A heavy hand descended on his shoulder.

"Dr Doig! The very man! Let me introduce another EngLit specialist..." Jim's thought that it was late in the day to introduce himself to anybody erased the name of the little grey man big shaggy Personnel had in tow.

"...from the College of Further Education. Our Dr Doig is leaving to become a gardener, over in Fife."

All hot brown eyes and a mouthful of over-long, over-pink tongue, the doggy Admin man was notorious for his Interest in the Arts, though that "our Dr Doig" sounded more like a solicitor referring to a junior partner – and how inappropriate now. *We don't want to lose you but we think you ought to go...*: Jim knew that was over the top but felt it summed up the University's attitude to him. His big blue baby-doll eyes were brimming pathetically from that "our Dr Doig" because it echoed the solicitors through whom he'd bought Margie's and his flat – what was Margie's and his flat for all of three weeks. If Margie hadn't left him – or rather if Christopher hadn't come back... If Christopher hadn't left the Findhorn Community, after *x* mystical years there, to work with the Woolwich... If the Tories hadn't won the '79 election...

"Didn't Wittgenstein work in a monastery garden between the *Tractatus* and *Philosophical Investigations?*" The man from the College of Further Education had to keep his end up when visiting the University.

"There you are, Dr Doig. I'm sure you'll be continuing your academic pursuits", breezed Personnel – as Jim always thought of him, though he'd a more discreet official title.

"I've to finish my book on Berryman – the American poet." Another of his crosses – total incompatibility between author and subject.

"You know, I think we've got a tiger by the tail."

Jim nodded at Personnel, wryly. Wonderingly – though these days people he scarcely knew on campus seemed surprisingly *au fait* with his CV. Then he realised from the direction of those doggy brown eyes that their owner was referring to the painter not the poet, and to one of her subjects, our mutual friend in the next but one picture, TO HELL WITH A HAND-CART. The familiar blonde confection of lacquer and speedy styling (premiers count every second the hairdresser steals despite the sovereignty of the image) crowned a towering lady in royal blue – a royal blue nylon overall, just the job for a grocer, say. With the handles pushing uncomfortably, he would have thought, against her breasts, the sturdy entrepreneur up-ended a hand-cart to tip medicine bottles, bandages, the odd bed-pan, nurses' caps, toys, textbooks, library books, *any* books into a pit below the bottom frame of the picture, at the viewer's feet. A book had fallen open at a picture of *tricoteuses* under the Guillotine.

"The bloody woman's even tried to hijack the Scottish Enlightenment." Another bull's-eye for the College of Further Education man.

Not that it was in Jim's nature to be competitive, and now he was silently musing that she might have tossed a few academic gowns into that hand-cart of national depths... The rays from her eyes, withering the viewer, caricatured how he'd felt... virginal... Blodwen's in that Tooting Bec bedsit, with himself naked, erect, crossing the lino and on to the carpet toward the bed where she was modestly tucked up. A short walk carefully engineered to put her at her ease – how many naked men had she seen, let alone aroused...? – but whose final few steps were almost impossible as he sensed not excitement, warmth, curiosity or shyness exuding from her so much as indifference, understandable when Maurice saw fit to make himself known.

Jim was dragged off Blodwen not by Mrs T. but Personnel, whom he somehow sensed to be suffering through a sixth sense of intuition, that is a change in the pattern of his breathing. His brown eyes were now leeches on the face of judgement: JUDGE... the picture between TO HELL WITH A HAND-CART and EARLY DAYS. At first glance, Jim wondered why this picture of a female judge in full fig and wig of stuck-on cotton wool should so pain Personnel? Perhaps he was affected by what in the last ten minutes Jim had come to think of as the painter's 'skin of wires' motif, here closely related to prison bars, covering half the face like the net on a Queen Mum hat. A silent cicada, Personnel was now rubbing one brown-corduroy thigh against the other – he could never be a *grey* Admin man, not with his Interest in the Arts. Jim gave himself a Brownie point for spotting brush-end scratching (*après* Picasso?) to extend the mesh or the shadow of its fear across the judicial right breast. And gave Personnel a judicious glance. The man didn't know where to put himself.

Then Jim realised that what he'd taken for coiled cotton wool festooned for a wig was a sanitary towel, an object last seen at even closer quarters when packing Doreen's suitcase. He noted that this was far from an orthodox feminist painting, given its suggestion that female judges might be equally susceptible to PMT (in which he'd been instructed by Miranda) as female criminals, who of course wouldn't have been criminals at any other time of the month. Then he remarked matily to Personnel, "Well, at least she spared us the blood."

Poor Personnel! This was truly one below the belt! This wasn't fair! That wasn't Art! His big brown eyes couldn't meet Jim's big blue baby-doll ones. Beautiful as pond water in half-light, his eyes sought instead the reassurance of his Hush Puppies, and he muttered that he must 'push on': this meant transferring his gaze to EARLY DAYS... The man from the College of Further Education, keeping his own counsel, pushed off. As so often, Jim felt unenlightened. The kind of man who'd never be called "one of the lads" and who drew in his skirts at most dirty jokes affronted by lack of wit rather than taste, frequently he could state a fact and people stared at him like an open sewer. He stared at the next canvas to drown himself in cobalt blue or viridian, though in whose suffering. Though SWING, first of three together entitled PASTEL PASTICHES (since like the rest they were oils, metaphorically pastel?), was surely an invitation to do just that, swing anywhere out of this world, that as ever was too much with him.

On the swing sat a slender, beautiful black man in white shorts and white open-necked shirt with the sleeves loosely folded back to six inches above those wasp wrists. Wasn't there something about that lilt...? So Jim laboured to tell the swinger from the swing. A trailing end from the painter's 'skin of wires' – here elaborated from the twigs of shrubs the better to ham-string a white woman in white skulking in the bushes and another white woman in green pushing the swing – connected with a loose end of Jim's wool-gathering and he saw Fragonard's *The Swing*. A froth of petticoats was replaced by the lissom black, and Fragonard's skulking and pushing men, respectively, by the woman in a futuristically shining white wet-suit – or cat-suit? – and the woman in a leaf-green sundress. Like a fly, Jim swatted off disquiet about the little silver object that the woman in white held in a pseudo-James-Bond stance. The other woman held him… and he wanted to bury himself in that leaf-green skirt. Yet, he was beside not even Fragonard's surf of petticoat but an Impressionist young lady, trailing *voile* was it? and pastel summer, wide-eyed beneath a wide straw brim, a Renoir?, with Rosalie at his side, pretty as a picture. The Royal Academy Impressionists' exhibition around '74? Except that Rosalie came later. If it was London, it must be Blodwen. But he could remember Blodwen only at the Hayward's early- seventies' Lucian Freud, looking askance at the female nudes… the beginning of the end? Post-Doreen, post-Steph, pre-Margie, pre-Miranda …and Thelma belonged to Glasgow. So he shuffled on.

THE MENTAL STAGE might have been the seat of memory, a stage cavernous as a skull or tomb with a tableau of *commedia dell'arte* figures, and a foam of white roses on the ground in front of Pierrot. With less surprise than recognition, you noticed the wires from the actors. They were held by two huge hands filling the upper canvas, forming heaven's vault in a gilded rose early evening light. One wrist foamed lace like Fragonard's girl's petticoats or effluent into a river, while the other was decently clothed in the ribbed cuff of a salmon sweater above a digital watch. Curtain-call for the performance, or the night?

The next picture was night for all the nostalgia-hazed, eighteenth-century sun gilding the tableau of embarkation. Where you might have looked to a statue of God not omniscient in classical incarnation, say Venus off right mobbed by *putti*, a streamlined missile was noseward heavenward. The blue-jeaned, motley T-shirted tableau in its shadow was familiar before he read the title: NUCLEAR CYTHERA, which left Jim casting about between Baudelaire and Verlaine to locate the Isle of Love – and forget the fallout. His bearings always impeccably literary as behoved his profession – ex-profession – he assigned the painting behind the painting to Query Fragonard along with THE MENTAL STAGE's, and hurried on.

To be desolated afresh. On a black ground, THE HIERARCHY OF NEED, at least six feet by six, showed a pyramid-shaped mountain in a plastic globe, like an old-fashioned toy snowstorm, drenched in green light. On tiered ledges, stick figures sheltered, cooked on open fires and, toward the top, made love or lust. Mid-way between that privileged apex and the deprived base because blessed with shelter and fire, one woman had no partner but bestirred herself as best she might. Among the couples, gender was often up for grabs in the universal shagginess, stick-figure scale. This was a change of gear after the PASTEL PASTICHES, and yet wasn't that green-lit mountainside reminiscent…?

"Jim! Jim!"

Isa, mercifully Archie-less, had him in her sights. As usual, she reminded him of the Joyce Grenfell song, "stately like a galleon..." Nicely slimming russet dress, but she'd tarted it up with a stole like lemon curd. "Fancy seeing you here, Jim!" She bore down on him, preceded by her breasts.

Though this school secretary lived and worked across the river, in Fife, he was never surprised to see Isa on campus. "I still work here. For the moment."

"Och Jim! You sound like you're being cast into outer darkness."

And where was that, if not off campus? Ask any of his colleagues. And as if he'd not long since located where. Perhaps 'replacement' kids always did. The possibility of a kind glance from Tracey was a frail crutch to lean on in a world of Isas-and-Archies and Personnel and his wife, not to mention the entire Department – University – town – world and his wife, plus assorted couples who at least had each other whether or not in the eyes of the world... Unlucky Jim! So much effort it all took, talking and smiling and faking interest in other people's interests and just putting one fucking foot in front of the other. And he spared an occasional thought for the lone disabled and for his pains felt guilty, which meant depressed...

"Newburgh isn't really outer darkness", Isa was rallying him. "After all, we'll be neighbours."

"That'll be nice", he said dutifully. His eyes slithered over the painted green mountain, fleeing the remembered green hill behind Newburgh backed on to by the gardens of Isa's and Archie's house and his future flat. When she had mentioned the little empty flat just along the street from them, it might have been the answer to a maiden's prayer. When she had translated his vague remark "I might get a few odd jobs in the village" into a full dance-card of Newburgh residents apparently eager to employ his hitherto-untried skills as a gardener, the maiden had ceased to utter prayers at least in Agony Aunt Isa's hearing.

"Did all the lecturers get an invitation for tonight?"

"God, no! What a waste of paper! A colleague who's interested in painting passed his on to me. I'm filling in time – I'm going out to dinner in ten minutes or so." An edited version. He'd ascribed both invitations to a *Be Nice To Jim Doig, He's Not Long For This Life Campaign*. And he feared he'd betrayed the pictures. "Though I'd have looked in at the exhibition next week anyway. I was struck by the poster: HUNG, DRAWN AND QUARTERED." He couldn't say the image had clawed him in. With nails.

"Not quite my cup of tea, though of course Edith's a friend."

He was hearing her say *some people might collect pictures or the shadow of their memory but I collect people*, when lest she revert to Newburgh, "I'm ravished by these pictures" he gushed on, astonishingly if truthfully and to postpone the future.

"Well, if you've a strong stomach." She rocked back as if to display hers, under autumn tints. "I drove Edith over. She lives near us. Well, near in rural terms. Five miles out of Newburgh."

He wasn't surprised to hear the painter lived near Isa. People always did. Soon he would himself, unfortunately. Earlier in the summer, when the future was a hazy possibility, he'd looked across the Tay to the low

Fife hills, duns and greens of good farming land, and fantasised *la vita nuova*. (And Tracey's Fife connection was only an element in that?) If you didn't have to take yourself with you, you could move.

"I had a full car with Jean, and Iain as well. You must meet him. He's a retired colonel. He's one of your clients."

So, a colonel on his dance-card to match his instinctive distrust of the military – which he knew rationally wasn't fair. Rationally? Fair? All's fair in love and war – shit. Wasn't the military's role in 1982 by existing to deter war – wasn't all defence these days an extension of the nuclear 'deterrent'? The Argentine surrender on Monday, ending, the colonial war for the Falklands?... Hardly front-line material even if what he might have called 'conscience' – if he were even less honest – wouldn't have complicated ... Jim went fumbling after his version of Clausewitz.

"Look, Jim. There he is!" Isa was waving at the phallic thistle rearing out of THE FLOWERS OF THE FIELD. A small grey head occluded the dog-rose.

"Oh dear, he's still talking with Jean. *They're* not doing much circulating."

In so far as Jim wasn't too oppressed by his personal problems to be amused, he felt wry at Isa's instinct to organise someone else's party – in this case, the University's party, or at least that of whichever hastily-convened committee was responsible for hiring out this hall for what would presumably be the first of a series of exhibitions in the new age of DIY university financing. (And wouldn't there be additional janitoring costs, even given the restricted hours of opening?)

"Who's Jean?" he asked, to punctuate the silence.

"Edith's friend. Just there, in that cream outfit. Look, there's Edith over there – behind that group behind Jean. Then to the right of the couple with the woman in that powder-blue crocheted dress. And to the left of the couple with the man in that off-off-white linen suit. *There!* There's Edith. You must meet her."

Perhaps Isa was staring at a slight figure with her back to them at the centre of one of the buzzier knots of people, who'd turned their backs on the images the better to cultivate their own. Edith's, of course, had entered the viewers' souls like iron – or at least what passed for this viewer's soul.

"The woman with long hair and a long patchwork skirt?"

"Yes. Come on. I'll introduce you."

"Oh no!" His ersatz Hush Puppies could have been quagmired. He shrank from the fecundity of the petite painter. If he framed a sentence, it was fatuous. And absurdly, the woman was somehow less real than the images from her mind, heart and womb that had blinded him, as the sun temporarily blinds you to other light. Out of the corner of his eye, he was erased by the scarlet pillar of sky off right in NUCLEAR CYTHERA. How had he barely registered it before? The colour of poppies.

"Well, let's have another drink. I'll fetch them."

For that relief, much thanks... not having to chit-chat to Isa for two minutes. All talk was now an effort. Essentially, that was why he was quitting. This was the first time in months... years...? that he'd gone somewhere he wasn't obliged to go. The poster of HUNG, DRAWN AND QUARTERED could have been the first time in months... years...? that he'd seen. The sibling HIERARCHY OF NEED's green globe glowed back at him like spaceship Earth to a moon-walker, reminding him how the world was too much with him.

Yet, he was lifted up... inched up by THE TRUE ICON. Washing clothes at a sink with her back to the viewer, a girl held up a small towel on which was imprinted the face of an androgynous Christ. In schizoid chiarascuro, she was caught between two light sources, an off-stage amber, perhaps a candle, gilding the crucifix on the wall, and white moonlight poured through the window above the sink to illumine the face. Then it was vouchsafed to him that the face was anybody but baa-lamb Jesus. This was the point... a true icon. He was glad his atheist soul hadn't knelt to a golden calf.

The bull-terrier glaring from the next frame with rouge smeared on that white face soon had him on the ground. He so wanted not to have seen... like Personnel a few minutes ago, seeking the consolation of his own toes. For diversion, he looked round to see if Isa had used the ploy of fetching another drink to stand him up. That surprised him, and he detected a pin-prick of hurt through relief at her silence? He himself could take *un mauvais quart d'heure* to disentangle from bores at sherry-parties: his favoured tactic was to pull out... home. Though perhaps people weren't hurt as easily as he empathised?

He homed in on Isa in front of THE FLOWERS OF THE FIELD, one glass in each hand, going at it hammer and tongs with the colonel. The phallic thistle was now sprouting from his grey hairs. Jim's roving eye lit on a woman with her back to Isa, talking with yet another male campus face on which after four years he couldn't pin a name. He remembered he'd just learnt the woman's name was Jean. Take off that well-cut cream trouser-suit and she would be a dumpy little personage... like himself. Up to a point. She was a nut-brown maid; her hectic brown colouring reminded him of Personnel. Though as Personnel was almost as notorious for being a 'Man of Sussex' as for his Interest in the Arts, it was unlikely that there were more of his immediate tribe in Dundee – and he'd only just married, belatedly if decently 'into' Scotland. Thoughts of the doggy man re-focused him on the painted dog opposite.

After the shock of recognition, with familiarity-as ever bringing a kind of acceptance, you saw that IN THE COMPACT showed the dog's face reflected in a powder-compact mirror. Clasped by proportionate bangled paws, the mirror filled the canvas like the plastic globe in THE HIERARCHY OF NEED. The litter of the dressing table was the mirrored set. Jim's critical faculties resurrecting, he saw in his mind's eye a famous Beaton photo of Fonteyn reflected in her compact mirror. Perhaps the liquid eyes prompted... Gratified to pick up the Goya pun in the painting, he was complacently wondering if that firm tested cosmetics on animals now.

"Oh the poor dog!" Even justified, Isa's yowl was painful. Even though her capacious heart tucked in beneath blowing autumn tints would shame us all, if she didn't meddle.

"What's the Latin mean, Jim?" She was staring at cursive characters thorned round the compact's lower rim.

"It's Spanish. *¿Que tal?* 'Can this be me?' She's referring to a Goya picture with two old women tarted up like teenagers. Goya's subtitle was *Till Death*."

He'd already drained the phial-like glass of standard University-issue medium-dry sherry she'd just handed him: *in vino veritas... que tal?* He saw the weekly half bottle of gin soberly doubled in the cracked glass in that attic in Leicester where it sat from Wednesday to Saturday each week for a couple of months, till he decided he couldn't afford this hangover from the few months of weekends it had illumined but which *were* Rosalie. Nobody as negative as he could become an alcoholic? Tautologically, he couldn't have afforded in any sense to put that to the test. In future, watery porridge would be his ambrosia: Maggie T.'s round.

"You *should* talk with Edith. You know about painting."

"Damn all. I've been to a few exhibitions, mostly when I lived in London, and I've looked at a few books of reproductions, including one of Goya!" Didn't he remember more vividly than the paintings the presence of whichever woman was soon to abandon him? Doreen, Steph, Blodwen, Thelma, Rosalie and Margie. Unlucky Jim!

"Let's swap glasses, Jim. I didn't think – I'll be driving back if Archie doesn't call in here. I've got his Metro cos my Mini's being serviced. He said he might get a lift back from someone in the office who was to drive over to Dunbog this evening. His morning lift has an evening class on 'Do Your Own Car Maintenance'."

To keep the blowsy creature alive, he could enjoy her drink without equivocation.

"*And* I need unclouded judgement. I've to love you and leave you and go and talk with Iain again. He's threatening to buy a picture if he can find one that tickles his fancy – and hasn't already got a red dot."

In a flickered second of sunlight between grey, Jim registered that if the Colonel were to invite his gardener into his house, say to pay him, he might have the doubtful pleasure of being confronted by one of these pictures in Newburgh. Part of him wanted to possess... himself. But how live with the image...? And now that he'd spurned salary not to mention pension, he'd be on iron rations for the duration... Though at thirty-two he'd no sense of tracts of time... till death.

Resolving the long-term in the short-term, as ever, he turned to the next picture to be thrown back on his future by the very title, FIFE DOVES, WINTER. Under snow, a shabby shed of a dovecote was linked through a rainbow parabola of tail feathers or flight to a grey woman bent over the stew-pot. The image hit home. He'd noticed a similar dovecote in one of the back gardens in the terrace below his flat in Newburgh, when viewing it with Archie and Isa and the solicitor. Archie had remarked that pigeons often used to be kept in North East Fife to supplement the winter diet.

He moved smartly on to THE COMMON STRAW. Two men in a kind of monk's habit stood in an outhouse behind a cattle trough where a baby lay. Never given to sentimentalising over children, to dash the tears diluting those deplorably blue baby-doll eyes he moved on more smartly to confront, in black and white, THE BURDEN OF SELF: Everyman stumbling up a hill, trailing stray nerves or the shadow of his wool-gathering.

The next few were portraits, perhaps mercifully blurred by his distance. His eyes strained to see, to know... but his Hush Puppies were quagmired again. His wise toes knew the worst scenario always happened, and cried off further harrowing. Yet it was unlikely he'd know any of the sitters – except conceivably Isa? – so hopefully he'd not be too harrowed. Though didn't you always see yourself... he transposed quickly from fiction where he'd identify with anybody, equal clay in the novelist's hands.

Then the rest of him froze like his premonitory toes in recognition of three familiar faces among the *verismo* cluster round the portraits. The two students depressed him at the best of times, since Margie had decamped, since Christopher had 'come back' ...because he saw them as love's young dream and at thirty-two feared he'd missed out on love's early-middle-aged dream. And now that he was quitting, whereas his colleagues irritated him with their thoughtful looks, thinking so much more than they *said*, as there was, like Margie... the students let it all hang out in emotional simplification, as if Maggie Thatcher were stood over him to drag the bread out of his mouth. The students wouldn't have hesitated to add his as-yet plump but indubitably martyred body to the premier grocer's barrow in TO HELL WITH A HAND-CART. Not that he'd taught either of these love-birds...

Heart-broken to miss the portraits despite his fear, he none the less took evasive action round the three *verismo* faces, fetching up in front of ALL OF THE POSSIBLES. All footsteps and feet – cut off at the ankle by the upper frame – again in black and white, the skin texture was used as the basic grid for the over-meshed 'skin of wires'. He saw these netted white feet as belonging on 'the passage which we did not take'.

Darker than the black and white of ALL OF THE POSSIBLES and THE BURDEN OF SELF, in an only ambivalently sinister context, the muted colours of FRAMED vegetated dun, tones of loam, sky- and lake-grey, muggy and trampled grass and the blue-grey iris of the eye that in a sliver of profile peered on the semi-rural through a door slit far right.

ELECTRIC returned to black and white for two figures separated by a fence... electrified by government or their nerves lying all over the shop in coils? The pair's cross-hatched shadows could rear. He could only snuffle. Partly for renounced Thelma, seeing him off in George Square after his last visit to Glasgow, Aryan blond bob haywire, her frenetic wave flowing into cursive "...can't think of marrying out... even though I'm not sure how much I can believe... Dear Jim, you mustn't..." snuffle, snuffle.

FAN revived colour in a 'pretty' picture of a woman twirling a fan with a painted woman, near a window open on a cottage garden of roses and hollyhocks. Till you focused the primary colours of the doubly-painted woman, intensified, you felt, by the woman who held the fan. Or was held in the unbearably yet irresistibly tightening revolutions of its twirl. And he felt. Oh yes! And he also felt quite pleased with himself still capable of arousal by Art, albeit if Personnel and his ilk had eyes to see, it would be seen as a deplorable response. More deplorable than snuffles. In fact, the bloody painter could have been loading her brush with his semen.

"Jim! So sorry about your predicament."

He turned into the black-polka-dotted cerise cravat of a Geography man. A lanky Geography man. "I hope They haven't been waving the big stick at you, Jim. That won't do. If They've been getting out the big stick, you should tell Them where to put it. I mean you're in the Union. We're not chicken-feed. If you make a big stink –"

"It's not like that. I'm leaving *voluntarily*."

"Who knows what's *voluntary* these days? I mean the pressure we're all under. Subliminally. I can't even think properly now – you can't expect plants to put out tender green shoots in smog. And we call this a university! When you think Devolution was *still* going to leave the Scottish universities answerable to London… But I do take my hat off to you, Jim, the way you've got the English Department out of a pickle. Sure as eggs is eggs. None of your over-fifties looked like budging. They were going to dig their heels in and sit back. *English was earmarked.* Where would your oldster colleagues have been then? Come to that, where are you now, Jim? *You* won't get any settlement. Not a penny! It's financial suicide for you. That's what it is! Financial suicide! And mind you, Jim, I don't think it's such a bad retirement deal They're offering the over-fifties. Nearly 50% salary, I mean it's not generous. But. You know, Jim, if I were a few years older I'd be seriously considering early retirement. Though of course as a family man… you're not a family man, are you, Jim?"

"No."

"And no spring chicken either!"

"No."

To evade the polka-dots, not to say the surprisingly keen eyes, he sought refuge in the pictures. His eyes homed to the wall of portraits, but he was too distant to recognise unknown faces. What could have been faces blurred together, as the women who could have rendered him an off-beat 'family man' had blurred in time, in memory. A twinge would surface – like a tinge of ochre impasto on an ear-lobe or thumb – and he'd acknowledge Rosalie again and later realise, or not, that Rosalie couldn't have said that, that wasn't her style, that must have been Blodwen?

"*Not* my style really, Jim." Geography's Adam's apple waggled above his polka-dots. "I find her a bit extreme."

"I find her bloody good."

"Oh." The Geography man set down his brimming sherry, with a sour little moue. "I thought white wine was the correct drink with paintings. Well. I suppose that Pierrot is rather sweet. Though I don't care for these black and white pictures."

He nodded at the final canvas, PIERROT AT HIS LETTERS, where the letters of the alphabet fell off the margin of the lackadaisical clown's page to run riot into another 'skin of wires': a net pinned to the sentinel Chinese characters either side of the scroll that the painting also comprised. Between these two framing ideographs, Pierrot's pen extended diagonally across the painting like a (teacher's?) stroke cancelling the picture. A white shape of a knowing eye – bar the black pupil, a stray polka-dot – subverted the illusion of silhouette.

Butterflied in that net of external nerves... Jim suspected he saw a different image from the Geography man.

"You know, Jim, we might as well be in China. I mean now they're attacking the universities, where will it stop?"

Jim was glad he'd apparently not heard about his future gardening in Fife.

"I'm off, Jim. I've had enough."

Jim's fingers curled round the other's sherry-glass, as the tan-and-cream dogtooth sports jacket topped by a polka-dotted cerise and fall of prematurely grey curls receded. He was drawn to the wall of portraits, but the trio he'd evaded earlier was there again or had never gone away. All the more conspicuous now the crowd had thinned dangerously. The booster sherry didn't make passing the time of day seem less of a rockface.

The vivid brunette Jean was smiling across the hall at him. Unaccustomed to people looking favourably on him, he turned to see in whose shade he stood. And found the painter practically rubbing shoulders with him, so that as she chatted with the Principal's wife and an 'arty' Pharmacology professor she was obscuring the half of HUNG, DRAWN AND QUARTERED that he'd left uncovered. Only somebody as fatuous as Cerise Cravat failed to awaken his compassion for his own loneliness outside coupledom. He swallowed the rest of the Geography man's sherry, so conveniently to hand.

And stood poised like a diver, about to plunge among the pictures again. His podgy body *un bateau ivre*. His eyes desperate to see again. Meanwhile, his eyes saw that except for die-hards like Isa a general exodus was under way, so the hall would soon seem as bare as Mother Hubbard's cupboard, with murals.

The hall or his skull overlapped the skull or heart or cunt or womb of the painter and he couldn't be expelled yet to dinner with the Boxer-Brownes. More than ever, the pictures had a come-hither look, now that he'd not have to dodge high foreheads and whinnied laughs to see. His eyes strained to suck the image. His nerves had tangled with her skin of wires and the net tautened as like an Angela Brazil old-school schoolgirl joining the crocodile, he tagged along out behind the crowd. Pierrot's mocking eye found him out as, unnecessarily, he closed the glass swing-door behind him, turning in his usual posture: on the outside looking in.

III

Looking out on the cliché moonlit Tay from his dark window, he saw a nocturnal version of the upper part of sunset BLACK GOLD – minus the oil rigs. He could read by moonlight the title-list hand-out from the exhibition. And the moonlight blanched the green phone, that had come with the flat, to a phantom …fitting, since the phone had become an invention for Margie to reiterate "Christopher has come back" – though she'd said it only three times. His eyes stripped back the moonlight from the Tay to the under-painting of the daylight view of the low Fife hills, duns and greens of good farming land, over the water… And he saw dawn's pinks and greens of the EARLY DAYS, which had also brought Tracey close. Still drained from the strain of his good-guest mask at the Boxer-Brownes' dinner-table, he saw that Tracey would prove another dead end. He saw the green-lit mountainside of THE HIERARCHY OF NEED, with the stick figures and the psychologists' graduated scale of human needs of food and shelter, and love. Since Margie, he'd supposed the way to avoid misfortunes really was to learn to stay home by yourself… Except what about earning a living and all that jazz? His elation at the pictures, dressing him as he'd walked round to the professor's house in Windsor Street, had fallen away on his installation in the airy drawing-room with the Boxer-Brownes' nubile sixth-form daughter and another couple. Yet, an Achilles' heel of his podge was still held by the painter. He sensed the vivid brunette Jean was her lover. But if there wasn't a woman fawning over her, there'd be a man, he didn't doubt. That was what was wrong with most artists, especially the novelists who'd once fed him. They wrote about loneliness but they hadn't known enough. Those who knew didn't survive to tell the tale. Catch 22. Most novelists' idea of loneliness seemed to be three years solo between two divorces. That painter had peeped over the edge. He saw the figure of THE BURDEN OF SELF stumbling up the hill, trailing stray nerves. If she'd gone deeper, she mightn't be here to tell the tale… Perhaps his deepest reason for quitting the University was that no novel touched him now. Possibly a not uncommon failing among English lecturers! But a society which produced more novels about the plight of women doing more than their fair share of the washing-up than about the plight of women (or men) who'd never had a partner was beyond his ken. Moonshine. That they should be so lucky! Alone, you were outside history. On the edge… The worst that history could throw at you was death and if you were alone (from necessity not choice, because you looked like the back end of a bus or your toes turned in or your tummy stuck out…) death was your permanent fall-back position. The couples could decide that suicide was a crime and then decide it wasn't, but the lonely always know their place. We know the way home. Of course, the most amateurish suicide would be a piece of cake compared with the kind of death history could throw at you… But most of their revolutions and movements were something else again. And you wouldn't quit even unwittingly iconic for a cause – but as a freak who shouldn't have been here at all, if only because you'd increasingly suspected you'd end up strung up. That was his reading of the pictures.

Val Warner

Anne Frater

Ceileireadh

Bha dìdig agamsa uair
a bhithinn a'cumail ann an cèids',
agus sheinneadh e dhomh bho àm gu àm:
òrain cianail airson an speur;
òrain bròin ag ionndrainn adhar,
agus 'caoidh cobhar nan craobh.

Cha dèanadh e 'chùis as m'aonais,
thuirt mi ri càch.
Cha b'urrainn dhà a bhiadh a lorg;
cha b'urrainn dhà e fhéin a dhion –
bhiodh e caillte ás m'aonais.

(Ged a bha e beò mus do rug mi air;
ged a rinn e a'chùis
gun prìosan mo chùram.)

Thuirt mi gu'n robh e toilichte
leis am beatha a'thug mi dhà,
's gu robh e airson fuireachd.

Cha do thuig mi carson,
an latha a dh'fhàg mi a chèidse fosgailt',
a thug e a sgiathan leis
a-mach air an uinneig,
a-mach ás mo bheatha...
gus am faca mi na ruidhlean
a dhanns' e anns an adhar,
's a chuala mi na puirt
a rinn e 'measg na sgòthan:
a'seinn a shaorsa
le òrain aighearrach.

'San diugh 's mise 'n dìdig,
ach tha mise
fhathast glaist'.

Airgead-beo

Tha 'ghrian a-muigh
agus airgead-beò a' sreap suas faisg oirre
anns an adhar:

'ga coimhead troimh'n ghlainne.
Nuair a thig na sgòthan
tuitidh e gu làr.

Anne Frater

Birdsong

I once had a birdie
that I kept in a cage,
and now and then it would sing for me:
songs of longing for the skies;
songs of sadness for the air,
and laments for the sheltering trees.

It couldn't survive without me,
I told everyone,
it wouldn't be able to feed itself;
it couldn't protect itself –
it would be lost without me.

(Even though it managed before I trapped it;
even though it got along
outside the prison of my care.)

I said that it was content
with the life I gave it,
and that it wanted to stay.

I couldn't understand why,
the day I left the cage unlocked,
it took to its wings
out of the window
and out of my life...
until I saw the reels
danced in the air,
and heard the jigs
sung amongst the clouds:
praising freedom
with joyful songs.

Today I am the birdie,
but my cage
is firmly shut.

Mercury

The sun is out
and mercury climbs towards it
in the sky:

watching it through the glass.
When the clouds come
it will plummet.

Mo chridhe a' leum
glaiste 'na do ghàirdeanan
'sa tuiteam

'nuair a gheibh e saorsa.

Sainnsireachd

Do ghuth 'na mo chluais,
faisg agus fann,
a' sainnsireachd.

Do chòmhradh air chall
ann am bualadh mo chridhe
'na chabhag a' riuth
gu do thaobh.

Nach bochd nach faod mise falbh cuideachd.

Feumaidh mi fuireachd
gus am fairich mi d'anail air mo bhilean
an àite d' fhacail 'na mo chluais.

Agus a-nochd
feumaidh do shainnsireachd
mo chumail blàth.

Geallaidhean

Thuirt thu gu'n robh thu gam'
dhion
agus thug thu dhomh
claidheamh maol;
thuirt thu gun éisdeadh tu rium
agus dhùin thu do chluasan
ris na bh'agam ri ràdh;
thuirt thu gur tu mo charaid
fhad's a cheangal thu mo làmhan;
thuirt thu gu'm faodainn 'bhi saor:
agus ghlas thu an dorus
le iuchair mheirgeach.

Ach gheibh mi a-mach
ge b'oil leat;
's ged is trom do shèinean
cha bhris iad mo chasan.

My heart leaping
locked in your arms
and falling
when freedom comes.

Whispering

Your voice in my year,
faintly, softly,
whispering.

Your conversation lost
in the beating of my heart
as it runs ever faster
to your side.

I want to go there too.

I have to wait
until I can feel your breath on my lips
instead of your words in my ear.

Tonight
your whispering
must keep me warm.

Promises

You said that you were protecting me
by giving me a sword
that was blunt;
you said that you would listen to me
but you closed your ears
to what I had to say;
you said that you were my friend
while you bound my hands;
you said that I could be free;
and you locked the door
with a rusted key.

But I will escape
despite you;
although your chains are heavy
they will not break my legs.

Kathleen Jamie

The Queen of Sheba

Scotland, you have invoked her name
just once too often
in your Presbyterian living rooms.
She's heard, yea
even unto heathenish Arabia
your vixen's bark of poverty, come down
the family like a lang neb, a thrawn streak,
a wally dug you never liked
but can't get shot of.

She's had enough. She's come.
Whit, tae this dump? Yes!
She rides first camel
of a swaying caravan
from her desert sands
to the peat and bracken
of the Pentland Hills
across the fit-ba pitch
to the thin mirage
of the swings and chute; scattered with glass.

Breathe that steamy musk
on the Curriehill Road, not mutton-shanks
boiled for broth, nor the chlorine stink
of the swimming pool where skinny girls
accuse each other of verrucas.
In her bathhouses women bear
warm pot-bellied terracotta pitchers
on their laughing hips.
All that she desires, whatever she asks
She will make the bottled dreams
of your wee lasses
look like *sweeties.*

Spangles scarcely cover
her gorgeous breasts, hanging gardens
jewels, frankincense; more voluptuous
even than Vi-next-door, whose
high-heeled slippers
keeked from dressing gowns
like little hooves, wee tails
of pink fur stuffed in the cleavage of her toes;
more audacious even than Currie Liz
who led the gala floats

through the Wimpey scheme
in a ruby-red Lotus Elan
before the Boys' Brigade band
and the Brownies' borrowed coal-truck;
hair piled like candyfloss;
who lifted her hands from the neat wheel
to tinkle her fingers
at her tricks
          among the Masons and the elders and the police

The cool black skin
of the Bible couldn't hold her,
nor the atlas green
on the kitchen table,
you stuck with thumbs
and split to fruity hemispheres
yellow Yemen, Red Sea, *Ethiopia*. Stick in
with the homework and you'll be
cliver like yer faither.
but no too cliver,
no *above yersel.*

See her lead those great soft camels
widdershins round the kirk-yaird,
smiling
as she eats
avocados with apostle spoons
she'll teach us how. But first

she wants to strip the willow
she desires the keys
          to the National Library
she is beckoning
     the lasses
     in the awestruck crowd...

Yes, we'd like to
          clap the camels,
to smell the spice,
to admire her hairy legs and
bonny wicked smile, we want to take
PhDs in Persian, be vice
to her president: we want
to help her
     ask some Difficult Questions

she's shouting for our wisest man
to test her mettle:–

     Scour Scotland for a Solomon!

Sure enough: from the back of the crowd
someone growls:

whae do you think y'ur?

and a thousand laughing girls
draw our hot breath
    and shout:

THE QUEEN OF SHEBA!

A Dream of the Dalai Lama on Skye

A summer wind blows the horn of Glen Brittle.
It's a hard walk, Black Cuillin
to his left hand; asks
the mid-summer moon
setting over Canna, *what metaphors
does the market whisper?
If the hills changed shape,
            who would tell me?*
She shines on ditches choked
with yellow iris: butter-lamps
in a temple corner; a snail-shell
in his moonlit palm:
the golden dimple of an icon's smile.
            He smiles too, notes
the private union of burn and sea,
as one by one, laverocks rise
irises open. When no one's watching,
he jumps lightly onto Soay
and airborne seeds
of saxifrage, settled
            on the barren Cuillin
waken into countless tiny stars.

A Perfect Possession

A L Kennedy

It hurts when we love somebody, because loving is a painful thing, that
is its nature. Today, even though we are sure that the pain will pass, it has
to be said that our loving is hurting us.

He is spending this evening in his room where we don't see him. It is
raining outside and he always likes to smell the rain. Often, we have

listened while he opens his window and lets in the damp and the insects and the draught. Downstairs, we can hear the rasp of wood when he tugs at the frame. He can be strong sometimes, even though he is small, and the window is loose-fitting and old, he can push it up quite easily. So he empties out the heat we pay for and he really doesn't think. We don't know where he gets that from, his terrible lack of thought, he simply isn't one bit like us.

Of course, no little boy likes to think and we expect to do that for him until he is grown and responsible. This is a burden to us, but a light and pleasant one. Loving someone means that you will do things for them, almost without consideration. We would catch him if he ran and fell, we would bandage him if he were bleeding and now we can measure his actions and think ahead on his behalf. On many occasions, we can stop him being hurt.

We don't think of these attentions as any kind of chore, after all, when he was so noisy and smelly and dirty, so very difficult to hold, we didn't abandon him. We knew he was a baby, not just some troublesome pet, and we kept him with us. For months, he made our lives extremely different, in fact he was quite a tyrant, but we didn't mind. We taught him to do better. Now we can really believe that he is quiet and clean as a matter of course. He sometimes makes mistakes, but then, mistakes are how we teach him. We learned by being corrected and that is the best way.

The worry of keeping him safe is another matter, that can be draining now and then. For example, we didn't know what to do about his window. He might have opened it up and then dropped out, so we had the bars put on, but still we had to fret because a fire could easily trap him in his room, what with his door being locked the way it must. Then there was the problem of his still opening the window inside the bars and doing whatever odd little-boy things he feels himself moved to do. His carelessness could have left us with rot in the window frame and perhaps he would catch cold. It was much better to screw down the window and put our minds at rest, because he will give us promises and then break them, which hurts us all in the end. Better to use the woodscrews than tempt him to lie at us.

He wasn't grateful for what we did, but that is very normal in boys; we understand. His spite didn't stop us saying that if he ever were in difficulties, or a fire did occur, he could bang on his door the way he does now and we would certainly let him out.

We are puzzled he still prefers not to be granted full run of the house. We don't know how many times we've asked him if he would like to be trusted not to break anything else, or to disturb us. Always he refuses the privilege, which we suppose shows that he knows his limitations: he is still dreadfully clumsy for his age. We make a point of sharing meals with him and having him sit at our table – it is so important he should have good eating manners when he goes to school. We suffer for the decision, but we persevere. It doesn't matter how many glasses he drops, and stains he makes in the tablecloth don't deter us; we will stop the silly shaking in his hands and eventually see him performing respectably.

If we let the child know our rules and what happens when he breaks them, it's only a matter of time until everything falls into place. More people should understand that and keep the incoming flood of modern and imported attitudes out of their homes. Today we all suffer at the hands of criminals created by sloppy care. A good child will be a good citizen and a bad child will not, as anyone can appreciate. Upbringing has to be just that – bringing up from the animal level to something higher, better, closer to God. Obviously, some races will always be nearer the animal than others, we must accept this as God's will, but if everyone would simply do their best then how much more pleasant the world would soon become. As it is, we are almost afraid to go out.

He never goes out without us, of course, and we can't trust him to strangers. This means we must be with him always which takes time and effort, but we would rather do a good job now than reap the sour rewards of slacking and idleness later. We tell him this and expect him to feel the same. Equally, we wouldn't leave him to the tender mercies of the television. If we sat him in front of an endless stream of filthy music and filthy talk, filthy actions, what would we get? We would get a filthy boy. He may listen to some radio, look at his picture book or amuse himself in any way he likes and enjoy the haven we have made for him. Our home is a clean home, free from tabloid sewage and the cheap and foreign pollution most people seem content to have wash around them all the day. We are not like that, we even sing him hymns to keep the air sweet in our rooms. It's such a pity we can't take him out to church.

We have the cares and troubles that come with the gift of a child. It would be very easy to give him material things and think that making him happy would make him good. There was even a time when we did offer him presents, wholesome gifts for a boy, and we were surprised when he broke them, or dirtied them, or pushed them aside. He could quickly forget we had given him anything.

This ingratitude and forgetfulness was hurtful, but because we love him, it hurt us even more to take the things away. Still, we have the bitter satisfaction of finding our judgements proved right. His will is undeveloped and can be swiftly poisoned by exposure to the material side of this world. A time came when he wanted something he could hug on to in the night and we knew what that meant. That was a warning. We had to take his pillow away because he would sleep alongside of it, in spite of what we told him, and that was dirty, that was more of the filth we constantly fight to save him from. It grieved us when he cried about it, cried in the night, and didn't understand the procedures to which he would have to conform. In the end he was persuaded to pray with us and became peaceful which was a little victory for us all.

Other little victories will come. We would love him to have birthdays and presents like other children. That would be such fun, but the way he is now, it would be quite impossible. We hope that he will change in time and become more upright and mannerly, a suitable example to others, and we are overjoyed to see that he is already much quieter than he ever has been. Sometimes we only know he's there, because of a certain feeling in the house and the ties that loving binds.

His extreme delicacy frightens us, naturally. Some mornings when we look at him, he seems so pale and thin, perhaps as an angel might be. His whole body is almost white which is clean, but not natural. No matter what we do, what methods we apply, he turns back to white again within days or hours, even minutes. He could have gone to school this term, had he been well. We will have to wait until he's stronger and perhaps reconcile ourselves to the likelihood that he may never go to a normal school. That would be a disappointment. That would make us sad.

Sometimes we have to ask ourselves if he is a judgement on us for our part in his conception. Children come from sin, they are the immediate flower of sin and there is sin in him. It would be idle to consider why this should be so and we believe only that, through him, we may find an opportunity to conquer sin again and again. This is more a privilege than a punishment and we treasure it. Many times in the night, we examine him for signs of filthiness, wetness of every kind, and often we are given cause for concern, or rather, we are challenged by sin. He has bad seeded in him and it comes out. Evil cannot help but flaunt itself and in the darkness it is most free to be manifest. How weary he makes us, forcing us to search and watch and search: a rubber sheet is not enough, an alarm is not enough, all our vigilance is not enough. Nobody knows what pains we have to take with the boy, purely to keep him up and away from his animal self.

And the animal brings on the animal, the beast. We find him tempting us as the devil tried to tempt Our Lord and we are uncovered as wanting. He offers us what he has and should not have and takes advantage of our tiredness, our weakness and our humanity.

We have to be strong for his sake, we have to pray and take action fearlessly for the sake of all our souls because we want him to grow up into a man we will be proud of. He will not be a fear and a stranger in our house because our strength and fortitude will not allow it.

Even tonight, when we think of our love for him and feel tender, we are undefeated because we know that tenderness is not enough. We must call upon our action and our faith and, with God's guidance, proceed.

Our child has sinned today. He has summoned an evil under our roof. What sin, what evil, need not be mentioned, we will not dignify it with a name. We need only say that he is ugly with sin and now we must call upon our God-given love to make him beautiful so that good may triumph in all our hearts. We will release him from himself and hear him thank us for it. We must.

Time after time and time out of time, we will purify him for the coming world and watch him cultivate his gratitude, piece by piece. When we are finished, he will be a good boy entirely.   *A L Kennedy*

The Husking

Helen Gilbert

This is the hymn they gurgle in their throats, but cannot sing
in words that truly sound.   Dante Alighieri, *Inferno*

She arrives at the boatshed just before dusk, the pumpkin in one hand and
a pair of long green gloves dangling from the other. The ferryman is just
leaving the far shore and she figures that she'll have plenty of time to dress
before he reaches her, so she pulls out the black cape from her knapsack
and buttons it around her shoulders, then reaches for the hat, frowning
briefly to find it slightly crushed, the tip of its cone bent and the brim
crooked in places. But it keeps her hair from her eyes while she smooths
her face into a mask of white paste and then etches it with red lipstick and
thick dark vertical lines drawn down over each eye to pierce her cheeks.

"Now all you need is the broomstick", she says to her watery image as
she focuses her attention on the river.

"Or Maybe a poisoned apple or two", the image replies.

She laughs and then sits under a tree on the bank, cutting a striking,
though not altogether odd, figure in the late October chill amid a flaming
landscape of maple and birch which burns cleaner with each fall day.

The ferryman seems to be dawdling, but she doesn't mind in the least.
It's easy to patient in a foreign language with a man you know will never
know you. And she's good at moulding emotions to fit the words she's
mastered, the one's she can pronounce perfectly, the ones that translate
without those traces of difference which allude to a world she does not
understand. So she waits, hands shifting idly among the fallen leaves.
Through the river's lens, she watches the sun sink into an ice cold cauldron.

Across the water, in the island's flat land, bonfires have already been kin-
dled and she can discern several figures backlit by jagged heat. Her blood
rises with a half-remembered childhood as she thinks of bushfires, her
tongue thickening with eucalyptus ash, burnt flesh, smouldering corn...

He scares me sometimes. Me big brother I mean. He's got a real hot
temper an' when he lets fly his face goes all red like it was gonna bust.
Then he yells louder than Uncle Frank an' that's sayin' somethin'. Uncle
Frank lives about a mile down the road. He's always havin' fights with
Aunty Dot an' you can hear 'em from here. Dad tells us not to listen 'cause
he reckons the air's blue with four letter words, but that don't worry me.
I hear plenty right here when Mum an' me sisters go to town an' everyone
forgets I'm around. I know lotsa other words too. More than me big brother
even. He stopped goin' to school ages ago. Now he calls me smarty pants
'cause even though I'm only little I'm never stuck for somethin' to say. I
read books about places all over the world, an' I practice big words like
perpendicular or some of them foreign words like parlay voo fransays, all
the time, an' when he gets really mad at me an' starts yellin' fit to kill, I
just put me fingers in me ears an' hum those words over'n'over.

The ferryman hums to himself as he ties up the boat. His eyes register no surprise at seeing a witch waiting to board. He pockets her fare and then steers the bow deftly through a narrow channel in the reeds. When open water slaps lightly against the gunwales, he maintains his course with one hand and turns to watch the woman, his breath spiralling across her eyes drowning in the black water. As he looks at her, the ferryman thinks of a loon calling across the marshes. He waits for her to say something.

It doesn't take long to get to the island at this point. Further up the Gaspé peninsula the St Lawrence yawns into an immense gulf where its waters turn back on themselves, folding and breaking, but here the river sucks arctic winds gently into eddies and the boat trip is smooth throughout. And silent.

After they dock, she stands hesitantly on the shore, watching the flickering fires.

"*Salut! Vous rêvez?*"

She turns quickly, starting at the figure at her elbow. He's wearing a wonderful black spangled dress, a thick shawl, and carries a rather long wand. A crown perches precariously on his tight curls."Let me guess... the fairy godmother – *la bonne fée*", she fumbles, for something to say.

"*Non, la fée Carabosse.*"

"Of course, the good fairy would be in virginal white."

He smiles enigmatically. She has no idea whether he understood her or not. "*Pourquoi le potiron?*" he asks.

"The pumpkin? I liked the colour; it matches my gloves."

He smiles again, white teeth flashing, then leads her toward the house, their path lit by the fires. As they walk, the figures she saw in silhouette from the boatshed materialise as elves, gnomes, wizards, goblins. She is surprised to realise that some of them are children.

Two small ghosts come running up with their hands out.

"*Donnez-moi quelque chose ou je vous joue un tour*", they chant in unison.

She looks at them blankly. Somehow you never expect children to have mastered a language that still trips on your tongue, that falters between the thought and the sound, or the sound and its image.

"Trick or treat", the fairy nudges her, producing candy from a false breast.

She hasn't brought anything so she smiles weakly.

The ghosts chant more insistently now, their disguises giving them licence to menace. A few gremlins join in, blocking the path. They sense they have power over her, this voiceless witch in the limp hat. She feels it too, but steps forward, fear laughing through the smoke in her throat.

I'm not s'posed to light the fire anymore 'cause I nearly smoked the house out when I burnt me big brother's war comics, but me big sister lets me do it when Mum's up the spud paddock. I like puttin' little sticks in the coals an' lettin' them burn at one end, then I take 'em out again and draw pictures in the air with the flames. Just watchin' fires is fun too. Your eyes get glued to 'em, an' you can forget about everythin' else. You gotta be careful, but, 'cause even when they've died right down you never know how much they're burnin' on the inside, or when they're gonna start right up again an' nearly blind you. Me big brother says you shouldn't look into fires in case you see a window into hell. I reckon he's just tryin' to scare me, but I always say holy words while I'm lookin' just in case.

The children's words echo in her ears as she passes the last of the fires and enters the house which is packed with more grotesque forms. Some revel in the music, some grope each other in quiet corners, while others chat animatedly, pretending not to notice. She wonders how you tell who is who and if it really makes much difference.

The fairy gets her a drink and introduces her to a few of the others. She strikes up a conversation with a dragon but their words get tangled up in the crossfire and he starts fondling his tail and leering at a group of sprites, so she takes her cue and wanders off outside, drawn by the smell of food to one of the smaller fires where someone has set up a pig on a spit and a huge tub of water for the corn.

"You've been here for three months and you still won't speak French", she grimaces to her image in the tub.

"Go back to your nice safe university", the image grins back, flames licking its face.

I've got a scar on me face where I came a buster off Trigger but I'm not scared of horses an' I don't cry when I fall off. Most of the time, anyhow. I've been riding' me own horse to school since I was in kinda an' I'm countin' how many times I fall 'cause Dad says you gotta reach a hundred before you're a good rider. I made sixty three last week when Trigger dumped me in the mudpool. I guess he was mad at me for makin' him jump all those logs. Me brother'd kill me if he knew. I'm not allowed to jump anymore 'cause the doctor cost five pounds or somethin' like that when I cut me face open. Me brother carried me home. Dad was on the plonk again so he wasn't much use an' me brother had to drive the truck to town an' I was bleedin' all over the seat. Blood doesn't worry me, but. Sometimes I get Dad's razor an' cut little slits in me fingers. I like it when the blood comes out in big round drops.

Shé wants to speak volumes, to bleed words into the air like nectar oozing from a cut stem, but she can't trust her mouth because she never knows what's going to come out until its too late. So she sips wine to loosen the vocal cords and melt the crystals of cold night air on her breath.

The air bubbles with children while masked figures come and go in the firelight. They are mostly men, shades dancing in the margins of her mind, leaping around the flames with blood-curdling yells that redouble as the children scream back in fearful delight. Emboldened by the wine, she talks to some of them, the sentences coming slowly at first, then more freely as she builds up a rhythm until words sizzle on her breath, making small hissing sounds like pig juice dripping onto hot coals. It helps that she can't see their faces.

I use'ta go all the time an' lock up the poddies with me big brother but now I stay at home when I can even though I hate peelin' veggies. Feedin' chooks is even worse. Mum asked me why I swapped jobs an' I had to lie 'cause she'd kill me if she knew the real reason an' I'd never be able to look her in the face again. Anyway, me brother told me not to tell anyone an' I bet he'd get real mad if I did. An' Mum thinks the sun shines out of his bum, that's what me sister says anyway, an' he'd never let her see what he's really like. Sometimes Mum makes me help him with the poddies, but I don't go near the shed any more if I can help it. I'm always scared he's gonna bolt the door then I won't be able to get away. I use'ta go there a lot. At the back there's heaps of corn piled up right to the window. I use'ta pretend I was Rapunzel an' the corn was me hair only it went from the ground up to the window an' not the other way round. Or sometimes it was the Yellow River of China, or Sinbad's Treasure. You know, if you kinda half shut your eyes an' look at corn when the sun's shinin' on it, you can see rainbows, an' it looks almost like real gold, or near enough if you got a good imagination. Mum reckons I got real beauty an' I reckon she must be right 'cause I can see the man in the moon, an' the man who hides behind the tree near our toilet at night, an' lotsa other things that no one else sees around here.

The corn roast has begun. She chooses a plump ear and pulls off the silky brown beard first, then the husks, one by one, until the grain is fully exposed. Gathering up the pile of husks, she flings them deep in the fire where they burn into papery cinders. Then she pierces her cob with a roasting fork and looks for faces of men in the flames as it cooks.

The other day he got me in the corn shed again only this time I got really scared an' started to yell so he called me a bitch an' let me go. I knew I shouldn't've gone there in the first place but I couldn't catch Trigger an' he told me to go an' get some corn ta make him come. Anyway, then he came in behind me an' bolted the door like he did before only this time he looked like he meant business. When I said I was gonna be sick he picked up his whip. I started to yell an' then he threw it down an' kicked me outside an' started breathin' loud. I shoulda just run home, but I'm always wantin' to know what's goin' on so I found a nice crack in the door an' watched him. Lucky he took off his pants. As it was, he made a real mess all over the corn cobs. I wouldn't wanna be the horses eatin' that stuff.

She butters her corn, sprinkling on salt and pepper, her teeth bared for the first bite.

I've tried climbin' out the window, but goin' up the pile's a dead waste of time. When you get near the top, the grains always spill everywhere an' suddenly you're back where you started. Anyway, its not much use tryin' to run away. An' it doesn't really hurt – not if you don't fight an' if you don't count the spewin' up. I spew up all the time anyway. Mum reckons I've got a nervous condition, whatever that is, but that's crap. I just do it to make everyone sit up and take notice for a change. An' nothin' makes 'em take more notice than vomit all over the place.

The corn hits the ground in yellow splatters as her stomach pulses thick fluid into her throat, rejecting the wine and the food and the grey smoke and the farm smells. She moves further into the shadow, hoping no one will notice her, finds a log, sits down, drinking in air to cool her stomach. A satyr comes up and asks if she's okay. She puts on a face to meet the mask she meets, finding the words to brush him off but not the tone. Language is like music – if you don't start in the right key, you're lost. So the satyr sits down and asks her where she's from, why she's here, who she is. And since she's already lost, she tells him more than he is able to know.

I'm makin' me first holy communion next week. I had to go to confession first 'cause the nuns say your soul's gotta be clean an' white an' that the devil gets impure little girls. I wasn't going to tell the priest about me brother until they said that. I read all about the devil, an' the river – Sticks or whatever it is, an' the ferryman, an' I don't want to be stuck there. Only person I ever heard got outa there was that prince who stole three golden hairs from the devil's chin an' he had a kind ole woman to help him. Anyway, so I told Father Kenny I sinned against the sixth commandment 'cause it didn't sound quite so bad sayin' it that way. I was scared shit he was gonna open the window to see who it was confessin' somethin' like that, but he never said nothin', just kept on prayin' an' never missed a beat. An' he only gave me three Hail Mary's for penance. That's nothin'. Anyway, I said six, just in case the devil was watchin'.

She hardly notices that the satyr says nothing, his face inscrutable behind the mask, while she cuts the air with her talk, the alcohol still singing in her veins, tuning the words, smoothing out the occasional stutter, honing the sounds to a fine pitch so that only a trace of discomfort remains, the odd dissonant beat in a symphony of words that translates her life, transforms it into sounds that are beautiful because they render foreign what is contemptible in the familiar, freeing her from old echoes as she speaks about her childhood in a foreign language because it seems easier, because it's less personal, because she can say the word that corresponds to "I" and it never quite means the same thing, and so she tells him about her country, about the farm, about her family, about her passion for horses and the words she used to practice when she wanted to shut out the world, and finally about her big brother and the corn shed.

I know I said I was never goin' near the corn shed again but me big brother was real nice to me for days an' he even promised to give me a good horse to learn jumpin' on at the pony club. An' he took me out ridin' an' never got mad an' never touched me neither. I figured God musta listened to me prayers for once, 'cause everything was going real good. But then he got me in the shed an' went an' wrecked things again. This time it really hurt but I still didn't cry even though I nearly busted a gut tryin' not to bawl out loud. After he let me go I got mad as hell an' said I hated him, an' I was gonna tell on him. I didn't really mean it, but I thought he'd belt me one for sayin' that but he just went red an' reckoned he was real sorry. Then he went an' got out his pocket knife an' asked me to cut him, so he wouldn't wanna hurt me ever again.

She's on her fifth glass of wine when the smell of hot dung sears the air and the satyr leaps on her, pushing her down into the darkness with his frenzied weight, one hand sliding under her cape and up her sweatshirt, the other fumbling with the zip of her jeans until her skin burns with metal and she thrusts herself away from his sour breath and cloven hooves, feeling the smoke burning in her brain, watching the children watching her, fighting against gravity, against his goat beard rasping on her skin, and most of all against her body, falling...

I dunno why I did it. I guess it was the devil makin' me fall outa God's good books like Eve in them bible stories. Dad was at the pub again an' everyone else was sleepin' an' I just took a whole box of matches over there an' got a bunch of husks an' lit 'em. Anyhow, the wood caught fire an' everythin' started burnin' real quick an' it went all red an' hot like hell must be. I only just got out in time 'cause I was too busy watchin' the fire an' seein' all kinds of animals an' people in there. Fires are like that.

In the log's hidden core, in its smouldering eye, the heat still glows from the ashes of Halloween on the island in the middle of the river where the ferryman waits. It is one of those crystal clear autumn mornings when you could drink the sky. Inside the house, human debris litters the floor. But the witch with the green pumpkin does not sleep like the others. She is leaving for the ferry, for the city, for the minutiae of her daily life. The wicked fairy guides her down the path and they talk about the party. She tells him how she spoke French for hours, how good it felt, how she almost believed she was a sorcerer poised at the edge of magic until...
"*Qu'est-ce qui s'est passé?*" he says, noticing the blood on her glove.
"Nothing... only I tripped over a satyr and it made my mouth bleed."
"Satyre! *Il n'y a pas de satyre. Vous rêvez.*"
"No, I didn't dream it. There was one there. I... talked to him for quite a long time."
"No." He reverts to English to emphasize the sound. "You are mistaken."
She fixes her eyes on the fields of hoarfrost, laughing away the taste of fetid corn on a blackened tongue, and continues towards the dock where the ferryman waits.

I'm waitin' for Dad to come home an' I'm sure not lookin' forward to it 'cause Mum says I'm gonna get the beltin' of me life. She reckons he'll be especially mad 'cause all the trees near the shed got blackened an' it nearly started a bushfire. You could still see it smokin' this mornin'. I don't reckon it'll hurt much, but – the beltin' that is – 'cause Dad never stays cranky for long. An' anyway, I got some leaves to stuff in me pants so you can't feel it. I learned that trick from readin' about Blinky Bill. I can't do it on Mum, but. She knows about that kinda stuff an' she's always threatenin' to send me to boardin' school when I do somethin' bad. But I'm not scared. Anne of Green Gables went to boardin' school an she met lotsa nice people there. When I grow up I'm going to Canada 'cause it sounds pretty good there an' I'm gonna learn French 'cause if you know foreign words you can say secrets out loud, only they're still secret 'cause no one else can understand you, an you won't get into trouble for sayin' bad things. I might even go and see what the North Pole's like. I heard you can see coloured lights an' rainbows in the sky at night time there, an' I read all about the reindeers an' the snow queen, an' I wanna see how white snow is, and if the cold really hurts bad, an' what it feels like if you get one of those ice splinters stuck in your heart.   *Helen Gilbert*

Janet McKenzie

On a Clear Day

She sees herself as a love-letter
In which emotions don't get out of hand;
A balanced blend of sex and sentiment,
Cliche-ridden, well-presented, bland.

Scarcely read, she still plays out her role
In the sleek volume of his life,
As a mere bookmark at the place
Of the sweet love-poem written by his wife.

Fright

Dim furtive sound – a rustle, mutter, sigh,
out there in dark. I know they wait and I,
haloed in searchlight, may go out to die.

A rodent panic gnaws me deep inside,
My limbs are water, but my mouth has dried.
With rictus smile, on to the stage I glide.

At Paphos

Little lizard in the bath at Paphos
spread-eagled, trying to lose your third dimension,
I see you,
clinger fingers splayed,
a sliver of salmon on a white china plate.

I've come hot-foot from ancient Kourion
where your much larger cousins,
unimpressed by pricelessness,
play in the Graeco-Roman Theatre,
hide in the Sanctuary of Apollo Hylates
traverse the mosaic face of Ktisis
at the Baths of Eustolios.

But, Smallfry, you adorn my bath
translucent, pink and perfect.
I move. You move
and dart down the drain.
How can I ever shower again?

Some Poems by Willa Muir

Willa Muir will be remembered as a writer mainly for her predominant part in translating Kafka and Hermann Broch with her husband Edwin; for her translations of the now neglected Hans Carossa; for her two published novels, and for her memoir *Belonging*. But she wrote a lot more, much of it unpublished – two novels, short stories, essays and verse. In 1931 she published lively translations of *Five Songs from the Auvergnat*; in the Muirs' rendering of Broch's *The Sleepwalkers* the extensive translations of verse in the final section are mainly, perhaps wholly, hers; and in the early 1940s she made versions of some poems from Czech.

She published a few original poems in periodicals, notably four in *Botteghe Oscure* XXIV (1959), about which Robert Lowell wrote to her:

> I am writing now because of your *Botteghe* poems, very masterful and firm and touching. I like particularly 'Solitaire' and 'Requiem'. They are all true and right for you and what I might have expected from your conversation.

Near the end of her life she published a slim volume modestly entitled *Laconics, Jingles and Other Verses* (1969), of which she wrote to me:

> I hope these trifles may interest and amuse you. They were written before Christmas, and meant to be a kind of farewell to my friends.

There are a few older poems among the recent ones there; but I do not think she tried to bring together in that volume all the best of her work. So I believe it is not going against her wishes to look for nuggets in the considerable amount of verse scattered through her notebooks and other papers in St Andrews University Library. Some of this is light-hearted doggerel, dashed off for amusement, but quite a few of the poems are typed, presumably with a view to publication; and some even of the ms. ones seem to have been carefully written – for instance 'Coasting down the steep of your forehead', of which two widely-differing drafts exist. The following selection gives a taste of the range and quality of her work.   *Peter Butter*

'Where have you come from...'

Where have you come from, shred of a daughter,   from
daughter I longed for and never bore?   *Laconics*
Here you are in my dream   (1969)
blown by what wind?

a shred, a wraith that cries in a piping voice:
"Don't leave me behind!"

Newly Wed

I felt in my bag for coppers
To pay the usual bus fare,
Then, three people away, I saw you buying my ticket.
That was no special treat, no taxi outlay,
But the small change of daily life.
In that moment
Less than an hour after we were married
I understood I had a partner,
A husband, not merely a sweetheart.
It was fifty years ago, that moment,
Never forgotten.

Solitaire

from
*Botteghe
Oscure*
(1959)

Alone, and for how long, who knows?
Alone unable to relax,
I lay them out in disciplined rows,
Anonymous card backs.
A bitter pleasure, this, to see
So many turn their backs on me.
But I have no cards up my sleeve;
Let me believe, let me believe.
Turn then, O turn propitious faces;
Promise me luck and recompense.
I know you have your proper places
And patterns that make sense.
There are four families in the pack;
To every queen a king and jack.
Let wives and sons and husbands meet,
Let every family be complete.
Trivial magic for great occasions?
Yet once again, O patience, patience!

Requiem

And so let the loud tongue fall dumb.
Cease to mock time with forced, unseemly jests;
Compose the aching limbs, protuberant bum,
Still more protuberant belly and slack breasts.
Lay them all down, relax the vertebrae,
And sleep, old wife, after your too long day.

Storm over Europe

The bairns are fairly louping in the womb,   From Mss.
Lunting and lamming oot,   and Tss.
Riving great dads oot o' the Christian sky,
And the Universe is feeling a wee bit sick.

She's retching and thrawing like ony ither
Uneasy mither,
While her unborn bairns, flauchtering inside her,
Are roaring *Soviet* and *Swastika* and God kens what else.

But does God ken?
Is He the Father
Is this His wark – I'll no say handiwark –
Is He the Father o' a' the stramashing,
Tearing, thrashing,
Buckle-swashing,
Louping, kicking, frichtened bairns?

He's got the wind up, onywey.
I can hear it ooing and drummling roond the hoose
In cosmic farts and rumbles at ninety miles an 'oor.
Puir auld God.
I'll wager He's in a taking.
I'll wager He's wishing He'd never been sae chief
Wi' Moses and Gladstone.
I'll wager He's wishing now He'd never cloured Wotan
Or skelpit Pallas Athene
Or stashed Isis below the belt –
There's naebody He can jouk ahint noo-a-days.

Puir auld God.
He's got the wind up richt eneuch.
Listen to yon.

[1933-35]

Pasques

I mind us rowin' Easter eggs oot on the links
amang the laddies' fingers an' the sodgers blood,
helter-skelter doon the brae, yallas, reids an' pinks,
an' us skirlin' like craiters gane wud.

We rowed ourselves after them, an' aince at the fit
we chappit them an' ate them: na, they were na fyled.
Thyme an' the saut sea wind relished ilka bit;
it was the eggs, no' us, that was hard-biled.

Virgo Ferox

My little smoke-grey cat, so plump and furry,
Rolls in the wanton gutter, fiercely growling
At Venus, whose lean servitors, taut yet wary,
Stand at a distance, miowling.

O little cat, O valiant little pussy,
Six months at most you have been here on earth,
While Venus, for uncounted aeons busy,
Brought you yourself to birth.

Cease, then, to growl; the struggle's too unequal.
They know it too, these tom-cats tatterdemalion;
Kittens (alas) are bound to be the sequel,
Battalion on battalion.

'Coasting down the steep of your forehead...'

Coasting down the steep of your forehead
careless and bold upon that durable bone
I check in the tangled brushwood of your eyebrows,
and slowly, slowly, like a heavy stone
fear rolls into my heart; for as I peer
over the rim your eyelids are so tender,
so palpitating, fluttering, unsure,
I have no certainty they will endure.

Yet even a tortoise dies within its shell;
and were you wholly armoured, with no pulse
of skin and nerves and vulnerable flesh
we could not love each other half so well,
being but mortal. On the verge
of this poised moment, while your eyelashes
like flower stamens brush my eager palm
I will not listen to a future dirge.

Coasting down the long slope of your cheek
to the firm jawbone, gayer now and bolder,
alive and yet undying, strong though weak,
I rest, it seems forever, on your shoulder.

[1947]

AN AULD SANG DIRLS AGAIN!

the CEILIDH HOUSE

The **H**igh **S**treet wis yince a hub o music, poetry an' talk.
The **C**eilidh **H**ouse pits back that tradeetioun.
Folk nichts – poetry nichts – an aye-bidan come-aa-ye

ilka nicht o the week a new stramash!

Cleik yer pals in fur a pint or a dram. Ye'll hae a waarm walcome.

Eldritch neuks and crannies fur smaa foregaitherings
Cellar haa fur middlin-scale occasiouns

The Ceilidh House, 9 Hunter Square, Edinburgh EH1 1QW
Heid Wanger: Cy Laurie
Tel 031-220 1550

Violet Erskine, as she then was, in Shakespearean pose, c1885.
(All photographs courtesy of Hugh Arbuthnott)

Autobiography in the work of Violet Jacob

Sarah Bing

The recent discovery and part-publication of Violet Jacob's diaries and letters marks a valuable contribution to autobiographical studies, in particular to those of women in the early twentieth century. The most complete self-penned portrait of Violet Jacob is found when all her works, fiction and otherwise, are viewed as a whole. Her son Harry's letters and photographs from France have also come to light over the past year. They were left in the possession of Violet Jacob's close friend Nancy Arbuthnott. A selection of Violet Jacob's correspondence can be found in Montrose Library, the House of Dun archives and the National Library of Scotland. Poems referred to in this article are found in *The Scottish Poems of Violet Jacob* (Oliver & Boyd, Edinburgh, 1944)

Violet Jacob was born Violet Kennedy-Erskine in 1863 at the House of Dun in Angus. She spent her youth in Scotland, being educated at home. In 1894 she married an Irish soldier, Arthur Jacob, and most of her married life was spent in India, Egypt and England – it was only when Arthur died in 1937 that she returned to live in Angus. The couple had a single son, Harry, who died, aged twenty, in 1916.

Violet Jacob wrote in a variety of literary forms. Her Scottish vernacular poetry received most critical recognition. She also published poetry in English, novels, short stories, fairy tales and *The Lairds of Dun* – a history of her family, the Erskines of Dun. From 1885 to 1900 Major Jacob was posted to India. While they lived there, and on a return visit in 1922–23, Violet kept a diary, and some letters also survive.

Diaries and letters form a literary tradition that is only recently gaining academic recognition, particularly in the study of women writers who often lacked the free time and academic education which would have enabled them to write in literary forms as formally constructed and therefore time-consuming as the novel or autobiography. These women still had the urge to record their thoughts and everyday experiences. 'Formal' autobiographical writing like memoir or reminiscence that seem to involve much self-analysis could, as Valerie Sanders says, seem a form of vanity to Victorian women. Instead they felt more comfortable writing letters or keeping a diary. To further deflect attention from their inner or emotional selves, women felt more justified in recording their family's development or observing a foreign country in a travel journal. Both these forms of autobiographical writing were employed by Jacob and, in both, exploration of her self is far from the central theme of the writing. Jacob tried to recreate India in detailed letters to her mother in Scotland. Jacob wrote her Indian diaries "to keep me from forgetting things I shall always want to call up in the years to come". Her aim was to shore up the memories of an extraordinarily happy time and create a record of the sights and people she encountered. Writing *The Lairds of Dun* was similarly a way of recording the knowledge of passing people and events.

It has been said that letters and diaries are marginal forms of autobiographical writing. Indeed Estelle Jelinek[1] states that she does not regard them as autobiography. This is too exclusive for a writer like Violet Jacob, who drew on her own experiences and emotions in all her fictional work. I prefer Sanders' wider definition of autobiography when she says "a writer's collected works might be regarded as autobiography, if they trace the development of an individual"[2]. Northrop Frye approaches the definition of writing about oneself from another angle. Finding it hard to separate autobiographies from any other form of prose fiction, he says:

> ...most autobiographies are inspired by a creative, and therefore fictional, impulse to select only those events and experiences in the writer's life that go to set up an integrated pattern.[3]

As well as seeing Jacob's letters and diaries as a background to her creative work, they are creative works in themselves.

This is illustrated when two of Jacob's short stories, 'Other People's Gods' and 'Fringe of the Forest', are compared with the account she gave in her letters and diaries of days in the Indian countryside. She wrote to her mother about a visit to the city of Ujjain:

> The impression of heat, crowd, dirt, violent colour and endless detail is extraordinary... [there was] a strange and very beautiful figure of a cobra cut in a stone that leaned against a temple wall.

In 'Other People's Gods' the character of Sands is fascinated by the kind of forgotten shrine that Jacob would discover when riding. Jacob would send a silent salaam to the Hindu God for whom it was built. Sands found an isolated shrine, next to the carved shrine 'was a little stone serpent placed alone beside the sculptured horseman'. Unlike Jacob, who would at most sketch the figure, the character she creates aims to steal the serpent and in doing so is unnaturally killed. The fictional work goes beyond the beautiful descriptions of the diaries to show the ideas that capture Jacob's imagination. As well as being sharply observant Jacob believes in the spiritual forces she senses in India.

Throughout all Jacob's work there runs an element of the supernatural, of a world beyond that of the living. In her fiction this first appears as variations on local myths. The haunting of mist-shrouded hills in *The Sheepstealers* was believed to be true by actual inhabitants. In a *Country Life* article Jacob recounts this and other local legends as they had been told to her. Many of her poems relate superstitions, like the one believed in by the terrified narrator of 'The Rowan'. The rowan is a tree believed to protect against visitations by witches:

> For I feel the long een set
> Like a gloom upon my heid,
> For the warlock's livin' yet –
> **But the rowan's deid!**

1. *The Tradition of Women's Autobiography: From Antiquity to the Present*, Estelle Jelinek, (Massachusetts: Twayne, 1986); *Women's Autobiography: Essays in Criticism* (Indiana: Indiana University Press, 1980)
2. *The Private Lives of Victorian Women*, Valerie Sanders (Harvester Wheatsheaf, 1989)
3. *Anatomy of Criticism*, Northrop Frye (New York, 1968)

The mystical saddhus of India "with that lurking spiritual horror" fascinate her, and embody the atmosphere of "sacrifice, fate, perhaps death itself; something that is always close, everywhere". This shows most clearly in the short story, 'The Fringe of the Jungle' when the heat is presaged by the dhak flowers whose "claw-like scarlet blossom" coincides with the Hindu festival of Holi, celebrated by rioting and debauchery:

> ...beyond these forebodings, the tree is sacred in their eyes, because the three divisions of the leaf represent the Hindu trinity of Birth, Life and Death – Brahma, Vishnu and Shiva. In essence the dhak belongs to Shiva, for its whole leaf is an emblem of the trident in the hand of the Great God – that God whose attribute is destruction; who waits among the shadows of every temple and village... whose meaning is not death alone, but Life-through-Death.

Like the majority of autobiographical works by women in her era, Jacob's letters and diaries only give rare glimpses into her personal emotions. Jelinek says that it is a fallacy that "the autobiographical mode is an introspective and intimate one and that autobiographers write about their inner and emotional life". The characters in Jacob's prose and poetry reveal more about themselves: it seems that Jacob feels more comfortable communicating deeper emotions behind the mask of a fictional persona. Jacob's writing of a diary could be seen as her first attempt at prose writing. The desire to communicate her individual experience is later more fully realised through the disguises offered by fiction.

Consciously or unconsciously, Jacob's diaries show similarities in form and content to other contemporary autobiographical works, especially those of women. Jacob goes to great effort to create the scenery of each place. This loyalty to detail, whether or not it is entirely relevant to the day's events is, according to Jelinek, a typically female trait. Violet Jacob's choice of subject matter also differs from the majority of male writer's subject matter:

> [Women] emphasise to a much lesser extent the public aspect of their lives, the affairs of the world, or even their careers, and concentrate instead on their personal lives – domestic details, family difficulties, close friends and especially people that influence them.

Jacob worked in a hospital for much of her first stay in India but beyond entries like: "20th January: Went to the married quarters and women's hospital" she writes nothing of what she does there. Similarly, although she was writing her first novel in 1899 she gives no details of its progress apart from: "11th June: Read the first seven chapters of *The Sheepstealers* to A. [Arthur Jacob, her husband] after supper."

Virginia Woolf saw the diary form as invaluable because it "sweeps up accidentally several stray matters which I would exclude if I hesitated, but which are the diamonds of the dustheap". Jacob too sketches scene after scene in her diary, capturing all her experiences, so that when she reads it later she will be able to see the most important moments. Diaries record fluctuations in the writer's moods that would otherwise be forgotten or go unnoticed. Just as the Modernist writer tries to record all detail, to avoid obvious narrative intervention and leave the reader to interpret the significant details, a diary yields significant autobiographical detail to the critic. Although obviously selected by the author, the diary is a more pure form of autobiography than memoirs written long after the event.

The diaries themselves focus on very specific periods in Violet Jacob's life. Firstly her going to India as a young wife and mother. All of the exotic East was new to her and a delight. The pleasure of her early days is expressed in her letters to her mother as Jacob tries to recreate for her the people and setting of her new life. She writes to her mother of amusing incidents as Harry grows up, for example when she is telling him stories:

> Sometimes I vary the Hindu mythology with the ordinary fairy tales and 'Cinderella' is the one that he particularly likes …"and there was the Prince Sahib dancing with Jane and Susan (for these are our names for the cruel sisters) and when he saw the lovely Cinderella come in he said, 'Go away, wicked Jane and Susan, I will not dance with you any more!'" "oh!" said Harry, thrilled, "and did he kick them?" When I told him it was not thought right for Princes to kick their partners I think he was rather sorry.

The second diary is written when Jacob is in her sixtieth year. The joy of returning to a place where they were so happy is tempered by the memories of their past:

> It was terrible to think how happy one once was …and how many dead, and how young one once was and how strong. I don't know whether all this is a greater pleasure or greater pain. My old love of the place wrings my heart and I see ghosts, though not where others see them. The best of all my life was here; youth, health, spirits and Harry, who began his life here and who ended it, a soldier amongst the soldiers who knew him here as a little boy, when the great test came.

The later diary is similar in volume to the first, although it only covers a period of five months as opposed to five years. This shows an even stronger wish to preserve her memories on paper. The emotionally demanding visits she makes lead to more personal writing than before. As a result of twenty years of literary endeavour her style of writing is also more mature. She is assured in her opinions and writes more expansively and fluently of her impressions.

The character of Violet Jacob that comes through from her diaries and other prose is that of a highly intelligent woman with a thirst for knowledge. Jacob was a keen botanist and taught herself about the flora of central India. Her paintings of the flowers in India are highly respected and are found in the Botanical Library in Edinburgh. In the search for unknown blossoms she often rode alone in the Indian bush, an unconventional pastime for a lady of the Raj. The disapproval of others was no deterrent. After an expedition she returns to write:

> This whole country appeals to me as nothing ever has yet; it is impossible for anyone who cannot see it to have an idea of it, and there are enough and to spare of those who can who have none either. I keep thanking God, like the Pharisee in the parable, that I am not as other men, and certainly not as other women in this matter.

As a child, Jacob's inquisitiveness led her "aye in and oot amo' the ploomen's feet at the Mains o' Dun". So, despite the fact that her family were of the Angus gentry, she learnt the dialect, attitudes and myths of Scots of every class. John Buchan, in his introduction to *Songs of Angus*, praised Jacob for "the living speech, with the accent of the natural voice" in her Scottish verse. Interestingly, the Hindu she learnt was that of the lower castes. This was invaluable to her on her wanderings but totally useless for polite society. This caused awkward situations on her return trip to India. At one dinner with the Begum of Bhopal she wrote:

> The Begum of Kurwai and her daughter came noiselessly in, and I was introduced to the former, who sat on my right. I did not attempt to talk to her, not having enough Hindustani to warrant my addressing a venerable lady of rank; but I was sorry for this as she interested me very much.

Jacob was fascinated by the people she met, she judged them all equally irrespective of their station. She saw the stately figure of the Maharajah, for example, as 'awfully and fearfully fat, and wearing a garment that looked as if it were made out of a grey eiderdown quilt'. This lack of awe leads to some interesting insights to India's native rulers, especially as Jacob, being a woman, is allowed behind the Moslem purdah. She sees purdah as a tradition that hampers the progression of any developing country because of the isolation of the women from world affairs. She sympathises with the men who are never allowed to flourish away from home due to the narrow views of their wives or mothers.

Jacob's love of life is closely bound with her interest in other people and an appreciation of the complexity of human nature. She was proud of her heritage and her family history. In a typically feminine, oblique form of autobiography she writes of other significant figures in her family and in Scotland's past. She depicts them in a highly entertaining manner, with an eye for their idiosyncrasies as well as their achievements. For example she used in her fiction the character of the 13th Laird of Dun, a respected judge yet a Jacobite supporter, and his more openly militant younger brother. They appear in *Flemington* as Lord Balnillo and James Logie. The novel is the fictional recreation of an actual event – the disastrous landing of a Jacobite ship, the *Hazard*, in Montrose harbour. Here, as with her own experiences, she is transforming reality in to art. War, over the centuries, ravaged the male line of the Erskine family, not least in Jacob's own day, and when she wrote *The Lairds of Dun* she would have been painfully aware that she had no male heir to carry on the family line was.

In *The Interloper*, there features the bizarre character of Lady Eliza Lamont, a keen horsewoman who wore

> a short red wig of indifferent fit ...a buff waistcoat ...covered a figure which even in youth could never have been graceful, and the lady's high-collared coat and riding skirt of plum colour were shabby with the varied weather of many years.

This is a description of Jacob's great-great-aunt Alice, the 16th Laird of Dun, which came directly from those who knew her. Alice spoke the broad Scots of her forefathers and was said to be "a mixture of homely speech and immense family pride". Alice's mother, alive in the late eighteenth century, was described by the family tutor as

> Well looked ...and converses with ease [but] rather masculine in her diversions, for instance she often walks seven miles before dinner, goes a hunting with her husband in the season and is a great salmon fisher.

There is evidence that Jacob inherited many of the qualities of her predecessors. Another feminine family trait Jacob highlights is the love of flowers, particularly from her grandmother. When in India, she wrote detailed letters to her mother about the flowers she saw and even enclosed some blossoms. When Harry Jacob first travels far from home it is to the battlefields of the Somme. Harry too sent flower cuttings to his mother. In July 1916 he wrote:

> There are the most wonderful cornfields in this country; *full* of poppies, cornflowers, corncockles, and these things I enclose, it is really lovely.

Harry Jacob's letters are in themselves a valuable record of the experiences of a young soldier. In an effort to stop his mother from worrying too much about him, Harry's letters from France rarely give way to the terror and misery he must have felt. The photographs he took (by smuggling a camera to the trenches) show the muddied and freezing conditions in which the soldiers fought. He only once mentions this, and in an understated way:

> Will you send me some socks please as mine are worn out and my feet are not in a very good condition at the moment.

It is only in a letter to his father, written days before his death, that the seriousness of the occasion is conveyed:

Harry Jacob, photographed in 1916

We all trust in God to bring us through safely and I feel that he will protect me for Mother's sake; don't let her get frightened about things, but I am sure she will be brave.

Violet Jacob loved her son dearly and had been a strong influence in his life. His letters show that, as when they had both enthused over Hindu myths, they still shared similar interests. He wrote poetry and sketched but had little belief in his talents. He wrote of amusing incidents among the soldiers that would appeal to her humour but above all he clearly shared her strong Christian faith. Harry wrote a poem to his best friend before he left for the Front and it ended with the lines, "of my mother and him shall be my last thought/ ere they number me out with the slain".

By the very act of writing Jacob was contributing to another aspect of her heritage;

Scottish literature. Her poetry best illustrates how she continues and adds to a tradition going back hundreds of years. It is said of Jacob that as a child in Montrose Library "she read avidly and revelled in the poetry of Dunbar, Ramsay and Burns". She skilfully employs the local dialect to explore again the old themes of nostalgia and exile, superstition, religion and, of course, love. Through the personae of the townsfolk and tradespeople, farm labourers and gypsies she artfully evokes the atmosphere of the north-east. She was frequently compared to other 'aristocratic' poets like Lady Nairne (who wrote of country folk with a similar sharp observation of character and dry humour). In a letter to Jacob, Charles Murray, a contemporary Aberdeenshire poet, called her Scotland's best poet since Burns. Helen Cruikshank wrote a poem 'To Violet Jacob, on reading her *Songs of Angus*' saying:

> I too lo'e weel the Angus braes
> Ye pent wi' sic a skilfu han'
> An' aften ha'e I langed tae write,
> As ye ha'e dune, o' my hame-lan'

Hugh MacDiarmid admired Jacob's work and included it in the anthologies of Scottish poetry he published in the 1920s. However he was not such an effusive critic. He called her "definitely only a minor poet" in a letter to Ronald Garden, but he did write that Jacob was "by far the most considerable of contemporary vernacular poets". As well as drawing from the past tradition of Scottish literature, Jacob and other makars like Cruikshank, Murray and Marion Angus, laid the foundations for the twentieth-century renaissance in Scottish vernacular poetry of which MacDiarmid was a central figure.

Jacob is sympathetic to all aspects of human nature (with one exception, narrow-mindedness). She treats the life of itinerant travellers, like the tinkers, sympathetically and celebrates their freedom. In doing this she does not hide the drawbacks of life exposed to the elements, scorned by many and relying on theft to survive (as in 'The Tinkler's Baloo') but also shows the romance. Christina Mill, the complacent heroine of 'The Lum Hat' is spurred on to marry and travel having been pitied for her limited horizons by a tinker's wife. In the same collection of short stories the eponymous 'Banny Firelocks', a more free-thinking heroine, is portrayed more favourably. It is not that Banny has lower moral standards than Christina, but that she is not shackled by limiting preconceptions.

Girls scorned for their sensuality and labelled as 'jaud' or 'huzzy' are not condemned by Jacob. In 'The Jaud' the disgraced girl in the clour'd and nettle-ridden grave is envied by the old woman who, superficially, seems to have had a fulfilling life. The old lady does not remember the girl's shame, but her beauty; "sae prood an' lichtsome an' fine was she" and thinks that despite her respectability and 'honour' it is

> Wi' envy I'm like tae dee
> O' the warld she had that was no for me
> And the kingdom that ne'er was mine

In 'The Jaud' Jacob rejects stereotypical Victorian roles for women epitomised by Mrs Ellis in *The Women of England*. Mrs Ellis sees woman as having little function outside her domestic role:

> Women, considered in their distinct and abstract nature, as isolated beings, must lose more than half their worth. They are, in fact, from their own constitution, and from the station they occupy in the world, strictly relative roles.

Once again Jacob is reacting against a limited outlook. In her actions as well as her writing Jacob refuses to conform. That she was an author at all made her "a little suspect to the military society of Cairo" according to Susan Buchan. She also smoked which, as Carol Anderson points out in her introduction to *Diaries and Letters From India 1895–1900*, was quite unusual for her time and greatly surprised some Indian women of her acquaintance. When out camping she and Arthur dressed alike in "topis, khaki clothes and leather leggings".

Love is a common theme in Jacob's fiction and is depicted in many guises, for example the frustrated love of 'Rejected' or the unnoticed girl of 'The Heid Horseman':

> For wark's yer meat and wark's yer play,
> Heid horseman though ye be,
> Ye've ne'er a glance for wife nor maid,
> Ye tak' nae tent o' me

or the excitement of 'Tam i' the Kirk':

> He canna sing for the sang that his ain he'rt raises,
> He canna see for the mist that's afore his een,
> And a voice droons the hale o' the psalms and the paraphrases
> Crying "Jean! Jean! Jean!"

Little is known of how Violet Jacob met her husband and whether she had suitors before him. She does not discuss their marriage in her letters or diaries but her romantic character can be seen in the encouragement she gave other lovers when she was older.

Love is not confined to the young, in 'The Guidwife Speaks' (from *The Northern Lights*, Jacob's last book of published verse), the handsome man the guidwife married has become a surly and taciturn companion but, to his wife, a companion all the same:

> An' yet, an' yet, I dreid tae see
> The ingle standin' toom; oh, then
> Youth's last left licht wad gang wi' ye –
> What wad I dae? I dinna ken.

In a letter to a friend, Jacob laments the endless moving and homelessness of their army life, then she confides that, being a 'nomad', she rather enjoys it. Montrose, the setting for so much of her poetry, is an active sea port and many of the characters in her poems long to go to sea. The boy in 'The Doocot up the Braes' yearns for the time when

> Dark still smoors the sky
> A Baltic brig will tak the tide
> Wi' a lad that canna rest!

Tom Falconer, a ship's mate in 'The Figurehead' finds it impossible, after all his travelling, to settle down with a local girl due to their now differing perspectives. However it is to Angus that Jacob returns to end her days. Her husband predeceased her by nine years. Although their marriage was clearly a happy one from the way 'A' is seen as companionable and supportive, Jacob hardly mentions him in her diaries. After his death, though, Jacob expresses her devastation. She wrote to the librarian at Montrose "no words can express how I miss him", but she realised that "it is not many people who can look back for over forty years of such happiness". She settles in Kirriemuir, writing:

> I always knew that, should I be left alone, the only thing that would keep me from breaking my heart would be to live in Angus.

On her second trip to India Jacob reflected upon the frustrations old age was putting upon her:

> There are so many things in life, quite harmless, that one cannot do now. I wonder if, for their sake, one would accept youth again. I think not; not even for the fulfilment of them all.

Her faith and her longing to be with those who departed the earth before her caused her, despite her great love of life, to welcome her end.

In his introduction to *Songs of Angus* John Buchan attributes Jacob's ability to recreate "a living tongue" to her being, at that time, an exile from Angus. He hears the note of longing "like all the poetry of exiles, a chastened melancholy". A sense of sorrow and the sense of a life beyond the present would have been affected by the early deaths of her father and siblings. Wistfulness and nostalgia were elements of her work before Harry's death, but after 1916 the sorrow deepened.

In *More Songs of Angus*, the first volume of poetry published after Harry's death, the poem dedicated to him is her most direct. In it she addresses him personally and in English, thus lowering the masks of language and narrative personae:

To AHJ

ast life, past tears, far past the grave,
   The tryst is set for me,
ince, for our all, your all you gave
   On the slopes of Picardy.
n Angus, in the autumn nights,
   The ice-green light shall lie,
eyond the trees the Northern Lights
   Slant on the belts of sky.
ut miles on miles from Scottish soil
   You sleep, past war and scaith,
our country's freedman, loosed from toil,
   In honour and in faith.

For Angus held you in her spell,
   Her Grampians, faint and blue,
Her ways and speech you knew so wel
   Were half the world to you
Yet rest, my son; our souls are those
   Nor time nor death can part,
And you lie proudly, folded close
   To France's deathless heart.

Death is seen here as a separation, not an eternal parting. Jacob shows the importance of the Angus people and countryside to her and Harry. She writes of his death with pride as well as sadness. This sense of honour is illustrated in her 1922–23 Indian diary when she talked with the Begum of Bhopal of the Begum's grandson's suicide:

> She told me about the tragedy they had when her grandson, the General's eldest son, blew out his brains. From her account he was a charming youth – O [Oswald Bosanquet] said the same – and his parents were inconsolable.

An autographed photograph from around 1915

He had recovered after an illness to find his wife had died. She asked me if I had any children, and I told her that Harry had been killed in the war. She said, "Then you know what it is." I told her that no one knew better, and she answered: "But your son's death was an honour to his country and his family, and our boy's death was for no use; it was different." I was sorry for her.

In the poem 'Glory' an Angus mother mourns her son:

> I canna see ye, lad, I canna see ye
> For a' yon glory that's aboot yer heid,
> Yon licht that haps ye and the hosts that's wi' ye –
> Aye, but ye live, and it's mysel' that's deid
> ...Deith canna kill, the mools o' France lie o'er ye,
> And yet ye live, O sodger o' the Lord.
> For Him that focht wi' deith an' dule before ye
> He gied the life – 'twas Him that gied the sword.

As shown in the earlier example of *Flemington,* Jacob never idealises war but she also never condemns it. In a sermon written for Sacrament Sunday in 1941 her Christian faith shows strong, despite and because of the war raging. Tellingly she rejects the notion that man is becoming more evil. Instead she points to all the good work and brave acts performed in war-time. She asks, "who are these heroes and heroines: Common folk" and says faith in God and human nature is the way to combat evil.

'The Lost Licht' from *Songs of Angus* tells the Perthshire legend of a child that can't be happy in heaven for the woe of his mother on earth. For Jacob all myths hold an element of truth. This particular legend helped her contain her grief over Harry in 1916. She wrote to a friend:

> I *know* he is so happy and I believe so much in the 'communion of saints' that I am certain that he is never far from me and I am also so sure that by giving way to grief I can cloud his joy that I try harder than ever to conquer it and to wait in hope and patience.

Part of Jacob's faith had always been a belief in life after death. When Harry died she felt his presence around her, as she wrote in a letter in 1917:

> He is *so* near me often

> Last night I was made so happy by feeling him beside me – I never know when it is going to happen and sometimes when I expect him to come I am disappointed and again, when I don't expect it, suddenly he is there tho' I cannot see him – but I feel it so strongly.

Jacob's final publication, *The Scottish Poems of Violet Jacob*, is dedicated to 'The comrade beyond'. Her faith in life after death is expressed in her verse in poems like, 'The Field by the Lirk o' the Hill' and 'The Brig'. The Brig is both a real one and the bridge between mortality and "the fields o' life/ and ye walk for ever there". For the person left on earth:

> And whiles a step treids on by me,
> I mauna hear its fa'
> But atween the brig an' the brier tree
> There gangs nae ane, but twa'

Violet Jacob's vision of the afterlife is best expressed by the quotation from Bishop Brent she had carved on her husband's memorial stone:

> And life is eternal and love is immortal and death is only an horizon and an horizon is nothing save the limit of our sight.

Jacob was a writer who drew from her experiences to create her fiction. She was fascinated by those she met from every culture and walk of life. She was proudly conscious of her heritage – her aristocratic background and Scottish roots. A passionate woman, she was deeply affected by the loves in her lives and personal tragedy. Highly imaginative and with strong spiritual beliefs Jacob believed in both the supernatural and life after death. Jacob was an observant woman and was quick to see the humorous in everyday events. All these facets of her personality can best be observed by reading her diaries and family history alongside her imaginative fiction, by recognising the autobiographical unity that connects all her literary work.   *Sarah Bing*

The Pond

Rosa Macpherson

I saw you in the park today. You were wearing grey wellington boots, a black raincoat, tied at the waist, and you were standing at the edge of the pond, looking in.

You didn't see me, although I was on the other side, on the bench, with the baby.

You are looking older.

If you want to know, Jack is fine and doing well, although there are times you still get in the way.

I have tried, for my part, to be a good wife. No, I have tried to be a good person; complete; you know, and I suppose I assumed that that would make me a good wife. You must be careful not to ask for too much. I learned that, even before I watched you today, watching the water on the pond.

Jack is still working at the University. His research is near completion: thank God; you know how tiring it can be. We have had to postpone our holiday three times this year. He is still smoking, regardless of the doctor.

Do you ever think of us? I ask because you have been in my thoughts more and more often lately. Today; at the pond, you completed my pain: the final jigsaw piece, slotted into place.

I hold nothing against you.

I kept the colours in the living room. Jack wanted to re-decorate but I saw no point. We have a new carpet though. The baby is often sick on it, but it is durable, thank God.

I never intended to steal your husband. I simply fell in love with him; with the shy grey in his hair; his smile. If you must know it was his hands that first drew me: those hard, calloused hands, on a thinking man. Like a fraud; an imposter.

He does not speak of you. He always gives me a disapproving look when I tell people I am his second wife. At University parties, where people do not know me. He never took you to those, did he? I cannot imagine why, although I must say it was a blessing for you. Ha ha.

Today, at the pond, I wanted to speak to you.

Jack would be furious if he knew. Anything beyond the microscope is beyond him. He cannot understand. He is very good with the baby. I'm sorry you never had children, but perhaps that was for the best, under the circumstances.

The first time Jack made love to me, he hid his face in my shoulder, and cried your name.

In the beginning I was never intensely interested in you. You were simply the woman who had walked in the rooms of my house; who painted my living room, and who once slipped into my body, and your husband mistook me for you.

You looked tired when I saw you at the pond today, as if you had simply put on your boots and your raincoat, without caring to check on the weather.

I heard that you had given up your job. When I told Jack he snorted, and turned the pages of his book, in much the same way he does whenever I speak of you. Does that surprise you? He wants to re-paint the living room but I insist it stays the way it is. We are sisters. You are everywhere and I do not know if I can forgive you. You are in the yellow curtains; in the hanging coffee cups above the kettle; in my bedroom; in the lilac laundry basket. Your face dissolves in mine, even without a mirror.

When Jack looks at me I don't know who he sees. He is still forever Jack, forever there. Only we change, you and I, on opposite sides of the pond.

I found your silver-flecked scarf at the back of the hall closet. It smelled of perfume when I held it to my face. What type do you use? Jack cannot remember. He has stripped you from himself so cleanly. This should please me. I gaze at his face, behind his smile, his eyes, and I see only love there. Much the same as you will remember.

You should not stand alone at the pond.

There is so much you could have told me, should have told me. I don't mean about Jack. I mean about us. You knew, of course you knew, that we would both eventually stand at opposite ends of the same pond, didn't you? That's why you let me in the way you did. No fighting, no trouble, no tears.

Just come in, your eyes said, that day I arrived too early and you were lifting your single bag from the floor. Just come in.

One day we'll both be standing alone, in the park. And all the Jacks will still be shadows, lying on us, whispering any name; and sighing, not for another, just sighing.

You knew I would stand at this same window, smoking, looking out towards the park, like you. That was a bastard thing to do, but I do not hold it against you.

I have put the cheese plant in the corner near the front door, since it has grown so. I'm sure you would approve.

Rosa Macpherson

First Fit

Mary McIntosh

He hearkened tae the kirk bells dingin oot the auld year. Guid bluidy affgaun this. Bluidy Bosnia, bluidy fowk, didnae bluidy ken whan thai wur bate. His gizz thrawed wi the thocht. The wup roon his airm seepit reid an the pine wis sair tae thole.

He skinkit his muckle-baned corpus intae the bolie o the bit waa that wis aye staunin, machine gun hauden ticht. He wisnae ower weel beildit but he wis siccarset fer a while. His braith cam in saft pechs, he wis fair buckled up wi the fecht. He creepit ahent the wrak o the hoose an gae a bit gley roon the waa, his lugs preened back fer ilka smaa soon. Nane cam. He wisnae shair whaur the lave o the forepairtie had ennit up, he thocht it micht hae been at the fowerweys whan thai had fauchten the tanks. He wis his lane an sair in need o sumbit tae lig his heid fer a while.

Hillocks o ribble lay afore him, here wa lair-stane waas wur aye staunin. The artaillery wis quait, but ootbye he cuid hear the tanks gurlin. Bastards, didnae ken whan thai wur bate. His mynd cast back tae the slauchter an he thocht he wid kink on the venim that wis in him. Redd thaim oot, that wis the anerly wey forrit. He mynded thir faces whan he had heichted the gun, het atween his fingirs, an the tyauvin whan the bullets skelpit intae thaim. He gleyed roon the stanes, heid sweyin bak an forrit, dreid wumplin ower the bak o his haunds.

Thar wis a spladge o orange i the sky aa shotten through wi a crammasie glowe, an he shiddered as the nicht creepit roon him. A licht flichtered i the ribble, he crawled ower aa his sinses alicht tae the jeopardie. Thar wis an ill-fittit trapdoor steillit intae the grund. He pit his ee tae the gaig. It wis the skimmer o a caunle, the low gien smaa licht. The har on the back o his craig prinkled at the pewlin soon cummin oot o that bleck pit.

He liftit the sneck cannily an lowpit doon the steps skirlin. Cauld swite haled oot o his broo an he brocht himsel up agin the waa, gun sweenging roon the cellar. The fousome guff wis like tae mak him boak but he chockit it back.

"Its jist us, thar's nae sodgers here." The wurds cam frae aneth a pickle cloots i the neuk. His vice wis shakkin. "Oot o therr, ye bastard, cum oan, oot." The hind-maist wurd wis a hairsh scraich. He delascht a roon o billits at the ruif. Aathing went quait. The air wis fou o the yowther an the wheesht dirled his lugs.

She rase up, bleck in the flichterin, the bairn close oan hir breist.

"It's jist us," she wis wheengin, "naebody else, jist me an the bairn. I cuidna gang wi the lave. I birthed ower sune, I cuidna get awaa. But thair aa awaa, lang syne."

The bairn wis claikin an she made tae gie it aisment. Peety, smuired ower the lang days, wis like tae brak in on his venim. He wis near tae greetin. "Christ, I didnae ken, I didnae ken", an he shawed hir the bluidy airm. She muived ower by him. "Ye maun hae that sortit", hir gizz wis pickit aneth the grey dirt. Aa o a suddent hir wurds cam strang. "It'll gang wrang else." She pat the bairn doon oan a pickle rags an heized his airm. "Gin ye dinna mynd, aiblins I cuid aid ye."

Sair taen abak, he yieldit. His haunds lowsed aff the gun an he pit his heid agin the waa an thocht aboot his ain wummin. She wis sauf at hame, aye sauf at hame. An he thocht aboot hoo it wid be if she wis deid, but he cuidna thole the notion. He gae a bit lauch, she wis in nae fuckin jeopardie frae thae bastards noo. He wis gaen wrang aa thegither, it maun be aa the bluid he had tint. His guid haund gruppit the braig i his belt. The wummin taen a stap backart.

"Dae sumthin", his teeth wur bared like a dug's. "Soart this fuckin lot oot." She crulged ower him an taen the watter boattle frae him. Her haunds wur canny as she sweiled the bluid awaa an rowed up his airm wi the blauded wup. He settled doon seekin tae get some ais frae the stounin. The bairn set tae keen aince mair.

"Shut it up, fuckin shut it up", the braig wis i his neive. He wis greetin, saut watter laivin fite runnels i the clart o his gizz. The laigh soon o the bairn's pewlin sabbed in his lugs.

He wis forfochen an aa the picters he had been seekin tae fauld awaa crooded intae his mynd. Simmer days, green gress, pikniks, watter gliskin bew i the sun. An the flooers that growed ilka year at the watterside, bricht reid, sweyin i the sowff o the wund. Nichts whan thir boadies had brunt het as they lay thegither, swite halin aff thaim wi the luferent that wis atween thaim, an he grat fer whit wis awaa, fer that hamit laddie, as the slauchter that lay atween him an the dour ill-faured man wha ligged in this bleck hole.

The bairn wis slaiken at hir breist. Hir heid wis boued ower it an he kinkit doon the better tae luik at hir. "Whaur's yer man?"

Hir sair een gleyed up at him. "He went awaa, tae fecht, he said." She muived the bairn oan tae her ither breist. "He didnae hae a uniform though, he took his anorak wi him. He'll no be cauld wull he? Aa that cranreuch ootside, he'll be cauld." She pit her gizz tae the bairn's. "I widnae like him tae catch cauld."

The veins in hir breist were bluachie agin hir fite skin. Anither picter cam tae him, anither lass, anither tyme, her een alicht wi the fainess o whit thai had makfurth thegither. He wis hertsair, weary wi the bickerin, the bluid and the wrack. He craved fer whit he had tint.

"Halt that an hap yersel up." He wis mislushious in his thrawness.

"I hae tae gie him the breist. He's hungert."

He heichted the gun, "Haud aff, I say, an hap yersel, ye luik like a hure." The bile wis soor i the bak o his thrapple.

She lifted hir breist and poued hir blouse ower it. He turnt awaa frae hir as she cuddled the bairn an stairted to croon. An auld sang o auld weirs, hard focht, an scowth sair cum by. The bairn at hir breist lookit up, een wide apen an hir douce tears faaed ower its broo. The wurds thirled in the smeik. "Fuck ye, fuck the lot o ye."

He rased the gun. It wis het atween his fingirs.

Mary McIntosh

Creating Ourselves
The poetry of Nan Shepherd
Mairi-Ann Cullen

The article, 'Poets, Penises...and Pints' by Lesley Riddoch and Mary Gladstone in issue 5 of *Harpies & Quines* must have struck a chord with many women readers struggling to find a voice and then an audience within the Scottish writing scene. The poet Helen Cruickshank put it succinctly in her *Octobiography*:

> I am not asked out to drinking parties and have never been in a Rose Street pub. I can't be a poet.

This problem has also affected the reputation of the Aberdeen poet Nan Shepherd (1893–1981). She published three novels and one volume of poetry between 1928 and 1934, yet she is best remembered as a perceptive critic and friend of Neil Gunn, and of the North East poets J C Milne and Charles Murray. Her own creative work, especially her poetry, has virtually disappeared from accounts of the literary ferment of the Scottish Renaissance.

Two of her novels, *The Quarry Wood* and *The Weatherhouse*, have recently been reprinted in the Canongate Classics series. If you haven't read these, rush out and buy them. They were an important milestone for me in realising, like Martha Ironside, heroine of *The Quarry Wood*, that "I can be my own creator." Nan Shepherd's novels are full of strong women characters and honest descriptions of female sexual longing; in addition, she uses perfectly-rendered Scots dialogue several years before Lewis Grassic Gibbon's *Sunset Song*. For these reasons, I looked forward to finding a copy of her book of poems *In the Cairngorms*.

Instead I discovered that *In the Cairngorms* is out of print and difficult to find second-hand. Fortunately there is a copy in the National Library, though sadly not in the Scottish Poetry Library. Most of the poems in the book are written in English and in a controlled, apparently detached, style that seemed at first to be far removed from the passionate, honest mind revealed in the novels. Nan Shepherd the novelist fell into obscurity because she was a woman; Nan Shepherd the poet has fallen into obscurity because she was a Scottish woman trying to write poetry in the English tradition. She is one of those Scottish writers who have been marginalised because she chose to write her poetry in English. In this context, it is not surprising that the two poems of hers anthologised in Catherine Kerrigan's *An Anthology of Scottish Women Poets* are both, atypically, in Scots.

In the Cairngorms is, in fact, an important part of our literary heritage. As the title suggests, most of the poems are inspired by Nan Shepherd's love of the Scottish mountains. Yet the mountains are only a starting point for her poetry. Her themes range through the intensities of intellectual and emotional life. In her poem, 'Strange gifts of pleasure has the mind', she expresses the "strange darknesses" of the soul, the suffering a woman has to go through to unmake the world around her before she can begin to be herself:

> Down and down and further down
> De-formed, annulled, unmade,
> She feels the whole creation drown,
> The ache of form allayed.
> The streaming seas, the ocean gulf,
> The rocks, dissolve away.
> Now she may recreate herself;
> Now is the primal day.

The slightly archaic language, the dramatic alliteration and stress-pattern, the tightly-controlled stanzaic form are typical of much of the poetry in the collection; so too is the use of the simple rhyme scheme *abab* to contain the complexities of her thought. The theme of recreating ourselves is developed further in her poem 'Embodiment'. This begins with a description of light among the mountains but at once goes on to state:

> Light was the principle of their making
> And light their substance.

Light, in this poem, is the only substance in the material world, a world that is still in the process of being created. Since we, too, are light and contain the "principle of making", we can "create ourselves in a form/ Imagined in no god's mind", a form perhaps as beautiful as the mountains she loves. Heady possibilities await the woman who dares create herself!

Perhaps her best-known poem, 'O, licht amo' the hills', is also a celebration of light, but it is, in addition, an expression of her sense of what the world would be like without it:

> O, licht amo' the hills,
> S'uld ye gang oot,
> To what na dark the warld'll fa'.

Her creative imagination accepted and worked on darkness as well as light; both the literal darkness of night or of rock, and the psychological darkness of physical and mental suffering. In her poetry, the recurring use of the simple words "light" and "bright" as in, for example, 'The Bush', or 'Lux Perpetua', is balanced by the complexities of meaning she attaches to them, and by the equally present awareness of the dark side of life and of the natural world. Her poem, 'Images of beauty and destruction' sums up this sense:

> The tarn, luminous verdigras, still as a jewel,
> No sound save, once, a thunder of snow from the corrie.
> No man so hot of blood but finds death in its water.

The use of the male descriptor, "man", is typical of many of the earlier poems in the collection, and is a vivid reminder of how hard it is to write as a woman using patriarchal language. A later stanza from the same poem, despite describing a woman's experience of the freedom the mountains afford, also uses this male noun:

> Here man escapes from the futile sense of safety,
> The busy and cheerful acts that invade the soul.

Yet Nan Shepherd's poetry is proof that she resisted the invasion of her soul: in 'Summit of Corrie Etchachan' she celebrates female intelligence and acknowledges her mind's awareness of

>...a vast, dark and inscrutable sense
>Of its own terror, its own glory and power.

In 'Crusoe', too, she imagines her spirit freely roving, then foundering on rocks but chancing to find "a quiet isle" where it discovers undisturbed thought:

>The dew of thought unbrushed from mile on mile,
>Thought that had known the primal dusk awhile.

The rest of the poem describes her spirit's joy as it explores this new intellectual landscape before time steps in and brings her back to the mundane reality of "forgotten toil and tears". Intellectual prowess was not an easy burden for a woman to bear: in 'Quiet over Lochnagar' she speaks of "the burning mind" learning to recognise the "secret stigma of its kind".

Many of her poems play on the four elements of earth, air (or light), fire and water. Often running water is used as an image of creativity as in 'Embodiment' or in 'The Flooded Meads' where the "loosened words pour down at last": sometimes it is an image of the release of sexual tension. In some of her poems light is imagined as a god, as male, while the earth is female. This is the case, for example, in 'The three great rocks of Beinn Mheadhoin' and is played on in 'A Girl in Love' – here the girl who people thought of as like the "dull earth" burns "like flame" under the influence of the light of love. Fire is usually an image of strong emotions, often of sexual desire, as in 'Fires' where it is the power that

>...snaps asunder
>The strange restraints of life for a soaring moment;

revealing the crumbling "walls of our self-seclusion" and the extent of desire.

Significantly, the last two poems in the collection reject the use of these images as a means of expressing the emotions of love. In the poem 'Not in a Glass', which begins "Let us have done with image", light, air, stars, flame, and waters, are all dismissed as false, as merely "veils of speech". The lovers are pictured starkly as being only themselves:

>I AM for each of us the ultimate fate,
>Betrayed, betraying, broken each for each,
>I take you, you me, accepting doom
>Of what we are, and yet – O profligate! –
>More than we are we give, and more receive.

In 'Real Presence', the same move away from image to reality, from essence to substance, from gods to real bodies is celebrated:

>No false gods now, the images o'ercast,
>We are love's body, or we are undone.

It is interesting, too, that both these poems pun on religious images of 'pure' love.

The victory for physical love is achieved at the end of a series of eleven poems charting the progress of a love affair. From the first realisation of the wonder of being in love, through the agony of masturbatory nights of longing expressed in 'Half Love' and particularly in 'Without my Right', the love continues despite physical separation until it has become a cut crystal memory in 'An Ecstasy Remembered'. But in 'Growth', the lovers have met again and found that love in the present is not safely controllable as it is in memory:

> I had not failed you had you been the same
> As that old self that at my bidding came
> In dream and memory; but now – but now –
> Anguished I break the vows I never swore
> And bear the shame for deeds I disallow.

At first ashamed and distressed by the physical consummation of their love, the poem 'Pardon' finishes with the triumphant statement "Go now, or stay. I have the whole of you." Thus, in the final poem of the collection, the poet is able to say with relief: "To such a clearness love is come at last."

Possibly this resolution of love's difficulties in her poetry reflected a similar breakthrough in her own life: for whatever reason, she published no more books of poetry. Nan Shepherd used a particular strand of the English poetic tradition to express her deepest emotions and insights. For us as modern women that style may be offputting at first, but her voice is individual, her insights important, her struggle to be an intellectual and creative woman worth remembering and cherishing.

Mairi-Ann Cullen

Deadheading the Rose

Magi Gibson

Check-up

Into the doctor's surgery I float
a skirt, a pair of shoes, a flapping coat
(this medicine man will know me only as
a well-coordinated set of clothes).

Perched upon a straight-back chair
I chat and smile, tell him all is well but
as I'm here, maybe he should take a look…
The doctor pokes and prods and stares

I disembody, hover in the air.
Finally he sinks back in his seat,
scrapes a blue-veined scrawl
across a pale pink sheet.

Against the ticking of the clock
I fasten every button on my coat
tuck his reassurance in my bag
note my appointment for a mammograph.

Mammogram

The waiting room is not – it is
the dead-end of a corridor
four chairs on their last legs
an abandoned *Woman*
and an empty paper cup.

Waiting for my turn to be X-rayed
I watch my hands grow old before my eyes:
brown liver spots spread wide,
white knuckle bones gnarl, arthritic

fingers curl to yellowed claws –
time telescopes so every second counts
a passing year – yet suddenly
I'm faced with mortal fear

that old age might elude my youthful grasp.
I turn my palms down on my lap;
the lifeline's length remains
an unsolved mystery.

NEXT! Like an omen of ill-will
the small word hovers in the air
I enter through the open door.
Undress! Pose!

I'm twisted, tugged at,
yield to every yelled command,
spineless as a bendy-doll.
I'm soft, pink, warm, alone. I stand

in a room of metal arms and legs
while robots' icy faces press
against my shrinking flesh.
No flashing lights,

no cheery shouts of cheese,
only the disconcerting click
the eerie whirr
of unseen cameras.

Salted Fruit

Outside there is a cutting wind.
From the third-floor window of the ward
I watch pipe-cleaner people curve
against its blade.

Wearily I sit back on the bed,
I turn the tinny headset up too loud:
its crack and hiss more welcome than
the Latin words and sterile platitudes

the doctors soothe me with.
The angry wind abates, snowflakes
float up past the darkening pane:
this is gravity defied,

they've turned my whole world upside down.
My cut breast aches.
The gods have sipped its salted fruit.
They liked its fleshy taste.

They will be back for more.

Friends

Friends come in waves
some lapping gently
into the flowered bay
where I'm marooned.

Others crash in merrily
washing me with smiles
splashing the stiff white sheets
with wet-lipped laughter.

We joke. We chat. We laugh. We dodge
the jagged rocks – death/cancer/pain:
social manners silently ordain
these words taboo.

We joke, we chat, we laugh.
Why do we find it so hard to accept
the one reality in life is death?
Will it prove fatal if we do?

Prep

A votive offering I have been prepared
by maidens in white lace caps.
With them my dark confessions have been shared
together we have prayed, we have wept.

Beneath a pulsing blood-warm shower
my body has been scrubbed and scoured
my tears diluted, will-power sapped.
In a long white gown I've been gift-wrapped
beneath a paper crown my hair's tucked back
around my wrist a bracelet's firmly snapped.

(for Saint Agatha it was not like this
no medicated scrub, no time for tears
only a long veil and an early grave
when Decius, envious of her sex and faith
butchered her breasts with vicious shears)

Since sunset they have held me to a fast
no food, no drink, no sleep, no rest.
Confined in silence in this bowered room
my eyes have trailed the black hands of the clock,

have trawled for shooting stars the velvet dark
(to make a desperate wish upon)
have thirsted for the first rays of the sun
the flickering of shadows on the wall

the signal that the strong-armed ones are come.
No make-up now, all gold and silver gone,
stripped of talisman and wedding ring
I'm helpless as a tiny babe new-born.

Grey shadows brush across my whitened face.
I sip the potion from the proffered cup.
They bear me to the sacrificial place.

Beneath the ice

Sinking beneath the anaesthetic ice
under a haloed ring of five full moons
I watch the white-robed high priests circle round
the sacrificial slab I lie upon

I am at the mercy of this masked mandala
I, who have no amulet
save the fiery jewels of my eyes

The masked ones' voices blur
mantras glide like dark owls on the air

I am at the mercy of these hovering mantras
I, who have no covering
save this paper skin

Unfazed by aphasia I float
a thankful prayer to Hua T'o

I am at the mercy of his sleeping potion
I, who have no magic of my own

The sacred scalpel shines, the slim wrist bends
red petals cascade from the feathered skies
I suck through every pore the heady scent
the priests lean forward and eclipse the light

> I close my eyes
> My choice is life
> I make the sacrifice

Amazon

Don't put her in purdah:
she is no devil woman
sent to spoil your view
of what the female form should be.

She is no less a woman now
no less the person you once knew.
Transformed to warrior Amazon
she will not flinch, she will stand proud
she'll bear her scars with dignity.

Don't put her in purdah:
the shawl of sympathy you fold her in
in time becomes a shroud – dead
petals clasped around a fertile head.
She will outgrow the shawl one day
like petals let it fall away.

Don't put her in purdah:
this woman's not taboo – view
her like a portrait by Picasso,
features might have gone astray
but the essence of the woman stays
enriched, enlivened, true.

Needles

Here comes the medicine man –
I'm his voodoo doll
(he holds me in thrall)
on his bed I lie, I watch him eye
the shining needles on his tray.

Here comes the medicine man –
in his hands I'm made of clay
he pierces with the silver of his voice
he punctures with the steel-blue of his eyes
he patches with pink plastic flesh
he punishes with needles pure and bright

the point being
my body has done wrong

Call me Eve, I caused the Fall of Man,
Mary Magdalene, I lived in sin,
I am Pandora, the most guilty one
I loosed disease upon the world
left Hope alone within.

Here comes the medicine man –
the needle glinting in the light
the point being
my body on its own can't fight
the point being
pushed into my flesh
the poison being
pumped into my blood

the point being hard to see –
they call this healing yet
it gives me pain, it makes me sick
it sucks my strength, it drains my dignity.

Recovery

In the raw light of a new day
I shred my patient's card.
Far in the east I see at last

fine filaments of light
flow through soft drifting grey.
The cutting wind with night has died away.
My scars are healed, but worries nag my head…

Where am I now? Alive, I think,
battered, bruised, buried in doubt
but not yet dead.
Have I escaped for good? Or am I on the run?

A victim, must I creep from day to day,
from one check-up appointment to the next
wondering if the cancer's been wiped out,
or has it, like a serpent, buried eggs

inside my spine, my brain, my other breast?
But this is not reality!
Cancer need not be Death's calling card:
a number nine bus or a speeding train

is just as likely now to end life's game.
The future's not the time in which we live
the present's where life's truly at its best
yet while we fret it drifts into the past.

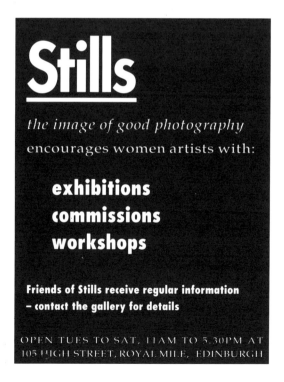

babysitting

Janice Galloway

Something he can't see hurts.

He kneels on the floor to pick up the fallen shell of flying saucer and it bites into his knee, making a noise. A soft, spreading crack. Wondering if it was bone, your own bone maybe being drilled at by something very small. He lifts the knee to look. Sugar. Little clear cubes sunk up the middles in the skin, the skin pushing them out again with stretching over the kneecap. Skin is like that. Mushy. Things get stuck in it. Gads. The sugar bounces out of its burrows, skites on the lino. It would be Allan. Allan in at the packet again and spilling it. The proof is there. A trail of wee white seeds comes out the cupboard to here, this sticky powder where the knee was seconds before. A drift of it silts in at the wood under the sink as well. And something else. Something with legs. A wispy black thing moves threads of itself against the skirting, half the body rising up then away again, back underneath. He looks till his sore eye starts to nip but it's definitely away, just slivers of biscuit and crumby stuff left, papery shapes that might have been onion skin. You see more things down here. Things you don't really want to see all that much. Anyway the knee isn't sore any more. He looks down. Pock marks. Most of the sugar has wormed its way out of the knee without him even trying. He could pick out the last bits with a nail. This filthy nail, black-rimmed where the horn separates from the quick, something grey creased into the loops of fingerprint. The blood bruise is still there. Going brown. At least it isn't a cigarette burn. They go yellow.

Tommy. A whine and a sniff was coming closer. The boy doesn't move. Tommy. The last bit of sugar gouges itself out the knee as the sniff blossoms out, rounding the hall corner. Allan.

Tommy.

The voice corkscrews up at the end, just the same. It never changes, the way he says your name, whether he thinks he knows where you are or not, not even when he finds you. He always sounds as if he's going to moan about something. The warm bulk of the wee brother sends out signals it's about to appear in the doorway. Starving. Is it teatime? Yesterday he kept it up till they went and took some of the money for penny things: toffee straps, liquorice ropes. Flying saucers. Allan ate them all in a oner and his face was black. The other day he was behind the settee with four sweetie cigarettes and it was ages before you found out where he'd got them. Finally he said David Armstrong from up the stairs gave them to him through the letterbox and you had to take them off him and fling them in the bin. He shouldn't have been taking things from David Armstrong. He was told not to take things off anybody. The putting them through the letterbox was worse than that though. He didn't know why but it was definitely not good. Tommy had to prop a chair in front of the door to stop the flap going up again or mibby Allan opening it from his side and shouting through. Being so wee, you had to watch him all the time. Putting the chair in and just giving him a battering every so often was easier than trying to talk sense because he was too wee to do what he was told and be trusted. Even obvious things like not talking to Mrs Morrison. You just didny talk to Mrs Morrison. She just got you into trouble. Somebody kicked her door once and she said it was Tommy and Dad told her to fuck off and then you caught Allan talking to her. She was a Nosy Old Cow and she gave you gyp. He'd been told but it had taken the leathering to get it through. Allan just hadny a clue.

Tommy.
  Allan is fat inside the doorway holding an empty crisp poke. One leg of the trainer bottoms up at his knee and the sock needing pulled up. Wanting to know is it teatime.
  Is it teatime?

A flake of crisp falls off the corner of Allan's fat mouth and into the rest of the bits on the floor. Sometimes you want to thump Allan for nothing. He just gets on your nerves.
  Tommy's knees peel off the lino and he sees the sugar. It isn't worth saying anything. He just starts walking. He walks through to the hall, past the living room door and through to the bedroom window. Allan's feet skiff off the carpet, following then he stands there clueless, crumpling the crisp poke over and over in thon irritating way while his brother looks out.

Grey and pink. It would be after five. There are no streetlights on yet but it is not possible to see too well inside the house any more. There is a time when it is harder to see before it gets easier and it is that time the now. When it gets darker, the orange sifts in from out there and you don't need to put the inside lights on at all. You can see ok without them. Anyway they only ever go through to the livingroom and the telly is on in there. It's still going full bung, making shouting noises and car brakes. Tommy can hear it. But it mibby wouldn't be a good idea to stick Allan through when he went out for the tea. He doesn't like it, being on his own with Dad through there. He does it all right if you force him but not without a carry on. So he just has to come. To be quicker. Tommy shuts his eyes and thinks about going out into the hall. About holding out one hand backwards and not having to wonder where Allan is. He is just always there, ready to take it. He will drop the crisp poke and fit his hand inside and let himself be taken. It's what Allan does. He needs watching.

David Armstrong looks like a ferret and hunches his shoulders up, watching. He kicks the wall where the chippy is, holding a bag in the one hand. Maltesers.
  How were you not at school?
  David Armstrong talks like a lassie and nobody plays with him. He was

never done out on his own, looking for folk. Tommy feels the eyes and refuses to look up, the crinkle of the sweetie bag in the other hand and keeps a good grip of Allan. David Armstrong always has something for eating but you're better off without it. Anything you got off David Armstrong was not good. Him and his mother both. You were better to tell them nothing. He would have given the sweetie cigarettes to Allan and then told his mother they'd been taken off him. He did things like that.

How no though?

The face a melted doll and the eyes watching. Able not to eat and just wait. He made you sick. One time they dug his rabbit up after it had been in the ground a week to see if it was any different and it wasn't only the eyes were kind of white and he said it was Tommy and Allan. He said they made him do it and started greeting and that made his mother think it was true. You took nothing off him if you could help it. Tommy flexes his hand tighter. Allan's bone thin and hard through the cloth and soft flesh and he whines. He doesn't pull though. He whines a bit with the soreness in his arm but he doesn't try to go over. At their backs, David Armstrong shouting Fuck off then. Soft as rotten fruit.

Inside the chippy is warm. It is always warm and smells of food. Mrs Mancini sometimes gives Allan a free pickled onion. This time she just looks. She looks at Tommy and twists the salt shaker.

You two here again, she says. Her face isn't right. Bertie, these two are here again.

Mr Mancini looks over the top of the glass cabinet, thin bits of hair greasy on his scalp. His face boils over a cabinet full of black puddings then goes away. Tommy holds up the three coins. Maybe they think he doesn't have the money. Nobody takes it. Nobody is looking because they are talking to each other, words he can't hear right: Mrs Mancini saying something about it being the umpteenth time, you wonder where it's coming from, twice a day and Tommy knows something. They're talking about him and Allan. And that doesn't feel good either. They should just get the food and get out. He wants to get back up the road and jam the chair back where it belongs. The back of the door is not safe. He wants home.

Fish supper and an extra bag.

He hears his own voice being sure about what he wants. Then they might get it and get out. Nobody can stop you if you have the money.

Fish supper and an extra bag.

Mr Mancini says something about nothing to do with him and the frying spits up. Tommy lifts his eyes. Mrs Mancini's hair appears over the top of the cabinet, the pink overall shifting into place behind the counter. She gives them a look.

Ok boys. Fish supper and an extra bag.

Her lipstick is a different mouth to the one underneath and neither smile. She takes the ladle out the pickles and stares at it. The chips come and she wraps them staring at where Mr Mancini must be. She picks up the newspaper bundle and reaches, still looking away.

See and say to your daddy I'm asking for him boys ok?

Ok. Allan is looking at the newspaper parcel, saying ok to Mrs Mancini. She claps eyes on him and stained teeth show. Red marks on the teeth like a vampire.

You need your face washed young man, she says. See and wash his face if nobody else will.

The pink thing she wears moves when she leans, handing over the bags. Tommy nearly takes it then remembers sauce. Look at him Bertie he's completely mawkit. Tommy does not listen and asks hard for sauce. She looks. She reaches to take the parcel back.

I don't know, she says. I don't know. A couple of chancers.

Fat fizzes up and more fish hurl themselves into the display case. Mrs Mancini holds out an opened palm for the money.

The house always feels colder after you've been out. He shivers through the shirt and reaches for the switch. Hard greasy plastic. It is not like real light that comes on. It makes things look sore. The wrapped bundle in at his chest, burning, he walks through to the kitchen. Hot vinegar hurts his nose. Allan follows close enough to tip the backs of his heels, the rubber bumpers of the trainers touching. In a minute there will be whining about wanting his bag. But there is something about the idea of washing his hands, cleaning Allan up a bit before he eats. He wants to make sure Allan looks ok. He puts the bags to one side of the sink where Allan can't reach and looks for the wet dish cloth. It isn't there. Tommy looks and the whining starts. The cloth isn't there. It isn't there because it's in the living room. The sound of the telly playing music and Allan starting to reach up for the bundle on the drainer. After. It'll have to be after. Letting Allan start up now is more bother than it's worth. Tommy watches the newspaper start to slide, Allan's face change as it edges into his grasp. He tears a bit off the end of the parcel and it nearly cowps. As soon as he gets the chips he'll want a drink. You were never done with Allan. They were nearly out of lemonade as well.

C'mon you. C'mon.

Tommy makes up his mind. He takes the chips before the whole lot falls and the greeting gets worse. They're not eating off the kitchen floor.

C'mon. Any minute and the wail will start. But all he has to do is go through, look like he means it. Allan will follow. He always does. He runs.

Blotches.

The telly throws grey blobs over the inside of the room, shifting all the time. The sour smell. He holds the bags up to his nose for the vinegar stink off the newspaper to make it ok. And it is ok after a minute or so but you always notice it on the way in. Allan stumbles in grizzling then shuts up when he sees unwrapping going on. Tommy handing him the extra bag and a piece of fish off his own. Cooling. The fish is cool enough to tear easy without hurting your hand. Tommy watches the trade of fish, bits

130

flaking onto the carpet. Allan picks one up and sticks it in his mouth, chewing. He should have got biscuits. There are no biscuits left and hardly any lemonade. They've run out of sauce.

Their father's legs flash patterns from the far edge of the divan: the news making webs. It makes the legs look as if they're moving but the feet are in exactly the same place. He might leave some chips in case though. Tommy bites the fish, looks down at the carpet. It looks as if it's moving as well. It isn't time for the light though. He might put it on later, after Allan was down, come and sit for a wee while. It is definitely getting darker since the start of this. Allan coughs suddenly and bits spray out but he keeps chewing. He's ok. The fat fingers glisten as the adverts change. After. He can get Allan through for a wash and into bed. It's getting too cold sleeping in here anyway, even with the two of them. That'll have to stop as well. After he's done with Allan he can come back through. He wants to sit for a bit. He needs to check for money in his pockets anyway. He wipes grease off his mouth, flicks his eyes up and away. It isn't a good idea, touching. It makes his mouth stop working. But it will be ok to come and sit, just sit in with his own dad and maybe talk. And if he's ok.

Inside the wrapper, the chips get colder. You see the fat on them going thick. You know you don't want to see his eyes open though. You don't want to know the colour of his eyes.   *Janice Galloway*

Catherine Carswell: Engagement and Detachment

Christopher Small

How far must you go from Scotland before you can write, especially if you are going to write about Scotland? Perhaps not at all: journals like *Chapman* exist to give such ideas the lie. But at any rate in the past Scotland like Ireland produced many writers who worked at ease only as exiles or expatriates – and who, partly in consequence, have had less than their due regard at home.

Catherine Carswell offers a striking example of a writer's need for distance, and of the different meanings that may be attached to the word. For her it was not severance, or even permanent geographical removal – no further, most of the time, than London. (Admittedly, that is a longer journey than most Londoners understand.) But distance nevertheless expresses something essential in her attitude to writing as such, of vital importance for her and of lasting interest for us still.

Her output, in published books at least, was not large. The need to earn a precarious living by literary journalism; personal catastrophes, the demands of other people, both family and friends, always got in the way. Craving privacy, even secrecy, she found in different places a room of her own, but Virginia Woolf's other requirement was beyond her. "All I need is to be financed for a year or two," she told a friend, and even that was out of reach. More important than the want of time and leisure was, as she confessed more than once, a strong inward rigour which made writing hard labour. She had a "conscientious objection" to work as such: "I have gone to the ant and considered its ways... I prefer to consider the lilies of the field." It was not dilettantism but respect for the task more profound than the self-satisfaction of "professionalism".

Three of her books have lately been reissued: her two "Glasgow" novels, *Open the Door!* and *The Camomile* (both from Virago, £3.95), and most recently her *Life of Robert Burns*, now a Canongate Classic (£5.95). The first two were originally published soon after the First world War (1920 and 1922 respectively), and the Burns biography nearly a decade later, in 1930. They can be read together in several ways, as books about aspects of Scottish life by a writer *from* Scotland; as expression of a particular point of view regardless of place; as illustrating the rewards and paradoxes of detachment. A fourth book, the fragmentary *Lying Awake*, underlines the last point of interest. It was written in bits and pieces over several years and never completed, being published in 1950, four years after the writer's death in 1946 at the age of 67. It seems high time, incidentally, that this also was reprinted.

Carswell was encouraged to write her life of Burns by D H Lawrence, already a friend and the strongest literary influence of her life. For Lawrence Burns was a Laurentian hero – he had contemplated and actually started a Burnsian novel, transplanting the poet to Derbyshire. Traces of this project (fortunately abandoned at an early stage) may be detected in her own biography; certainly what she shared with Lawrence was enthusiasm. But it was not at all a desire to remake Burns in her own image. It is tempting to see in her dedication, "to D H Lawrence, my friend, and Donald Carswell, my husband" a differentiation between two kinds of support. Donald Carswell, a deeply sceptical man, shied away from enthusiasm, especially for his fellow-countrymen; his own best-known work, *Brother Scots* (1927), a collection of nineteenth-century essays in the Stracheyan manner, is almost crippled by iconoclastic irony. But he did respect learning and scholarship, and he did admire Burns, even if he expressed it backhandedly, remarking that "for a' that and a' that" was "the only approach to a bad poem that Burns ever wrote." (Catherine and Lawrence didn't agree.) She herself, enthusiastic for her task, was generally scrupulous in research: her speculations, discussed by Tom Crawford in his introduction to this new edition, are at least arguable today. But, as he also says, that is not the point. The obstacles she struggled with were not merely those of "documentation" but of quite a different kind. As she told another friend, Florence Marian McNeill, "it is a damned difficult life to write, even adequately... an essay – yes; a long formless collection of facts – yes again. But to build up the life fully and in its true proportions – well, I'm not sure that it can be done, still less if I can do it."

So stated, it is a tall order, and it is clear that, however strong her misgivings, her ambition was indeed to achieve something beyond "adequacy". She hoped to make a new thing – a "fiction", as Tom Crawford says, with the intimacies and insights of a novel, but one true both to ascertainable facts and human experience, both full of traps, as she well knew. More facts have accumulated since then, and views of human experience have perhaps altered somewhat; but it is still dangerous to display, and accept, the contradictions and "crosses" in anyone's character; much more so when the subject is a national institution.

Catherine Carswell knew that the attempt to realise Burns both as man and Bard was likely to cause trouble. When the book was almost finished she wrote again to Marian McNeill: "How *furious* they will be to have RB brought out of the mist they have loved to keep about him!" The extent and virulence of outrage on publication – from moves to impose a boycott by the Burns Federation to a sinister letter signed "Holy Willie" and enclosing a bullet – may be difficult to understand today; except, of course, that orthodox fury and threats of violence to offensive authors are not unknown yet. To Mrs Carswell it cannot have been altogether a surprise; it wouldn't be fair to say that she courted such reactions, but they were part of her expectation in relations between artist and public. Her friendship with Lawrence has provided ample example long before. The notorious rumpus over *The Rainbow* and consequent breach with the *Glasgow Herald* (which provided her, as a regular reviewer, with a substantial part of her small income) is instructive in more than one way. When the novel came out in 1915, and the orchestrated fury of the virtuous and patriotic broke which led to prosecution and banning, she reviewed it for the *Herald*; and, foreseeing objections to her (measured) praise, contrived to bypass editorial sanction of her copy. The subsequent row ended her connection with the paper, an episode often used since to beat the *Herald* about its conventional, pusillanimous head. But it was entirely predictable: if it reflects dull-minded authority on one hand, on the other it shows just as much, and much more interestingly, the quixotry, the positively reckless daring, of the woman who provoked it.

The same impulse and disregard of consequences when friendship and truth were at stake moved Carswell to further rashness soon after Lawrence's death in 1930. Exasperated by the egoism and emotional exploitation of Middleton Murry's memoir *Son of Woman*, she wrote her *Savage Pilgrimage* to set the record straight; it remains the most clear-sighted and truly-felt first-hand impression of Lawrence that we have. But Murry threatened a lawsuit and the book was withdrawn: though eventually reissued in revised form it is still hard to get hold of.

In responses like these it isn't difficult to see a lifelong personal trait, as much physical as intellectual. By her own account in her posthumous memoirs Catherine was an agile and adventurous child, addicted to climbing the tallest trees up to the tallest branches, "trusting my passing weight to a twig." In the novel which contains much of her Glasgow childhood, *Open the Door!*, there is a similarly athletic incident, daring overcoming fear: the 12-year-old Joanna is afraid of jumping but forces herself to a formidable leap from a window sill simply because it is risky. "'If I'm killed it can't be helped!' was the thought that flashed through her mind as a solution." Ready interpretation may occur of teenage acts and fantasies of this sort, and doubtless Catherine Carswell was aware of them; but the habit persisted. Towards the end of her life she would "set herself" deliberately to vault a fence; on a particular occasion, already in her sixties, she jumps, baggage in hand, from a moving train which had passed her station.

But taking risks and launching out into the air were not only bodily adventures. Writing itself was risky, dangerous, difficult – to be undertaken, in part, for these very reasons. She disliked writing – and who among writers doesn't know "the awful feeling that one would rather do anything than write"? – but she also confessed that "I love, if not writing, having written. Writing interests me more than any other activity." The fact that she felt herself ill-equipped drove her to it; she counted herself among those "unfortunates", as she believed, "who can accomplish in any degree only by addressing themselves to the unattainable."

Stephen Dedalus, launching himself unsupported at the highest goal and the dizziest experience, "not yet fallen, still unfallen, but about to fall", proposes a future for himself, of course, in much grander terms, but there is a resemblance. It is possible to fit together Catherine Carswell's two novels and find in them not only a vivid view of a particular ambience and place – Scottish middle-class life in the late 19th and early 20th centuries – but, in their conscious overlap, a combined *Portrait of the Artist*.

Open the Door!, Carswell's first and (in the words of her son John) "mind-clearing" book, is directly autobiographical, following closely in the person of Joanna Bannerman the childhood and early adult life of the actual Catherine Macfarlane. Circumstance and feeling are the same: the child of a well-doing Glasgow businessman, brought up in comfort and affection but also in an atmosphere of all-pervasive piety; well-to-do and well-connected but also, without hypocrisy, "unworldly". Both parents were hereditary members of the Free Church, grandfathers and uncles on both sides having "come out" in the disruption; father and mother, reinforced by the Moody and Sankey revival, were sincerely (and in the latter's case, passionately) religious. For this reason if no other they and their children were fully aware, in their Glasgow bourgeois security, of the other Glasgow, the huge flood of desperate poverty on which (as the lifelong Socialist daughter much later observed) there floated "us and our like in arks of safety, industry, prosperity and hope."

Both influences were important. For the parents the poor, deserving or undeserving, were to be saved. For the child who watched the wild freedom of a Glasgow Saturday night in the 1890s – "a sordid splendour, a wholehearted ruinous contempt which, for the moment, excluded other considerations in at least one beholder" – they were to be envied. Reflecting upon her upbringing, in the novel and in her later memoirs, Catherine Carswell was looking back on a system of beliefs both restricting and of permanent value; her childhood had been "unfettered" except by that "never unkindly religion by which my parents lived", but which imposed fetters nevertheless. She had escaped, and she honoured what she had escaped from.

The title and most of the key images of *Open the Door!* (from 2 Kings IX, the instruction by Elisha to one of his prophetic messengers, "open the door and flee, and tarry not") are aptly scriptural. At another crisis in her young life (the episode corresponding to the author's disastrous first marriage) Joanna remembers Psalm 124, of which the familiar metrical version, "E'en as a bird out of a fowler's snare/ Escapes away, so is our soul set free", has been "the master symbol of her life. But if escape and flight are continuing themes, they are subordinate to one another, the search for love and truth. Flight is as much towards as from, and Joanna is compelled at this point to a flight in reverse.

After her first Icarus-aspiration she "must go back to Glasgow and learn how to live." The novel's second part has another epigraph, this time from the New Testament, and referring to a different release, "...open a door of utterance" (Col. IV 3).

At this hinge-point, halfway through the novel, one can turn to its successor published two years later, *The Camomile* – avowedly a sequel, though in fact rather more of an appendix, and of a revealing kind. It is set entirely in Glasgow, and some characters reappear (Joanna Bannerman herself is briefly mentioned). But the new heroine, Ellen Carstairs, whose letters and journal tell the story, is no less an aspect of the author, specifically of the author as artist. Ellen intends, as did the young Catherine, to ⌐ a musician, and like her has had a training in Frankfurt; back in Glasgow she finds piano-teaching unrewarding and turns more and more to writing. Writing is what the novel is about: the camomile – the plant described by Falstaff, "the more it is trodden on the faster it grows" – is the chosen emblem of writing persisted in against difficulties.

Ellen meets every discouragement and, again like her creator, takes to writing in secret, renting as cheaply as possible a room of her own for the purpose. Her only moral support is from a former teacher and colleague, unfortunately wrong in the head, who perceives her talent; and from an obscure scholar and spoiled priest, same but even less respectable, who advises her, lends her books, and finally helps to get her published.

Whether or not this "Don John" has biographical foundation – Walter Raleigh, who taught and befriended Catherine during his time at Glasgow University, seems a rather unlikely original – his function as high priest of literature to the young self-doubting votaress is decisive. She asks herself, "Is writing – serious writing – simply a mistake for women?" He doesn't supply a direct answer. But as one for whom "Books really live and matter" he lifts the question out of gender to a different level altogether. Poor, shabby, doubtfully clean, inclined to drink, visibly a failure, he stands for "something more precious and important than success"; he "uses no such words as 'sacrifice', 'Conscience', or even 'truth' ...yet my whole soul bows before him in passionate respect." When he dies, more or less of inanition, he leaves his books and papers to Ellen; one is left to doubt that he also leaves her his vocation.

How successful Catherine Carswell was in this calling is, by her own definition, beside the point; as is also the common complaint that, had her talent received more encouragement, had more scope or leisure for its use, more would have come of it. She may have desired such things from time to time, but she made no grievance of their absence. She required and secured for herself some solitude in which to work, but in no sense did she think of it as shelter. On the contrary, it was escape from shelter that was necessary. Joanna returns to Glasgow to "learn how to live"; Ellen ends her part of the story with the resolution "I shall leave Glasgow", and it is in order to write about it: "One can never write till she stands outside." The contradictory impulses are brought together in a curious formula: "It is true that if I had to choose between writing and life I should choose life. But then I couldn't do otherwise, for without living myself I knew I couldn't write..." This apparently banal statement is perhaps the nearest that Ellen or Catherine Carswell herself, could come, simply, to state her complex apprehension of reality – primal, "hard", "dark", even "sordid" – and its realisation in art. The first comes first, but the second is a task that can't be shirked.

To perform this task, distance is needful. For Catherine Carswell it had different aspects, which included an actual going away and, in any place or condition, self-detachment.

She made her home, or homes – for she was a frequent flitter – for the most part outwith Scotland, but she did not renounce a Scottish context. Writing her *Life of Robert Burns* she wished, more consciously than any previous biographer, to set it in a social frame, but something else was more important. In the preface to the 1930 edition she distinguished her approach to "matters of fact" and of deduction: in the latter, she said, "I have relied upon my own conception of Burns formed by years of unremitted study, and upon what knowledge of life I have through my own experience." "Ultimately" (she said with reference to another Burns biography) "it is the impact of a writer's life experience upon the necessarily imperfect record of another's life that gives the value."

Such an opinion, shocking to those who confuse detachment with objectivity, and don't perhaps understand the full meaning of either word, is certainly operative here. It does indeed giver her book permanent value; it justifies and gives real, fresh force to her peroration, in terms often used but here with uncommon conviction, that in Burns, "because none before had combined so many human weaknesses with so great an ardour of living and so generous a warmth of admission", Scots could see "the Poet of his Country – perhaps of mankind."

To receive without flinching the impact of a life experience requires a certain toughness. (Catherine Carswell knew herself to be "of the tough and not the tender tribe"). In a writer it also requires detachment: only so, by a radical removal of self, as she told Marian McNeill, is it possible to transmit the impact, transformed into art, "one's own word of truth" and not anyone else's. This good advice, not new, she strove to follow herself. When D H Lawrence told her, "You are the only woman I have ever met who is so intrinsically detached, as essentially separate and isolated as to be a real artist and recorder", he saw only one side of her self-removal. The other, beyond the simple egotism of the artist, gave her access to the truth of others, even hidden from themselves – so that Lawrence on another occasion confessed "Something makes me state my position, when I write to you."

Posterity, perhaps, repeats something of this half-reluctant tribute. Who or what is Catherine Carswell for Scottish readers today? She left so little: she never produced the masterpiece that makes itself known, in her own definition, by the conviction it imparts that "in that blessed space of time the world and all life becomes perfectly good." But she also knew that failure itself, fully apprehended, may be a person's "special word of truth". In the reflections of her last years, laying awake at night, she knew that "truthfulness alone is worth my effort". She preserved standards of discernment, integrity, and impassioned disinterestedness rare at any time in a nation's literature. Under her regard – in surviving photographs usually in exquisite profile, looking somewhere else than at us – we become, nevertheless, impatient and shifty. But even nervousness may be a sign of prevenient grace.   *Christopher Small*

Sheena Blackhall

A Thing of Beauty is a Joy Forever
Birse Farmer, circa 1963

Heich simmer makks the hochs a love-juice cauldron.
Dauchlin astride a sunshine-drookit dyke
I heard an engine purr, an iron bawdron.
The bowfin o a coo's-lick touslied tyke.

Syne suddent, frae ayont deep-shaddaed trees
A fairm-cheil drave his combine ower the lan
The jetty curls upon his broo ableeze
Wi sun, as ony bonnie Grecian Pan.

Braid showders, glistenin broon, the loon, bare-backit
Sat square abune the corn like a young God
Riding alang the barley-rigs half-nyaakit
Watched bi a lustfu virgin, and a bawd.

Reid kerchief lichtly wippit neth his chin
A mou wad sook the hinney frae a bee
Sweet fusslin, ower the birrin chariot's din
He smiled full on me, wi a bull-black ee.

Twa birdies flichtered, coortin ben the corn
Syne drappt tae couple, aa pretensions tirred
Their birdsang like the soundin o a horn
Biddin me cast ma bairnhood tae the yird.

He raisse tae cry his tyke, the stoot claith held
The fite swan o his secret manhood trussed
As faist's a muir-fire wi a breem is melled
I kent the gnaawin thorn-stob o lust.

Januar

The year birls on its axle.
Rikk frae a wintry reef,
Is a ribbon o grey frae a cauldron –
Furled like a cassen leaf.

Hyne in the wast, cauld cailleachs,
The ghaists o the Grampians lie.
Back o the ploo far the bare, birks, boo
Is blaik as a tinker's gley

A keekin glaiss o watter,
Is the puil that the dubs rise roon,
Far the elfin green o the chitterin breem,
Casts its drookit likeness doon.

Straicht lines o Black Watch sodjers,
Haudin their bayonets heich,
Are the fir wids raxxed ower fairmlans,
Far the leaden lift hings dreich.

Januar – spinnly branches
Wi their fingers aboot tae brier...
Throw the snaw an haar, o steen-cauld glaur,
Gie birth tae the bairn-new year.

AIDS

The act o luv brings daith insteid o life
The plague o Aids strikks silent as a scythe
The Reaper skitters skulls mangst bits o bairns
Takks flooers frae luvers' hauns, tae hansel cairns.

Paradise Lost

The joy has gone from the light.
Oh may the dark
Carry me down to Lethe
Like an Ark.

Toun Blues

Gairdens are stane Bastilles
Waas spiked wi shards o glaisse
Far fat-arsed corgies
Fyle smaa squars o girse.
Gin ye stravaig tae a park
The warld an its wife are there
Tirrin a creashie sark
Tae the tinny birr o trannies,
The lawns, shaved flat's a bap.
Gin ye stravaig tae the beach
The sea wull wash a condom
Ower yer sannies.
Served wi a satty plap.

Like human hutches,
Each wi'ts ain wee run
Wir gairdens thole dreich doonpish,
Wattery sun
Glimsks ower a toun wi granite biggins happed
Ilk knowe an howe ceemented ower an capped
Wi forests o street lichts;

Rowth o fowk rin reaming ower the cassies
The lift is blae wi rikk
Cars, breenge an birr
Wi seagull-drappins
Clartit ower their chassies
As sweir an contermaschious as Auld Nick

The days are threidbare
Fur the indiginous Scot.
The nichts hing doon like bats,
Frae a thoosan semis an flats
Clashes the claik
O fremmit ile incomers
Makkin wir wyes an heirskip
Seem a wake.
Gaels, claw respeck and siller frae fat cats
Oor lan, an leid, is
Cairtit aff bi rats.

Owl

Silent, the hunting owl slips from sight
A Jack the Ripper, melting into night
Swallowed up in the
Manacle-menace of gloom
A cloud enshrouds him
In the sky's grey, open tomb.

The shuttling wind clacks in the hedge
The road is mushroom white
In the dead-cold
Of an outworn winter day.
The snow is spread like a napkin
Down he comes to dine
A dropping stone
He'll vice a vole away
(How sweet the wine
That thuds beneath its pelt)
Hovering death, he
Arcs his lovely breadth

Like Two
Great
Waves
That beat an eternal shore
See the barn-owl soar
A graceful glider
Glib as a gibbet
Spreading his wings
Like a Franciscan's cloak
His eyes,
Two points of pitch
Supple as smoke
He targets a beating heart
That starts like a hare
Within a mouse's breast –
Which like a vine
Will soon be
Plucked and pressed.
A stifled squeak... His seeking beak...
The steel trap of his talons
Hoists his cargo high's a crane.
A closed book
A story, suddenly
Run out of ink
A head
With no more think
From his wooden berth in the coffin of a tree
Hear ye the owl's decree
"The meek shall NOT inherit the Earth."

The Lighthouse

Agnes Owens

"Let's go somewhere else", said Megan to her brother Bobby playing on the beach with his pail and spade. "Let's go to the lighthouse."

"I don't want to", he said, without looking up. At three-and-a-half years he had the face of an angel, but his appearance belied a strong determination to have everything his own way. So thought Megan, aged ten.

"You can stay if you like," she said, "but I'm going and I just hope a monster doesn't get you."

At the mention of the word 'monster' he began to look over his shoulder. It was only recently she'd been telling him about monsters and how they ate children. She'd even shown him a picture of one in an animal book, which was actually that of a gorilla, but it had been enough to make him refuse to sleep with the light off and even with it on he would waken up screaming.

"I don't want to go to the lighthouse", he said, running over and butting her in the stomach with his head.

"But I do", she said, skipping off lightly over the sand.

"Wait for me", he called picking up his pail and spade and trailing after her.

Together they walked along in a friendly way, going at a pace that suited them both. The day was warm but with a bit of wind. Megan almost felt happy. By the time they'd come to a part of the shore that was deserted except for a woman walking her dog in the distance, Bobby had stopped to gather shells.

"Throw them away", said Megan. "You'll get better ones at the lighthouse."

He emptied his pail, then asked if the lighthouse was over there, pointing to the sea wall.

"Don't be stupid. The lighthouse is miles away."

He said emphatically, "Then I don't want to go."

Megan lost her temper. "If you don't start moving I'll slap your face."

At that moment the woman with the dog passed by. "Is that big girl hitting you?" she asked him.

Before he could speak Megan had burst out, "He's my brother and I'll hit him if I want."

The woman studied them through thoughtful narrowed eyes. "Do your parents know you're out here in this lonely place?"

When Megan said that they did the woman walked on with the dog, muttering something under her breath which Megan suspected was some kind of threat aimed at her. She hissed to Bobby, "See what you've done. For all we know she could be going to report us to the police and you know what that means?"

"What?"

"Mummy and Daddy will be put in jail for neglecting us and I'll have to watch you forever."

At that he let out a howl so loud she was forced to put her hand over his mouth. "Be quiet you fool. Do you want that woman back?"

He quietened down when she promised to get him an ice-cream.

"Where's the van?" he asked, looking around.

"Over there", she said, pointing in the direction of the lighthouse. At first he believed this, running beside her eagerly, but when they went on for a considerable length without any signs of an ice-cream van he began to lag behind.

"Come on," she said, "or we'll miss it."

"Where is it?"

"Don't ask stupid questions", she snapped, thinking how it wasn't fair that she had to be saddled with him all the time. "You're a silly bugger anyway."

"I'm telling you swore."

"Tell if you want", said Megan, thinking her parents couldn't say much considering the way they swore.

"If you don't come…" she began, when he started walking again, and just when she thought he was going to act reasonable for once he stopped in front of a rock.

"Look! There's fish in there", he said.

Grumbling, she went back to investigate. It was true. There were tiny fish darting about a pool of water within a crevice in the rock.

"Aren't they pretty?" she said just as he threw a stone into the pool causing them to disappear. She shook him by the shoulders.

"You have to spoil everything, don't you?" she said, letting him go suddenly so that he sat down with a bump. But he was up on his feet quick enough when she said, walking backwards, "A monster's going to get you one of these days the way you carry on."

After a good deal of tramping over dry sand that got into their shoes and made their feet sore, Megan suggested they climb up over the dunes on their right-hand side to see if there was a better and quicker path that would take them to the lighthouse. He didn't answer. She suspected he was still brooding about the ice-cream, but he followed her anyway which was the main thing.

Climbing up the sand dunes wasn't easy. They kept sliding back down. Bobby did it deliberately thinking it was funny. Megan was glad to see he was in a better mood. Finally when they got to the top they found they were looking on to a golf course, stretching for miles and nobody on it except a man in a grey tracksuit, who, when he saw them come over, said: "Better watch out you don't get hit with a golf-ball. It's not safe up here."

Megan asked him if he was a golfer, though she noticed he wasn't carrying any clubs. When he told her he was just out for the day collecting golf balls she began to wonder if he might be one of those strangers they'd been warned not to speak to.

"Bobby," she said loudly, "we'd better get back. Mummy and Daddy will be looking for us."

"But I thought..." he began and was cut off by Megan pulling him back down the sandy slope. When he got to the bottom he said that he'd wanted to stay up there.

"It's not safe", she said.

"Why not?" Then as if it had nothing to do with anything he let out a tremendous wail.

"In the name of God what is it now", she said, in the same tone her mother used when totally exasperated.

"I've left my pail and spade", he said, pointing up at the sand dunes.

She felt like strangling him. "Well, I'm not going for them." But when he began to wail loud enough to split the rocks, she said she would go if he came with her to the lighthouse.

"I don't want to", he said, stamping his feet in temper. "I want to go back to that other beach where Mummy left us."

It was then she decided she'd had enough of his tantrums. "Go then", she said, giving him a shove so that he tottered on blindly for a few steps. "I don't want to ever see you again."

When he turned round she was racing along the beach at a fair speed. He called on her to come back, though it was doubtful she heard him above the cries of the seagulls. Even if she had she probably wouldn't have stopped.

On arriving at the lighthouse she saw there was no way to get close to it as it was surrounded by water, not unless she waited until the tide went out and that would take hours. Sullenly she looked up at its round turreted shape thinking it was much more boring from this angle than it had seemed from a distance. She wished she'd never come. The sea was stormy now with the waves lashing over the rocks. The whole venture had been a complete waste of time and energy she decided. Suddenly her attention was riveted to what looked like a body in the water. For a split second she thought it was Bobby, which would have been quite impossible considering the distance she'd covered. Nevertheless it was a great relief to discover this was only a mooring buoy. She laughed at her mistake then she began to feel uneasy. She could picture him stumbling into the sea for a paddle thinking it was all shallow water. It was the kind of stupid thing he was liable to do. Panic swept over her. What if something terrible happened to him. She should never have left him like that. Without another thought for the lighthouse or anything other than Bobby she began running back to where she'd left him, praying that he'd be all right.

From a distance she saw him hunkered down digging in the sand. He must have gone up the sand dunes to get his pail and spade after all, she thought. She slowed down, her legs tired and aching, then to her dismay she saw the man they'd met on the golf course. He was hovering a few yards behind Bobby poking some debris on the shore with a stick.

"Bobby", she called out sharply. "Come over to me at once."

He either didn't hear this or pretended not to, but the man did. He looked up at her and began to walk smartly in their direction. Galvanised into taking some kind of action she ran forward to reach Bobby first. In fact she'd almost got to him when she slipped on a stone covered in seaweed and went down, the back of her head hitting off its sharp edge.

Her eyes were staring up at the sky as the man and Bobby crouched beside her.

Bobby said, "You shouldn't have left me. I'm telling Mummy."

The man pulled him back. "Leave her alone. She's in bad enough shape." Then he put his lips close to her ear. "Can you hear me?" When her eyes flickered he put his hand over her mouth and nose and held it there for a considerable time. After that he turned to Bobby saying, "We'll have to get an ambulance. You can come with me." Bobby said he didn't want to get an ambulance. He wanted to go back to the other beach.

"All right", said the man, taking him by the hand and dragging him towards the sand dunes with Bobby protesting all the way. Finally his cries died down when they vanished over the top.

Later on in the afternoon a strong breeze sprung up along the shore lifting clouds of sand into the air as well as the strands of Megan's hair drifting across her face. Seagulls came down to stand on top of her and poke her with their beaks. Then as if not liking what they found they flew off again into the horizon, whilst imperceptibly and gradually her body sank into the sand making a groove for itself. A passer-by might have thought she was asleep she looked so peaceful.

But no one came all that day and on the same evening when the sun went down she was by this time gone with the tide.

Agnes Owens

Tessa Ransford

Tantus Labor No Sit Casus
(Let such labour not be useless)

I stand as Mary below the cross: *stabat mater.*
I have seen the pure, sacred body of my loved–one
taken up on the a nails, hung to prolong his pain.

I see the clarity of his temperament and every delicate feature,
the lines around eyes and mouth, the brow, the bones of his feet,
head and hands, the lean and kindly stretch of the arms,

the body I used to wrap in the silk of my embraces,
the head I used to take to my breast
and cradle on the curves of my womb

the one I held in familiar, daily caress
has been lashed on high and made to believe
there is freedom in such suspension.

Lords of the universe and queens of all that is green,
tender, innocent and loyal, gather your graces
and save this man, this one you created, vulnerable, perfect.

I name the relief worker, forced to watch
while a child died of starvation:
the eyes of the long–dead boy could never be extinguished.

I name Stella, who shone like her name with compassion,
who expended her life in rescuing refugees
ravaged and mutilated from Europe or Asia.

The temple of the body is to be revered,
for this is the body we dwell in, our home,
our communal shelter in daily endeavour,

in fullness and in welcoming proud humility
a I opened to him the doors of my dwelling,
my lowly lintel, my own magnificat.

let such labour not be useless, let
my fingers take up the pen and compose
the music of pain and lasting lament,

my outrage at this defilement, this scoring, scarring
of my beloved, his neck where I rested
my lips, my head, and stroked

his every part to touch, as if to restore
his childhood with gentle endearment,
the innocent godly shape that grew within him

and lives, despite the molestation of violent deaths
and of slow, unloving cruelties;
that grows and grafts a new and fragrant flowering

out of such loving, the labour the universe suffers
to bring forth, after aeons, exquisite persons
whose limbs, with each finest hair, are numbered and noted

and now have been crucified, have been torn
in their seamlessness, to be broken
and yet redeemed, reborn in each generation
by lingering, sorrowful, watching, maternal love.

Golden Images

Please leave this mask of gold upon the skull
the buried old, fast–plated to the corpse.

In the name of science don't strip it off
or tear apart the body and its sheath

of treasures, ornaments and familiar
daily objects, belongings that were used
or rituals, sacred totems we worshipped.

While ancient peoples buried works of art,
statuary, jewellery, airless and untouched,
alone, unseen around a royal corpse

we shoot our wealth to space, to the illustrious
moon, or blow it up in bombs made of the sun.

What is the empty mask, the golden mould
detached from the corpse it was designed for>

It is a shell to be wondered at, admired
for craftsmanship, commercial tradery.

We try to live by images alone and cast
aside the mortal person, the decay.

A photograph is all we cling to now
for we have buried what was real in the heart.

No one can excavate the treasure there,
steal through the wings of goddesses or across
the silent forepaws of the guardian hound,

who sepulchre my memories and keep
them safe-preserved and gleamingly attached
to the actual person, to the ones Love,
whether they are living yet or dead.

A Stable Relationship

In a stable relationship one person
is often the horse, the other the owner.

One person is kept in the stable
and taken out only in harness.

The stable door is divided and
allows the horse to look out.

The harness gives freedom of movement
but none of direction or speed.

Horse and owner often enjoy
the deepest trust and intimacy.

But horses have been known
to break out of the stable

and to bolt away, dangling
an end of broken halter.

The Case of the Intellectual Woman

Tessa Ransford

Even in writing this title I ask myself if I should have written *The Case **For** The Intellectual Woman?* The answer must be No. I am not trying to defend her, but I would like to discuss her as a phenomenon which our society in Scotland or in the UK generally is not entirely happy with. I am neither social historian nor feminist theorist. I hope that others with specialist knowledge in associated areas will contribute to the discussion. I shall have to limit the "case" to a small part of even my own knowledge and experience. I shall have to generalise.

The Late Show presenter, Sarah Dunant, interviewed in *Scotland on Sunday* on 18 July 1993 by Kenny Farquharson, fervently disclaimed the attribute 'intellectual'. "I swear," she says, hand on heart, "I am severely not Miss Intellectual." We are told "You get the feeling that 'sassy' is how she would like to be described." We are informed also that she is "painfully thin." Could this represent another anorexic statement of dis-ease with herself? The headline reads NOT JUST A CLEVER DICK.

Why should she be ashamed of seeming intellectual, as she is supposed to be on *The Late Show?* I could understand her being worried about seeming more intellectual than she is, but appearances count in the media as we wearily acknowledge. Would she worry if she appeared younger than she is, or more sassy? Obviously there is a problem only if the "seeming what she is not" is negative rather than positive. In this respect "intellectual" is considered a negative. "Intellectual" has become largely synonymous with "pretentious" and in women it indicates that they are non- or less-than-sassy. In the case of men, however, it is certainly possible to be thought 'sexy' – shall we say? – *because* they are intellectual (seeming or otherwise).

What does the attribute "intellectual" mean? The dictionary relates it to the exercise and training of the intellect, which is itself defined as "the faculty of perceiving, knowing and thinking". Intellectuals in a society are reputedly the first to be eliminated under a dictatorship. They are those who think for themselves, educate themselves, who do not accept their opinions secondhand, who question, turn things round, suggest alternatives, make connections, hold opposites in balance, keep openings in their minds, can change their minds, will reserve judgement, take risks in being wrong and often take the consequences – although the consequences of not thinking the same as everyone else can be severe even if one is eventually proved right!

In Robert M Pirsig's book *Lila*, the author tries to define different kinds of 'quality'. Dynamic quality changes things, whereas static quality maintains and stabilises them. There is in Teilhard de Chardin's analysis a need for a morality of movement and a morality of balance. Both are necessary. Inevitably there is continual struggle and tension between them, archetypally between father and son, priest and prophet, the pack leader and the loner, dogma and research, experience and experiment. Pirsig describes how we have several quite independent systems working simultaneously within the individual and in society. Analogous with computers we, too, could be said to have hardware, software and the textual input. The intellectual component is dependent on the existence of the other systems and yet leads them on.

In Vera Brittain's *Testament of Youth* we witness the determined struggle of a young woman to be allowed to go to Oxford, having overcome the difficulty of getting the education she needed to pass the exams. She does succeed, but war breaks out in 1914 and she abandons Oxford to train as a nurse. She volunteers for France, working in terrible conditions in hospitals at the Front. She returns to Oxford after the war and is amazed and saddened that the majority of students seemed to want to ignore the war as if it made no difference to academic life.

Vera Brittain, an intellectual woman, cannot remain at Oxford studying academic subjects while her friends and relations are being killed and the world completely changing around her. Similarly she cannot then forget the war and go back to studying as if nothing had happened. For the intellectual everything is related. There are distinctions but not divisions between one field of study or activity and another. Indeed most of what happens is in an energy circuit of some kind. We cannot make things happen, but we can try to make the conditions in which they could happen or the other way round: we can avoid the conditions that harbour disease, for instance. The intellectual is instinctively and faithfully ecological, seeing and making connections, *latching* or *latticing* and open to the energy fields within which we are all sustained.

The intellectual is usually also a practical thinker. If one line of thought or experiment does not work, he or she will try another before spending time tinkering with the broken-down system. The intellectual is usually a rather optimistic and positive person, "full of ideas" as we say, "full of energy" and also *generous*. The intellectual so loves ideas that he or she wants to share them and is not in the least possessive of them. Ideas are always the offspring of cross-fertilisation and it must be possible for this to happen within a culture and between cultures for intellectuals to flourish. Intellectuals often "borrow" ideas from others, throw them out for discussion, recreate them in new ways. They are freely open to and with ideas. Ideas belong to humankind. They are the sphere in which we specifically belong as humans. They are as water is to fish or air to birds. They are not for censoring, cornering, privatising, possessing, selling, buying or marketing.

In George Eliot's *The Mill on the Floss*, Maggie Tulliver is a sensitive, passionate, intelligent young woman. She meets a deformed man, Philip, who offers to lend her books and discusses them with her. She is forced to meet him clandestinely to exchange books, because society made it impossible for young men and women to meet on any other basis than the marriage market. He assumes she loves him. It ends in tragedy.

How many, many women have been attracted to men whom they hoped could feed their enquiring minds, only to be expected to give their bodies in return? Women make attempts to band together to share intellectual pursuits, whether in colleges or coteries, but then become inevitably divided from each other by domestic life with husbands and children. They may have to depend solely on husbands, teachers, clerics for any contact with the outside world and its intellectual life.

Of course all this is changing: continuing education; the Open University; freedom to choose to remain unmarried other than in "spinsterhood", widowhood, or the nunnery; freedom to choose to be childless; careers and returning to work – all the many advances achieved by the Women's Movement have made it a little easier for women to live a more consciously intellectual life at the cutting edge of things in society. (It has often been possible to live in more or less "quiet" dependence and domesticity and do some lonely or "private" reading, writing or studying in between home-making and child-rearing. Unemployment on a large scale makes intellectual pursuits for their own sake and for enjoyment far less rare among men and women, who, until recently, may have felt they had to wait for retirement to begin seriously reading and thinking.)

The arts are often branded in the popular mind as being for intellectual types. All the arts, whether the visual arts, music, dance, drama or poetry and prose fiction, are manifested in a variety of form and style. With poetry, where words are the medium, there is, no less than with the other arts, a wide range of form and style. One poet will work most effectively with the sound of words. Another will vividly conjure images, scenes, colours. Yet another will make verbal puns, witty juxtapositions, humorous plays on words. One may tend to listen with an inward ear and another will recreate the dialogue of others. Not all poets are particularly intellectual or even particularly literary or articulate. Indeed these may be in the minority and by no means therefore "better".

On the whole, however, I think it is fair to say the poems come from the poet's *mental* life. This is not to say a life divorced from experience any more than mind can be divorced from body. Those who find ideas more interesting than food also have to eat. If this were more generally understood there would be less need to explain again and again that poems are not autobiographical on the level of "this really happened". Whether it did nor not is of no relevance to the success of the poem. Poems are more like a *mentograph* on the level of "this idea – or this skein of ideas – was part of me. I lived in this idea or coil of ideas."

A good reviewer of poetry will help the reader to appreciate or criticise the poems. Often, nowadays, the fact that poems are by a woman is taken as sufficient to commend them, regardless of whether that woman's poetry is interesting or well-made or not: "a real woman's voice"; "an authentic woman's point of view"; "a feminine understanding and compassion". Often the more the poems appear to "expose" the physicality of being female the more they are acclaimed.

I find such remarks essentially meaningless. I am a woman. I have an intellect springing from a view, a voice, an understanding all my own, created through my own life experience. I do not necessarily share it with anyone else, man or woman. When I find someone, in the past or present, in the neighbourhood or far off, on the page or in conversation, with whom I can share an intellectual life, develop ideas, open up new revelations, I am excited and happy. I may note but I hardly notice if that person is male or female (George Eliot, for instance) any more than I notice the colour of their eyes or skin, what they are wearing, how old they are. If I find them in a book I don't need or even want to know what they look like in order to respond to their ideas. Meeting the author can be of dubious value, satisfying nothing much more than curiosity.

To hear poets reading their own poems is also to hear them *interpreting* the poems and can be of immense significance. But for this we do not need to know personal or domestic details or how many prizes they have won or what they had for breakfast. When considering poems for *Lines Review* I read the poems, not the name or biographical details of the author. If it is a poetry magazine, poetry is what it should publish. The only positive discrimination I might make is in favour of those resident in Scotland. I consider that, in a Scottish magazine, unless it is a special issue, more poems should be from Scotland than from elsewhere. This is part of the process of taking responsibility for our own poetry and not expecting other nations to do so on our behalf.

On the other hand we should believe passionately in translation. Poetry is in itself an act of translation: from the unwritten textual field into specific words. But the language medium must be a medium not a barrier.

Translation revolves the turnstile and lets the poetic ideas through into another language and its field of ideas.

There are certain well-worn thought-grooves in the Western mind. One of these is dualism. It is a constant "mental fight" to avoid that trap. It is useful only as a tool for analysis in a "suspension of disbelief", because experience is not dualistic but holistic. The intellectual, therefore, need not be thought of as half-human or set apart from the majority of humankind.

I think if Leonard Bernstein rehearsing the orchestra and singers for *West Side Story*. Elitism and populism need not be estranged. I have been accused of trying to popularise poetry, something essentially elitist, and of wanting to "take it out of the universities". This is far from the case. I am extremely elitist and believe poetry to be a high and difficult art. However I also believe that it speaks for and to human beings and that everyone should be able to find and discover a kind of poetry that is meaningful to them at any particular time or stage in their lives. I compare it in this sense with music or painting.

Intellectuals are not necessarily poets or creative artists at all. They appear in many guises and one of these is in the female body. Germaine Greer is struggling courageously to win back respect for intellect and personality in women, as no less valuable than youth and beauty. As the poets tell us, youth and beauty, fertility and fame fade very quickly. *Carpe Diem*. Let us grasp the flower of the intellect, which transcends the limits of space and time. Is Helen of Troy a beautiful woman or a beautiful idea of a woman that launched the ships of many thousands of poems? "What is the good of knowing about Helen of Troy if nobody else does?" asked a nine-year-old. The answer is that she is a timelessly fertile idea. Let us value our intellectuals and not dismiss them as pretentious, even if they sometimes appear so, male or female. My ideas are as important to me as my breasts and my poetry as my children.

All too often women are forced to choose between the life of the mind and the life of the body. The intellectual woman is in serious danger of decapitation in our society, now as in the past. Her head is of value only if cut off from her body and her body appreciated only if cut off from her head. Though this is most clearly manifested where women are concerned, such a disabling lack of co-ordination between the mental and the physical runs right through every aspect of life in Scotland as experienced by us all at present no less than in MacDiarmid's or Patrick Geddes' or Mary Queen of Scots's day. Truth, after all, is beauty – as Keats was laughed to scorn for saying by those pedantic Edinburgh reviewers of old. Intellectual women are a sign of culture in a society as trees signal an oasis in the desert. They represent the "Spirit of Beauty", hymned by Shelley, "that dost consecrate/ With thine own hues all thou dost shine upon/ Of human thought or form.".   *Tessa Ransford*

from
A Scarecrow for all Seasons

I overlook, from my field,
A residential school
With children who wear helmets,
Not to look cool

But because they cannot stand
Without falling down:
A general sickness in man, but
more
Pronounced in them.

I never saw them froth
At the mouth, as is said.
They looked, to tell you the truth,
More alive than dead.

Despite this, they are carried
As human corpses are,
Away, not to be buried,
But somewhere, somewhere.

one of a selection of poems by David Cameron
published in **Scottish Child** December 1992.

Scottish Child - the celebration of childhood in poetry and prose
Annual subscription rates - £15.00 individual/£21 organisations

For a free sample copy or to subscribe, write or phone

Edinburgh:
Scottish Child,
130 St Stephen Street,
Edinburgh,
EH3 5AD,
031-220 6502

Glasgow:
Scottish Child,
Maryhill Community Education
Centre, 35 Avenuepark Street,
Glasgow G20 8TS,
041-946 0009

Baby Doll

Jane Harris

Heather was convinced her chest was getting bigger. She inspected every angle in the mirror. Admittedly, the difference was fractional, but if she held her breath, tensed her stomach muscles and turned slightly to one side, there did seem to be some development, particularly if she leaned forwards about an inch. It was hard to walk once she'd found the optimum position, but just possible for short periods. She decided to try it out at school on Monday, in break, to see if anyone noticed. It might stop the boys that hung out in the smoker sheds shouting "Hey-you-wee-lassie-with-nae-tits!" and "Haw! Ironing board!" every time she went past.

She blew herself a kiss, dismissing the whole shower of them.

"Flat-chisted", was what her mother said. She'd said it only once, out of the side of her face: "She'll be flat-chisted."

To a neighbour for Christ sake. A betrayal Heather had never forgotten.

She cupped her hands beneath her chin and stared hard at the mirror, into her own eyes, trying to make her face disappear.

Disparu.

Disparaitre.

"Have you not found one yet?!"

The voice from the bottom of the stairs. Had Heather's father been there, he'd have shuddered and made a face like he'd swallowed vinegar.

"It would cut tin", he'd have said, then he'd sigh, pressing his fingers to the sides of his nose. "Voice like a laser beam."

"Just looking, Mum!"

"Try both drawers!"

"Yes!"

"Behind the underwear!"

"Fine!"

"What's that noise?"

"Nothing! I banged my foot on the wardrobe!"

Heather gave the dresser another kick and yanked open the top drawer. There was always the same smell in there. Musty and sour, a mixture of old talc, stale perfume and the biscuity tang of worn tights. She could never quite decide how she felt about looking through her mother's things. She sniffed tentatively and decided that although the drawer was redolent of her mother, it lacked any warmth, making Heather feel as if she was raking through the effects of a corpse. 'Redolent' and 'corpse', currently her second and third favourite words, were to be used whenever possible. Her very favourite, 'nauseous', couldn't be employed on this occasion, as the drawer didn't make her feel sick, only vaguely daring.

She stared in at underwear, curling limply around itself in sweet knots, casting up the stiff, dingy cup and frayed seams of a Wonderbra. Once in a while, when her mum ventured out to the Over 35s, Heather would dip into this drawer, and fantasise with forbidden items. She'd pose before the mirror, pouting in brief nylon slips, wadding sock balls into the cups of already-padded, underwired silk bustières, for a fuller figure, for maximum uplift. Occasionally, she'd brush a stripe of blusher down her breastbone, for cleavage enhancement.

As recommended in her mother's magazines.

And sometimes, she'd root through the rusty shortbread tin of discarded cosmetics at the back of the drawer, twisting up lipsticks and sorting them into colour sequence, from Pale Frost to Mulberry Meow, or Virgin Plum to Scarlet Lady. She was amazed at how each waxy cylinder was always worn down to exactly the same shape. Once, she'd read an article, that claimed it was possible to divine a person's character from the state of their old make-up. According to the pictures accompanying the article, the delicately-curved remains of her mother's lipsticks meant that she was sweet-tempered, likeable and unselfish by nature. Heather reluctantly concluded that there could be no truth whatsoever in this particular theory.

She was allowed some make-up herself now. Brown mascara, with lash-thickening fibres. One green eyeshadow, plus applicator. One blue eyeshadow, 'for a wee change'. Clear nail varnish. And an eyeliner, the existence of which she concealed from her mother. For what it was worth, she even had her own bra. A skinny white cotton garment she barely filled. "A trainer bra", her mother had said as she produced it from the wrapper, adding, when she saw Heather's crestfallen expression: "It'll have to do."

Heather had snipped off the label to save face in the school changing rooms. To be the owner of an AA cup size was too mortifying for words.

She raked through the drawer and pulled out a high-collared nightie with a raised paw-print motif and the words 'Cat Napping' embroidered on the front. Pushing this aside in disgust she rummaged again, surfacing with something more promising. A seventies-style baby-doll nightie, with gathered bodice and several layers of nylon that tumbled to mid-thigh. Lilac, unworn for years, since the Sunday her father popped out to B&Q and was never seen again. A garment from pre-history, old enough to be almost fashionable.

Heather held it against herself, trying it out in the mirror.

"You're not taking that."

"Aw, Mum!"

"No!"

"But the other one doesn't suit me."

"And this does?"

Her mother gave her the small, tired smile, which conveyed that though Heather was being ridiculous, she could expect no more from the child.

Heather glanced again at the mirror, this time, doubtful.

Her mother ran her tongue across her front teeth, gazing past Heather at her own reflection. "It's far too mature for you, dear."

"But I'm thirteen!" On the verge of tears, Heather resisted the temptation to stamp her foot. She stared glumly into the mirror, twisting the gauzy layers of the nightdress around her fingers so that the nylon snagged on her nails. "May as well wear my own nightie then", she said, sullenly.

Her mother snorted. "You will not wear that bloody thing. Falling to bits. What'd they think?"

"Ple-ease?"

Her mother sighed and Heather sensed she was weakening. "It's just for one night."

There was a pause, while they stared at each other. Her mother seemed to be weighing something up. "Okay", she said at last. "It'll be freezing mind, a caravan. This time of year."

Heather grinned, reached out to touch her elbow. "Thanks, Mum."

She could never quite bring herself to hug her mother. That faintly acrid smell, the cigarettes, the Rive Gauche and something else, an undertone of something fleshy, repelled her. She patted her, like she might stroke a nervous horse. For the first time, she noticed in the mirror that they were almost the same height.

"Thanks", she said again. "Look, if it's cold I'll keep my socks on."

Her mother moved away, as if she had more important things to be getting on with, laughing, saying:

"That'll be a sight for sore eyes."

Later, Heather lay in bed, listening to the television blaring in the living room. After a while, she threw back the covers and stepped softly across the half-light in her room, taking care to avoid the creaking floorboards. She stopped in front of the mirror. Her figure glowed, lilac, pale. She could just make out the dark line of her hair, and the blank grey oval of her face. She turned, looked moodily across her shoulder, like one of the models in the magazines, turned again. In this light, she decided, she was almost desirable. She pressed her hands to the flat of her waist, pulled the material taut against her skin. Then slowly, she stroked up across her belly, cupping her breasts. Her breathing grew softer and faster. She sensed, in her groin and thighs, a feeling she'd felt before, this time stronger. With one hand she lifted the hem of her nightie, bunched it at her chest. The other hand moved down cautiously over the curve of her tummy, towards the dusting of dark hairs across her pubic mound. She stroked, uncertainly, enjoying the tingling sensation it gave her. As usual, her mouth went dry and when she started to feel breathless, panic-stricken, she had to stop.

Sighing, she dropped the nightie's hem, negotiated the floorboards and slipped back into bed.

She woke with a grinding in the pit of her stomach and, after breakfast, added a pack of sanitary towels to her overnight bag in the hall.

"Heather! Not like that!"

"Like what?"

"Like an advertisement! Nobody wants to see your STs. Hide them in the bottom of your bag."

"Why do you always call them that?"

But her mother had disappeared into the kitchen.

Disparued.

"Christ!"

She pushed the towels out of sight, smoothed the lilac nightie into place on top of her bag.

Her mother bustled out behind her when they heard the car horn. Heather skipped on ahead and climbed into the back. Her mother hesitated on the pavement, puffing at a cigarette. The car smelled of new carpets and plastic. Cath sat in the rear seat, a book open on her lap, twirling an oily strand of hair round her finger. As far as Heather knew, she was Cath's only friend. It wasn't just the nervous tics, the vacant expression, the fact that Cath was a renowned swot. There was something odd about her, that made other girls avoid her. They'd been friends for a couple of months, yet Heather felt, somehow, that they were still strangers.

"Hiya." Cath glanced up as she got in.

"New car?"

Cath shrugged. "Yeah."

Mr Weir swivelled in his seat. "'A haven of high-tensile steel'", he said, then jabbed a button on the dashboard and the car window rolled down. He poked his head out. Heather's mother blew a cloud of smoke, nodding in her direction.

"Don't take any nonsense."

In the passenger seat, Mrs Weir laughed. "Oh, she'll be no trouble."

Mrs Weir always spoke with her eyes shut, so she couldn't see the person she was talking to, as if the sight of them might interfere with her train of thought.

"Make sure she buys no rubbish, Mr Weir." Heather's mum patted a lock of hair into place. "There's three pounds in that purse."

"Enough for fish'n'chips and a sticka rock, eh?" said Cath's dad. "And please, call me Archie."

"We'll be back tomorrow night", said Mrs Weir addressing her husband's shoulder, her eyes clamped shut. Mr Weir turned the key in the ignition.

"We go to church in the morning", he called through the window. "But Heather can take herself down the beach if she wants. Cheerio now."

Heather's mother ducked, mouthing something as the car moved off. Cath lifted her head.

"What's she saying?"

"Dunno."

"ST. Something about ST."

Heather shrugged, her face scarlet. "No idea."

Cath's dad demonstrated how the cigarette lighter worked, though he was quick to point out that neither he nor Mrs Weir approved of smoking. He showed Heather how the push-button radio moved automatically from channel to channel. Then, much to her embarrassment, he began singing teuchter songs, "to get them all in the mood." He jogged his wife's elbow, encouraging her to join in the chorus. Mrs Weir clicked her tongue.

"Och, away you go Archie." She fluttered her eyelids at the gearstick. "You sing, girls."

Mr Weir smacked the steering wheel cover with his hands. "Aye! SING UP, Heather! You've never smelt the tangle o' the isles!"

Heather squirmed, muttered an excuse about not knowing the words. Beside her, Cath turned pages steadily, a finger intermittently twiddling her hair, her mouth firmly stoppered with a thumb.

While Cath's mum went shopping in Largs they spent some time on the beach before driving out to the Weirs' caravan. Mr Weir produced a ball from his pocket and taught them how to throw overarm, like cricketers. He scraped a straight line in the shingle and tossed the ball to Heather.

"Have a shot", he said. "Run into your throw, but try not to cross this line."

Heather retreated, then ran towards the mark on the beach, circling her arm and as she reached it, threw the ball. Caught by the wind, it veered in an unexpected direction. Reluctantly, Cath stuffed her book down the front of her anorak and trudged off to retrieve it. Mr Weir sniffed.

"Not bad. Try again."

He stood behind Heather, guiding her arm in a slow arc, one hand firmly on her shoulder.

"Put the weight on your back foot as you throw. That's it."

He pulled her against him and squeezed her hand till it hurt. This time when she reached the line and released the ball, it sliced through the air, bounced off Cath's head and landed in the shallows. Cath rubbed her temple and Mr Weir chuckled.

"Better", he said.

Later they wandered around gift shops while they waited for Mrs Weir. Heather trailed after Cath, gazing dumbly at tartan tins of shortbread, thistle keyrings and tea-towels printed with maps of Argyll. She saw nothing she wanted to buy, except a polished hunk of crystallised quartz. She was currently going through a geological phase, fascinated as much by the names of stones as by their appearance: mica schist, igneous, garnet, gneiss, lapis lazuli. The amethyst was almost five pounds, too expensive, so she had to be content with admiring the size of it, stroking its gleaming purple surfaces. She found Cath hovering at the edge of a crowd of boys who had gathered around one of the shelves. Heather watched as one of them squeezed the shoulders of a miniature monk. An erect penis jerked up out of the monk's vestments and the boys sniggered, punching each other, darting quick glances at the girls. Cath gazed at the monk, balefully.

Behind them, Mr Weir cleared his throat. "Chips, ladies?"

He was smiling blankly at a point high on the wall behind them, as though he couldn't see the display of lewd monks. He inclined his head towards the entrance and they followed him.

Outside, he handed some money to Cath.

"A bag each, pet-lamb."

She smiled up at him and he ruffled her fringe like he often did, before she set off across the road to the chip van. To avoid having to make conversation, Heather pretended to be interested in the advertisement cards in a newsagent's doorway and was surprised when Mr Weir stepped up close beside her saying:

"What's this, what's this?"

He slipped something out of his pocket and pressed it into her hand. It felt cold and very heavy and when she looked down she saw she was holding the amethyst. She shifted her fingers and the uncut underside rasped against her palm. It was as big as her fist. She looked up. Cath's dad was smiling quietly down at the pavement. It was hard to know what to say. Gratitude seemed appropriate. She swallowed.

"Brilliant! Thanks very much, Mr Weir."

He winked at her, then his gaze drifted across the road to Cath, who was standing, her hand in her hair, in the chip queue. Heather thought he looked sad, until he coughed and said, still staring at Cath:

"Stick it in your pocket, eh? Our secret."

Then he strolled away, whistling, to examine an ironmonger's window.

They parked in the car park near the campsite office. Mr Weir pressed something on his key ring which made all the buttons on the car interior snap down. An alarm device chirped three times. He spun the keys round his finger and dropped them into his pocket as if it was a holster.

"Central locking", he said, pausing to wipe at a speck of dirt on the windscreen.

A little wooden sign, with the word 'Dunroamin' burned into it, hung above the caravan door. Inside, the air smelt of damp and pepper. Cath showed Heather the narrow bedroom they were to share.

"Bagsy top bunk", said Heather.

Cath shrugged. "Go ahead. I can sleep in it any time." She pointed out the toilet block through the little window then sat on her bed, staring at the pages of her book. Heather folded the lilac nightie carefully and placed it under her pillow. Mr Weir popped his head in to say there wasn't time before tea to do any exploring, so they played Scrabble while Mrs Weir cooked. Heather hated Scrabble. She could never see the point of games, particularly when she was losing. Mr Weir won most points, using all his letters, with a 'Z' on a double letter square. Heather, annoyed, disputed that 'paralyze' should be spelt with an 'S'. Mr Weir stood up to stretch his legs, adopting a cowpoke twang:

"Not in my dictionary it ain't."

Later, Heather sat on her bunk, listening to the sounds of Cath and her parents getting ready for a quick stroll before dark. She had pled tiredness in order to have some time on her own and Mrs Weir had closed her eyes and addressed the gas cylinder:

"That's the country air for you."

After they'd gone, there was silence. Through the tiny window, she watched the huge salmon-pink globe of sun slip down behind the treetops into where she knew the sea must lie. While the family were at church in the morning Heather planned to hunt for garnets. She remembered the amethyst, fumbled for it in her pocket, testing its weight in her hand, watching it glow dimly like a brittle lump of purple toffee. With a twist of tissue, she tried to brush out the dust that lay in every recess, before hiding it again in her jacket. Then she undressed, and was admiring the way the ruched bodice of the nightie bunched at her breasts, so that they looked bigger, when she realised she hadn't changed her sanitary towel.

She poked her head out of the caravan door. There was no one around. Her mother would have made her get dressed again, but she slid her bare feet into wellies and skimmed over the damp turf, clutching her toilet-bag, holding the nightie fast against her legs.

The toilet mirrors were made of shiny vandal-proof metal, giving her the appearance of being afloat in liquid mercury. She changed her towel and skipped back outside. It was only as she sped round the corner onto the open ground in front of the gent's that she glimpsed a group of men with fishing rods, chatting at the entrance. Instantly, she considered slowing to a walk and making her way across the space, nonchalant, though just as quickly she changed her mind. But in that second of hesitation, she lost her footing and slipped on the dew-soaked grass. Her legs flew up in the air and she landed on all fours, the nightie tossed up around her waist.

She lay, stunned, her face burning. Behind her, the men fell silent. Her hands and knees stung. And then, with her heart thumping in her ears, she scrambled to her feet and fled, the cold air nipping her eyes, boot-rubber slapping at her calves, the sanitary towel chaffing, sliding around in her time-of-the-month pants like a great dry turd.

"Nice walk?"

"Alright. You in bed already?"

"Mm."

"What's up with your hand?"

"Just a graze."

Cath picked up her toilet bag and wrapped a towel round her neck. "Going for showers. See you in a bit."

She stepped into the living area and a moment later Heather heard the caravan door bang. She sat back against the pillow. Through the window she watched Mrs Weir and Cath picking their way across the grass towards the toilet block.

Mr Weir appeared in the doorway.

"Hello! In bed already?"

"Yes."

He stepped into the narrow room and leaned against the wall, so he was beside her, his face level with hers. He smiled, parting his teeth. "Comfy?"

"Yes, thanks."

Heather's face grew hot. She hoped Mr Weir wouldn't notice. She'd never sat in bed and had a conversation with a man before. Indeed, she'd hardly ever had a conversation with a man at all. What was she supposed to say? She rubbed at her neck, though it wasn't itchy. Her voice sounded hoarse.

"...How was your walk?"

Mr Weir didn't answer. He seemed a bit dazed. He stared at her throat and she wondered if he was noticing how flushed she was. She wished, not for the first time, that she was one of those people who didn't blush. Mr Weir blinked.

"That's nice", he said. He reached out to touch the sleeve of her nightie. "Quite the young lady." He rubbed the material between his thumb and finger. Heather looked down at his hand. So close, it seemed larger than life, like the hand of a giant. Dark hairs, sprouting from black pores, curled over the wrist. The skin was knotted with thick indigo veins. A man's hand. Then, the fingers tilted her chin. Mr Weir was smiling at her, as if he knew what she was thinking, making her feel that she had to smile back. There was a sudden, uncomfortable prickling in her armpits. Mr Weir winked.

"Hey", he said. "Can I have a look?"

He dragged at the sheet, exposing the tops of her legs.

"Very nice", he said, touching her on the chest. She drew breath, opened her mouth to say something, but Mr Weir made a little sucking noise.

"Shh", he said and slid his hand down inside her nightie. She felt him press her nipple between his fingers.

She swallowed.

"Hey", he whispered. "Our secret." He shifted, leaned against the bunk and breathed out. "That's it. Very nice." His breath warmed her cheek. "Now", he said, closing his eyes and putting his hand up inside her nightie. He stroked her thighs then she felt him hesitate as he touched the edge of her pants. His eyes snapped open and he prodded, frowning when his fingers found the lump of her towel. Then he looked at her as if she'd let him down and said: "That's no good is it?" He made a sad face and sighed, patting her softly between the legs. "Never mind, pet-lamb", he said, ruffling her fringe, the way he always did with Cath, pulling down her hem. "Hey", he said, making her look at him. "Hey." He pinched her cheek. "Our secret, eh?"

He tousled her hair again and moved away from her into the living area, closing the door behind him, humming one of the tunes he'd been singing in the car.

She woke up, hot and sticky between the legs. The sanitary towel had shifted in the night, and blood had seeped through her pants, blooming on the pale nightie in places, like red petals. She sat up and a crimson amoeba stained the sheet.

In the bottom bunk, Cath slept, her thumb in her mouth, fingers wrapped around her nose. Heather dressed quietly and tiptoed into the living area, clutching her nightie. It was warmer there and a fuggy, stale smell hung in the air. She peeked through a crack in the curtain of the bed recess and saw Mrs Weir's perm and the thinning hair on Mr Weir's head resting side by side on the pillows. From the shape they made beneath the blankets she could tell that they lay close together, in each other's arms. Watching them, Heather felt a suffocating pain like a physical weight in her chest and she bit down hard on her lip.

Nauseous.

She crept outside the caravan and stepped into her boots. The cold air made her breath vaporise in front of her face. Stuffing the nightie down the front of her jacket, she hurried across the frosted ground towards the toilets, scuffing her feet, leaving dark green trails in the silver grass.

A woman was brushing her hair at the mirrors. Heather locked herself in a cubicle, disposed of the towel and rammed a wadge of toilet roll into her pants. She had meant to rinse out her nightie, but when she emerged the woman was still there, so she stepped outside and headed past the site office towards the road without any clear idea of where she was going, or what she might do. The car park was coated with a powdery frost. As she pushed her hands into her pockets, the lump of amethyst grazed her skin and she took it out, picturing herself hurling it into the ocean, enjoying the swift curve as it whipped through the air, turning, turning and finally smashing into the waves, throwing up cold white spume like chips of glass.

She passed Mr Weir's car. A thin sweat of condensation coated the expanse of windscreen. Heather froze for a second, glanced over her shoulder and retraced her steps, the amethyst heavy in her hand.

What could he say?

Taking a deep breath, she scraped a line in the frosted ground a few yards in front of the bumper. Then she took a few paces backwards and as she reached her mark, shifted her weight on to her right foot and drew back her hand, like a bowler.

The tide was out. She picked her way across the dark, greasy rocks and stood for a while on the beach, staring at the opposite shore. The sun rose from behind a cloud, momentarily lighting up the water. To her left, a chain of small boats bobbed like loose teeth in the silver of the sea. She waded in until the waves lapped dangerously at the top of her boots.

Taking the nightie from her jacket, she dropped it into the sea, and watched it shift back and forwards, dragged by the current, its skirts flowing delicately outwards as if it was some great bruised jellyfish, bleeding into the shallows. She let it float and walked away along the shore, splashing in the tide, watching her footprints move and change in the shale at the water's edge. She groomed a small section of beach, picking through the pebbles for garnets, listening to the harsh cries of seagulls and somewhere, behind the trees, the wailing of a car alarm.

She imagined the look on his face.   *Jane Harris*

Elizabeth Burns

The Alchemist

His presence is, as always, alchemy
in the gun-metal grey of ordinary days.
Just by being here, he can extract
gold-dust, turn all things
to his skin-colour, mango.

While he's in town the rain lifts:
late autumn seems as warm as summer
and we picnic on cheese and olives.

He brings with him golden-coloured gifts:
whisky, a pumpkin, oranges,
glass goblets from Mexico
brimming with wine and light.

He makes butter-tasting biscuits
in the shapes of stars
and one, enormous, too beautiful to eat
he calls 'The Flaming Sun'
and decorates with flecks of orange peel.

He pulls everyone onto the dance floor,
entrances all of us, men and women both,
with his smile and his gold-leaf skin.
Not knowing what it is to be rebuffed,
he throws out embraces with extravagance.

He's like some kind of sun-god
and we the lesser mortals circling him.

He smiles on us: we bask in his glow
having discovered, in his presence,
traces of fine gold within ourselves
drawn, imperceptibly, from dross.

without words

in the dream there were no words for this
I held the blank paper out to you

and in the poem there are only those
that say, this was morning time
and that there were, perhaps,
light-tipped fingers in half-sleep
and that the pale blue May sky
was falling through the window-pane
washing over each inch of flesh

Sculptures at Glenkiln

a king and a queen
on a hillside

clouds in their eyes
damp grass at their feet

they sit side by side
gentle and content

smaller than life-size
hands clasped

tiny fingerbones
intricate toes

scooped curves
of shoulderblades

folds of their robes
making laps

bronze flesh
mottled by weather

as they survey
as far as eyes can see –

the misty valley
and the reservoir

the firwoods
and the farmhouse

brown bracken
and bare branches

winter fields
and white skies

the wide-winged
kingdom of Glenkiln

The box

At night in the windowless room
you are there in my dreams, you
and your son, dead at fifteen,
you and your unthinkable grief.

Pitch-dark in this box-room
airless and damp. I wake, gasping,
waft my hand for a breeze,
thinking, I am in a coffin room

and do not know which way I lie
or where the door is – can't escape.
I twist round, panicky, groping
for the cup of water, not found –

and think of you, so motherly, so loving
and the dark box closing round you,
no chink of light, and the bad dreams
churning and churning –

Days later, glimpsing an image
of a mother, her boy on her lap,
I know something's awry with such love,
something's upsetting, not right –

and it's you, and the death of your son,
a remembrance, almost a warning:
of the gut-pain of motherhood,
of its sudden, wrenched endings.

Proof

The ghost
brings a poem
and a pot of marmalade.

The painting
of the roses
falls off the wall.

Look, says ghost-child,
elfin,
laying down her jar –

See the poem,
turn it over,
for a life you never had.

Then she's gone,
wisp. Was she ever
here?

Yes.
There's the jamjar.
And on my finger

a lick of orange,
her sweet tart
winter fruit.

At the dentist in the 1990s

Two types of fillings now:
one plastic, tooth-like, beautiful,
one containing mercury, tasting of metal.

Fill out the forms: sign here
if you are poor. This is how
you choose your filling.

Tick your sexual preference.
Whose tongue has touched yours?
Have drugs ever entered your blood?

The dentist is prying
in your mouth. The dentist is wearing
rubber, as a precaution.

A needle deadens pain.
Implements intrude in soft flesh.
Tears prickle. Blood comes.

'Rinse out your mouth' says a voice
handing you the cup
of tainted water, pinkish.

Feel nothing when you bite your lips.
The mouth of the dentist is speaking.
It is a white-toothed, shining mouth.

It has not known abscess or decay, nor
the lick of poverty. It smiles.
Says it's going private now. It lives

in a new country, gleaming as its teeth.
Lives in a continent, white as its coat.
It's grinning like the Germans

who took the Polish Jew
gave him a local
cut out his tongue with shears.

'Rinse out your mouth' says the voice
but the water is strange-coloured,
queer-tasting. Rinse, rinse,

take the anaesthetic, get numb
to the pain. Ask no questions.
Keep your mouth closed.

Stramullion

Elizabeth Burns

"Standing-up-and-fighting-like-a-man is a good deal easier than sitting down
and writing like a woman."

"We're daring to say, 'I, a woman, have made this' and not letting anyone tell
us we can't do it."

These are the voices of women involved in an Edinburgh women's
writing group a dozen years ago. Frustrated with the lack of outlet for their
work, and for feminist writing in general, they decided to borrow some
money, set up a women's publishing house, and produce their own work.
The publisher was named Stramullion (an old Scots word for 'strong
woman'), and its first publication was the poetry anthology *Hens in the
Hay*.

Focusing on that first collection, I want to look briefly at Stramullion's
history, and also at some of the preoccupations of women's writing over
the past decade or so.

Looking back now at *Hens in the Hay*, (1980), it seems that there are
themes emerging which have recurred in women's writing throughout the
1980s, a period which has seen the opening up of subjects previously
considered taboo in the largely male preserve of poetry.

Firstly there's a newly focused anger at the constraints within which women are expected to live. "I'm not playing at being... verb to your pronoun... mortar for your pestle" says one of Chris Cherry's poems, and Ellen Galford in 'A woman wanted to study Kabbalah' tells how the woman is forbidden access to learning and mysticism first by her mother, then by her husband and finally by the rabbi, who tells her "such matters [are] forbidden to idiots and women". And Stephanie Markman's prose-poem 'Spectogram' celebrates a friend's defiance: "YELLOW is for your afternoon jugband dancing, kicking your legs, two fingers at the world..."

As well as anger, there's a sense of exploration here, as the women write about their lives, their friendships, their discovery of common ground: "we have different experiences/ But we belong to the same country/ We speak the native tongue", as Lorna Mitchell writes, echoing the American poet Adrienne Rich's 'Dream of a Common Language'.

Discovering our "common language" as women can mean an end to a certain kind of isolation as a writer. As one of the women in *Hens in the Hay* says in the introduction, being with other writing women has helped her "to accept my own experience as interesting and valid – and to accept that I'm not totally crazy or presumptuous in wanting to [write]." Another adds, "we all as women have common experiences and the more we share these, the more we can accept ourselves and each other."

Quoted in a more recent book (*Sleeping with Monsters*, Polygon, 1990) the writer Rosalind Brackenbury tells how "I was brought up to think all poets were men", and, as a student, "The poets I knew were men... they wrote completely incomprehensible things... that didn't seem to fit in with my experience at all." But now, as a poet herself, writing is "an act of power": "It's saying, 'My experience is valid and what I want to say about it is valid.'"

It's this confirmation of women's experience as "interesting and valid", as a subject for poetry, which has been vital in the past decade or so, for the broadening out of the narrow confines of what constitutes poetry – and in particular women's poetry: as recently as the 'sixties, the poet and critic Theodore Roethke was saying that women's poetry suffered from "a lack of range – in subject matter, in emotional tone – and lack of a sense of humour" together with "other aesthetic and moral shortcomings".

To accept ourselves as not being "crazy and presumptuous" (let alone unaesthetic and amoral) can mean a physical as well as mental acceptance; an acknowledgement of our own bodies, not as the stuff of male fantasy or muse, but as ordinary, fallible flesh. This has become one of the tenets of the women's movement, and a significant theme in recent women's poetry. As one of the *Hens in the Hay* poets puts it, she's not the kind of woman who "comes wrapped in pretty tissue... doesn't eat garlic..." It's a theme picked up by poets in Stramullion's later poetry anthology *Fresh Oceans* (1989) where poems titled 'Anno-Wreck-Sick' and 'Sweat' explore the unnatural shapes and smells into which women find themselves forced. Others deal with subjects such as first menstruation and miscarriage.

On another level of defining the truth about what happens to our bodies, Stramullion's first non-fiction title, *Incest – Fact and Myth* broke new ground in exposing the sexual abuse of children.

Defining this new, more truthful reality – where women are possessors of their own minds and bodies – is also reflected in a re-telling, a reclamation, of history and tradition. It's a theme that recurs in Stramullion's publications: a calendar highlighting women's history in Scotland; Stephanie Markham's subverting of traditional poetry in *The Rime of the Ancient Feminist*; and two books which record a woman's view of history – the novel *Moll Cutpurse*, set in Elizabethan London, and *Grit and Diamonds*, a record of the '80s in Scotland. And in *Fresh Oceans* there are several retellings of history, from poems giving voice to the Daphne of Greek myth and the Devorgilla of Scots legend, to the 'Unspoken words of a North Uist woman, 1901'.

Wider in scope than *Hens in the Hay*, *Fresh Oceans* contains the work of almost forty poets, writing in English, Scots and Gaelic and gives a sample of the range of contemporary women's poetry in Scotland.

A pivotal poem in the collection is Margaret Elphinstone's 'To my friend who is a woman and a poet, like me'. "No man ever said I was a poet," the writer says, but

> You called me a poet,
> and took me in your arms, laughing
> with the terror of it.
> ...You called me a poet.
> You – the poet –
> So now I will believe you...

This need for self-confidence, for support, for someone to tell us we are poets, seems a particularly female need. Such a lack of confidence may appear disingenuous or even naïve; yet it is not so long ago that women were being told they could not or should not be poets ("A 'woman poet' is a contradiction in terms", it was argued in the late '50s). And to look at anthologies of that date, or even later, it could be assumed that there were in fact no woman poets.

To believe in our voices as poets and to begin to mark out a place in the tradition in the face of such denial takes a certain amount of courage and defiance. It has also meant a need for friends who "call us poets" – and for some women, it has meant being part of women's writing groups, such as the one which gave birth to Stramullion, or the one which has produced its latest book, *Pomegranate*.

The haunt of the male writer – the pub – has often been closed to women (for reasons of childcare, for example), or they may deliberately have chosen not to be part of its culture. (It's hard, though, to avoid the connections between drink and poetry in a country whose greatest modern poem celebrates 'A Drunk Man'; and where the vital role of whisky in the creation of Scottish literature is fulsomely praised.) For women, a writing group may be an alternative place for finding a literary culture.

Certainly such groups, during the last few years, have helped encourage a grass-roots level of writing and often of readings and publications. Pomegranate, for example, which began in 1980, has since given numerous readings and performances, and offered support and criticism of their work, to over twenty women. Their new collection brings together the work of past and present members of the group as a celebration of its continuing existence.

Its publication marks the closing of a circle begun with the *Hens in the Hay* group, for this book is Stramullion's final publication. Stramullion's decision to cease trading comes largely as a result of the financial constraints of being a small, voluntarily-run group in a time of multinational publishing and recession. Its ending does not deny the validity and usefulness of such a space for women (and perhaps the need for another Scottish women's press to continue the process?) But being an unfunded group committed to publishing work outside of a tradition (and to working in ways outside tradition – with collective decision-making, for example, and profits being used solely to fund future projects) has not always been easy, and Stramullion has far from fulfilled all its original aims and dreams. Yet hopefully it, and the women writers who have supported it, have had some small impact – either politically, in the case of non-fiction, or, with its prose and poetry, by going some way to what the original founders hoped for when they said: "Why did we bother? ...We hoped we might encourage other women to write, to feel good about writing, to share and publish their poetry too."

I'd like to conclude by looking at the opening poem in *Hens*, Chris Cherry's 'Winter', which seems, with its emphasis on solitude and independence, to symbolise what a separate existence, a physical or literary space for women, can mean. The poem begins with warnings:

> Just wait until winter, they said,
> Oh, you'll have a hard time of it then...
> When the frost crazes the window
> And you're cold, in isolation
> Holding fast to ideals...
> You'll know what's good for you...

The poet acknowledges that there is hardship in her chosen way of life – "I knew there would be times like this" – but there is also joy and wonder: "The day is the light with its waxing and waning,/ filling the house, sharp in the morning... And in the afternoon... mellow...The room is at one with the valley now."

Looking back on this poem about independent living and survival, it can be seen as something of a prophetic statement for the women writers of the '80s and '90s who were to follow, for despite the harsh surroundings and the dire predictions, we have begun to forge out a place for ourselves and our work.   *Elizabeth Burns*

Second Shift

A WIDER PERSPECTIVE ON WOMEN AND THE ARTS

Second Shift is the new magazine devoted to women and the arts. In 48 pages of original writing, criticism, features and reviews, Second Shift covers the latest and best work across a wide range of art forms.

COMING IN ISSUES 3 & 4

new fiction by Moy McCrory **Jane Rogers** on housework and *Mr Wroe's Virgins* **Zanna Beswick**, series editor of 'The Bill', looks at women writing TV drama **Ann E. Imbrie**, author of *Spoken in Darkness* talks about friendship and small town murder **Sarah Dunant** on the female private eye **Elspeth Barker** on Paula Rego **interviews** with American duo The Indigo Girls and jazz singer Claire Martin **the textiles** of Alison King **the Second Shift poetry competition** and much more...

£2.50 FROM GALLERIES AND BOOKSHOPS

SUBSCRIPTION RATES (four issues)
Supporting subscription/Organisations £20
Annual subscription £10 Unwaged subscription £8.50
Please make cheques payable to Second Shift and send to:

SECOND SHIFT
12 HOLYOAKE COURT, WHITEHILL ROAD
CAMBRIDGE, CB5 8NB

Janet Paisley

Old Man's Chair

This is the arm chair where he sat;
old leather, worn, stuffed with hair.
She will burn it now he's gone.

And if we had no memories
that would be that. An old man's chair,
a puff of smoke, a childhood done.

But what will we do with remembering
when it uncurls, and crawls
between us – keep silent still?

Or will we talk, and turn, re-make
the summers that we sat in,
break each other's hearts then heal?

Or has he won?

Clearances

A meenut mair, a meenut
fur the heather is in bloom,
the ptarmigan is cryin
an the yella's oan the broom.
Moss an bracken green the hills
an ah wad taste again
the icy sparklin watter
as it tummles tae the glen.

Aye, there's sour smoke ahint us
fur oor cott's been torched by men
brocht ower the sea fae Ireland
tae clear us oot oor hame.
Ma blood was spilt fur Scotland,
in foreign fields ma brithers sleep,
noo sons are torn fae kinfolk
so Argyle kin fatten sheep.

Sae, awa. This high wild place
kin staun as testament tae aw
oor Heilan lords. It's their disgrace.
Ah'd see them burn in hell, ah swear,
tae gain a meenut, a meenut mair.

Bonfire

He sweeps the leaves
into a pile of autumn gold,
crisp brown, pale yellow,
burnished rust.
He does not speak
though we could almost touch
and if I talk
he will refuse to hear.
I do. He does.

So I keep picking apples.
Next door, he twists a paper torch,
touches flame
to what was green and spring
and now is dust.
He is husband to his wife
but I have none.
And worse, I earn my living
doing something strange
with words.

The rising smoke ghosts
other women from my past,
and has not changed.
I feel the heat, smell
my flesh begin to burn.

Saun

ye cannae staun
in saun
cannae git gaun
gits in yer claes
an atween yer taes
steys there fur days
bit rins oot yer haun

ah cannae staun
saun

Prematurely Beached

You might have walked here
but the tide was early.

You might have laughed
as they laugh, carelessly

turning card over card,
making jokes of each hand.

You might have turned the wind
round your dark head, found

the ripple of cloud building
darker banks in your eye.

And the head hard, splits free,
turns, exultantly free

suddenly from scissored flesh,
in the shivered wake of pain.

But you,wet knuckle unwound,
foot-birthed a short step.

You might have breached here
but death heard, hurried on.

Graffiti

Johnny Scramble,
nae preamble,
draws oan waws whin naebody's lookin,
yaises aerosol cans,
rins awa fae polis vans.
Coarnered yisterday, he wis.
Ken whit the stupit eejit dis?
Pents hissell tae match the waw,
thocht they'd no see him at aw.
Johnny Scramble's jist a ful,
noo he's in the hoaspitul
whaur naebody hus oney peety
fur sich a rare case o Graffiti.

Togetherness

When all the words are put back in the chest
we'll carry it, two-handed, to the garden.
There, we'll bury it and hurry back inside.

There will be no cross to mark the spot,
the grass will grow and cover it. No one
will ever know what lies hidden there.

We will forget, a few feet from our door
lies every word we ever said. Silence
will sleep between us, undisturbed.

And in some future time, others will come
and, digging to reclaim the wilderness
to make their garden, will strike a store

of words that have been spoken once before.

While Pruning

Why now, while pruning, do you return
in the soft silk of a dying rose? The touch
of skin on skin has faded, not quite gone;
a ghost impression of the living thing.

So this rose, full-bud, half-opened lies
limp yet fragrant in my hand, dying.
Dying, sure, its petals never spread
waxing white bloomed in the sun. Perfumed,

as breath it taints the evening air, taunts
me with the might-have-beens. Tonight
nothing's clearer than this fresh green cut;
dead thorns draw blood. Could I have told

it was the love you kept that came between us,
the love you gave me that I couldn't hold.

Four Success Stories

Alison Smith

Of the four writers dealt with in this article, three were in their teens and the other in her early twenties when *Woven By Women* came out in 1980; none of them had published anything. Now they're known for their groundbreaking originality in style and voice in their chosen areas of poetry or fiction. Each was first published in small presses in Scotland before being snapped up by larger publishers. They've all enjoyed early success, winning deserved attention and garnering press and literary prizes here and in England, and the very promise of new work from any of them is exciting, bound to be challenging and sure to be important in any literary forum. Only thirteen years on from the original *Woven By Women* it would be unthinkable to produce a magazine looking at Scottish women's writing without focusing attention on each of them.

Janice Galloway

Probably the most astonishing and fêted Scottish novel by a woman for years, Janice Galloway's debut novel, *The Trick is to Keep Breathing*, was first published in 1989 by Polygon. Galloway, really the first woman to take advantage in her fiction of the pioneering styles of Kelman and Gray, was born in 1956 in Ayrshire; she gave up working as a teacher three years ago to write full-time and moved from Ayrshire to Glasgow. She began writing in the late 'eighties and with her formal ease and strength of voice was soon recognised from the short works she published as outstanding, signed up by quick-witted Polygon who commissioned her to write the novel. *The Trick* is an unremitting, dark and painful work with some of the stylistic relentlessness of Kelman's *The Busconducter Hines*. But Galloway goes where no man, except perhaps Gray in *1982, Janine*, has stylistically gone before, deep into representing the psyche of someone – importantly a woman in her case – whose world and self are falling to bits.

"I had an affair with a married man. He left his wife to come and stay with me. Things were difficult... Then we went away and he drowned." This is the psychological landscape of *The Trick*, a brief story almost monosyllabic here in its surface simplicity, at the back of a terrifying, complex and desperate journey into the self. The ironically-named Joy, a drama teacher in her late twenties, undergoes what one doctor in the novel calls 'reactive depression' after the death of her lover; she has to deal with the "tilting, adjusting, redistributing pieces" of herself and her world, and the novel tilts and adjusts as she does. Galloway's craft strips back the everyday surface of life to reveal sheer chaos, to demonstrate that what we call 'reality' is merely the flotsam of a deeper, darker place by far.

The Trick has a repeated visual motif, a set of letters or numbers – "ooo" – in the places chapter numbers might be, suggesting that you're yet again reading Chapter Nothing, or encountering another moan of pain, is the only suggestion of structure in the novel. Throughout there is an acute awareness of the roles people play to keep things coherent, and the most courageous thing the novel does is examine in first person the self-hate, the self-dismissal of Joy Stone as not just her sense of coherence but her very identity breaks down. "I'm not a proper woman," she says, "sometimes I think I don't exist", and the two statements are linked; her lack of role as a 'proper woman' has left her not just wondering who she is, but *if* she is at all. So the novel provides an unspoken attack on accepted 'coherence', the meaning and order of things. Here though, Joy is in the state of not knowing what her identity is especially when she's separated from the men who define her; whether to do with the hope that she can be "embraced, entered, made to exist" by sex, or the sense of disconnection brought on by bereavement, or the 'shock' she experiences on finding she is not indispensible to the first man she lives with:

> I don't need you for anything, he said, loud and flat. I don't need you for a thing.
> I racked my brain to find something to prove it wasn't true. I came up with the only answer left.
> Look, I'm going to make us something to eat. At least I can do that much. You need me all right. You need me because you can't cook. You can't fucking cook. …
> He went out slamming the door but I made something anyway. Pasta with seafood sauce, garlic bread, olive and pepper salad: his favourites. I didn't have favourites: I liked what he liked. …
> He came back an hour later with a carrier bag. A Chinese take-away. For one. He ate it without looking at me but I heard the message loud and clear.
> SHOVE YOUR FOOD
> It took me a month to find somewhere else to live. He was right. He didn't need me for a thing.
> I don't think I ever came to terms with the shock.

Ostensibly dealing with the initial trauma and aftermath of bereavement, *The Trick*'s achievement is to suggest that there's a frightening, inescapable nihilism lurking beneath the acceptable construction of female identity. It's a painful read, a claustrophobic and compulsive novel, and although there are the first tentative steps towards healing and understanding at the end, it's really a novel to drown yourself too, exceptionally powerful in its bleakness. Joy's saving grace is her ferocity: she is intelligent, articulate, fierce in her strength of irony, but in the end the warning is that none of these things is any defence against "the arbitrariness of things" or the deadly limitations of women's given role.

Galloway's collection of short stories, *Blood*, was published in 1991 by Secker and Warburg. In these, as in the novel, Galloway takes apart and ironises figures and places of supposed authority, the systems and those who make them work. People often fall foul of systems, expect help and guidance from them and get the opposite. In the short stories, too, there's the clash, similar to that in *The Trick*, where the psychological worlds meet the external worlds of her characters. Death, violence and fear are at the back of many of these stories, especially the fear that's to do with gender. In the story-drama of the silent woman, 'Scenes From the Life no. 27', the world's noises, offstage, are almost all hostile to women, and the short story 'Fearless', where a child stands up to a local monster by kicking out at his shins, is a fighting-back right-on-sister story to combat this hostility.

But the title story, 'Blood', spells out the real problem, again with utter bleakness – that Galloway sees gender as inescapable and women as physically defined by their own blood to the point of being silenced by it – the central character has had a tooth removed and is bleeding profusely at the mouth, unable to speak, silenced by a sanitary towel given by her dentist to stop the flow. Even with the frankness and reciprocation of desire in a story like 'David', where a teacher and former pupil have differences of age and rank smoothed away by sheer lust, the woman is left at the end of the sexual act,

> wondering
> what else to say
> what else to say

in what can be seen as a desperation, reduced to a powerlessness by it.

Clearly Galloway is driven by the question of gender; her writing unwraps huge social dilemmas, shows you the state of things without offering any notion of what to do about it. Of course, the clarity with which she reveals the questions, the dilemmas, is a start toward the understanding of them. But there's a peculiar passivity in her work that's all the more peculiar for coming from work of such passion and strength.

Galloway's language is kept flat and hard in her fiction, as far as humour goes she deals in deadpan irony and the odd one-liner, and for the most part avoids sentimentality. Her outlook is inexpressibly bleak. This is fashionable, acceptable, even expected as part and parcel recent and successful Glasgow fictions. The three older characters in Galloway's stories, the decrepit pensioner in 'Scenes From the Life no. 26' trapped in her front room with a humiliating health visitor, and the grown-old couple in 'Later he would open his eyes in a strange place', have nothing to look forward to or plan in their lives except death, preferably suicide since it's more dignified, since you're more in control that way.

A L Kennedy

There's a sense in which Janice Galloway's writing freed notions of voice and experimentation with form, opened doors and made it possible for writers like A L Kennedy to be appreciated. That these two differ fundamentally as writers can be seen by comparing Galloway's doomed pensioners with Kennedy's lively, crippled but determined old woman in her warm and unsentimental story 'Star Dust', who says "I have come to the conclusion that I deserve better things, that's all", ignores her disability as much as possible, starts taking photographs of those around her and imagining movies for the people she sees to star in:

> I have the idea that the ordinary people should be in the films… they would get their chance to be wonderful… my films are only silliness, I know, but I enjoy them and they help me set things right. I want there to be something to say I was here, that all of us were here, and that sometimes we have felt we were discontented. I wouldn't choose anyone special, like a spy, or a general, who might be remembered, or famous for anything else. I would film

an ordinary person, their story, because they have good stories, too. Someone should remember them.

Kennedy examines the hard times and lost lives of people, but emphasises the determination to survive, even possible routes to survival. The impetus for her writing is the giving of voice and articulacy to ordinary people who have been silenced by their ordinariness, the calling for due recognition of the complexities of their lives – the pensioner in 'Star Dust' goes on to reveal a hidden and dramatic love affair of her youth and the shattering choices she was forced to make. Kennedy's stories suggest the lostness and the importance of these 'small' lives and their 'small' dramas.

Born in Dundee in 1965, Alison Kennedy studied English and Drama at university and has done a variety of writer-in-residence, youth theatre and community work. She was the youngest writer included on *Granta's* Best of Young British Novelists list, even before her first novel was published. Polygon once again had been quick off the mark to sign her after she began publishing in small magazines short fiction with an unhackneyed voice and an off-centre sense of form; *Night Geometry and the Garscadden Trains* (1990) won several prestigious awards.

Her stories load the ordinary with meaning and sensuality and are often written from unexpected perspectives. Perhaps the most challenging aspect of them is this 'off-centre' sense, her tendency to end them in a way which catches the reader unaware, can suggest a whole new story about to begin or under the surface of what's just been read. The title story, for instance, seems to change voice suddenly in the last paragraphs, open up rather than come to a close the way a more conventional story would:

> But the silent majority and I do have one memorial, at least. The Disaster. We have small lives, easily lost in foreign droughts, or famines; the occasional incendiary incident, or a wall of pale faces, crushed against grillwork, one Saturday afternoon in Spring. This is not enough.

This paragraph comes right at the end of 'Night Geometry and the Garscadden Trains', jolting what was otherwise a sardonic farce about sex and infidelity into becoming quite another story with larger seriousness and repercussion on a grand scale. 'Tea and Biscuits' and 'The Moving House' are also stories with this break-out into an unexpected end, where it becomes apparent that a different story was being told than the one you thought you were reading. "This is not enough," says one character; another voices the need to "set things right". Similar demands echo throughout. "I deserve better." "Someone should remember." There's a moral drive in Kennedy's work regarding the status of the "small lives, easily lost". 'The Role Of Notable Silences In Scottish History', one of the strongest and funniest stories in the collection, uses a high irony style to protect and present its vulnerable core. The story could be about the role and power of the storyteller, the person whose job it is to lie, to "make things up"; it's a story about the need to record, more precisely to fictionalise, people's very un-notable lives, the final deadly irony being that this process is all in aid of providing them with their death notices:

> Go to a place where history is stored and listen. Hold your breath. Hear how still it is … It is the sound of nothingness. It is the huge, invisible, silent roar

of all the people who are too small to record. They disappear and leave the past inhabited only by murderers and prodigies and saints ... Only a lifetime from now, you will be part of that silence and nothing more. I don't like that. The means Kennedy has of counteracting this promised "nothingness" are twofold: to emphasise the voice that can so adamantly say "I don't like that" and can work against it however inadequately; the other to meet the hopelessness head on with humour and anarchy. These are stories written at an extreme of precision, fast-thinking, dizzyingly witty. The motif of lost or trapped children runs through several of them, and there's a sense of impending violence. In her work the peculiarities of the individual are made at once laughable and understandable, and her female characters are always individuals before they are women: "when she was young, her mother read her stories and she'd liked them. Not because she was a little girl, but because she was a human being" ('Cap o' Rushes').

Kennedy's first novel, *Looking for the Possible Dance* was published this year as a Secker paperback. Some reviewers felt it was a 'short story writer's novel' in that it's constructed out of several separate strands of story. However, it could be said, I think, that the sense of open-ended resonance which characterises Kennedy's short stories is harnessed by her here and made to work in a set of parallel connected stories which draw together to complete and sustain the novel on several levels. It's a skilfully controlled piece of work, another show of Kennedy's versatility with form.

All at once we're reading of Margaret's planned move down south away from Scotland (a journey which frames the novel), her time at university, her time at work as a 'Centre Assistant' at the Community Link Centre and the sexual harassment from her boss Mr Lawrence, her close relationship with her father and reaction to his death, her relationship with Colin who wants to marry her, Colin's own shocking story, and the story of James whom she meets on the train, all alongside a parallel commentary on the state of the nation and people. The novel's opening sentiment echoes the back of this – Margaret's father's desperate advice not to waste her time, to find the important things in the mess of living: "you'll grow up ... do things and run about and you'll think that what you're doing is important, but it's not. Being alive is important. Everything else is a waste of time."

The novel is set in Glasgow, among people whose sense of wasted lives, defeat, is bound up with their hopeless and often merry determination to fight back at the petty systems and authorities stamping on their souls, as Kennedy puts it. She demonstrates a cause and effect principle: people who encounter violence and brutality in the system, from school onwards, will be led to be violent and brutal. Her vision of Britain as full of disempowered people is a specifically political vision:

> Laws were being tightened around them: there were battles with the miners and then the travellers at Stonehenge. Things were being destroyed, very openly destroyed ... they lived in a country where pointless gestures were all they had left to make. There was almost a nobility in that.

People are shown as powerless in matters national and societal, and Kennedy also examines what constitutes power and right action in matters close to the individual, in personal affairs. The novel functions, with a refreshing directness about sex and the language of desire, as an analysis of the troubled relationship between Colin and Margaret in all its claustrophobia and attraction. It examines the difficulties of being single in a world of couples and the equal difficulty of maintaining independence while in a relationship. It is also about people's responsibility to others, how you learn to let them go, to live with them.

Although this novel can make you laugh and is full of characters as spirited as its protagonist, Kennedy is expert in pathos and her ironic omniscient narrator surfaces just enough to tell you that the future is probably pretty bleak. But the key to her work is the holding of the oppositions of hope and futility, neither quite cancelling the other out. Margaret, at her most desperate moments, "looks for the possible."

The one strand which brings the separate themes of the novel together is that of Margaret meeting her travelling companion on her escape-train travelling south from her country, away from responsibility. James is a physically handicapped "man-boy" with whom Margaret has a written "conversation" – because James can only speak through a machine, which isn't connected. Kennedy gives yet another silenced person a voice, reveals yet another hidden secret self through the written word. "WRIT TO ME" says James to Margaret on paper. Through this it becomes clear that the novel is concerned with taking responsibility that's in even the simplest communication. Taking responsibility will hurt you, damage you, even almost destroy you – Colin takes responsibility for the people threatened by loan sharks and is literally crucified for his actions. Now Margaret is leaving Scotland with the idea that if she returns she'll be forever responsible for the damaged Colin. Meeting James on the train indicates the richness of such responsibility, as well as revealing that such responsibility has to be accepted in a humane world.

It emerges from *Night Geometry and the Garscadden Trains* and *Looking for the Possible Dance* that Kennedy is a generous moralist. Her moral stance is a helpless or perhaps hopeless one, one that works in the teeth of its own defeat, illustrated in the determination and need of the powerless ordinary individual, always at the centre of her work, to do something about it. It is exciting that such a voice has emerged, one of formal skill, moral impetus and one with such power to entertain; there is no other voice quite like it in our fiction today.

Jackie Kay

Jackie Kay says she first started writing, late in her teens, "because there wasn't anybody else saying the things I wanted to say and because I felt quite isolated being in Scotland and being black. ...I started out of that sense of wanting to create some images for myself" (*Sleeping with Monsters*). Hers is a necessary art in its genesis, one which provides a correlation between poetry and drama and those not served or acknowledged by them, those of us who have not had 'images' created for us.

Born in 1961 in Edinburgh and brought up in Glasgow, Kay studied English at university and now lives in London. She's best known for her poetry, work as Tour Co-ordinator for poets with the Arts Council of Great Britain and for television and film work; her writing has featured in films and documentaries on a range of issues including pornography, AIDS, gender and racial issues, and transracial adoption, the latter of which is the subject of the set of narrative poems in her first collection for Bloodaxe *The Adoption Papers*, which was awarded a Gregory prize.

Kay is a playwright too – her first play, *Chiarascuro*, was performed by the Theatre of Black Women in 1986. In a highly-charged poetic language it explores the stances taken on lesbianism by four black women. Her next play, *Twice Over*, performed and toured by Gay Sweatshop in 1988, was the company's first play by a black writer. It's the story of seventeen-year-old Evaki's discovery, after her grandmother's death, of letters and diaries that reveal Cora, her beloved Nan, to had a happy and passionate secret relationship with her friend Maeve for the last fifteen years of her life.

The play tracks Evaki's reactions and those of her friends:

"I went round schools, asking kids what they felt … And they said that les-bians were big bulky people who worked on building sites and were dirty and swore! … The idea of an older lesbian disgusted them more than any-thing they could possibly speak of. …that's what gave me the idea … that I would have a granny who was also a lesbian." (*Sleeping with Monsters*)

For a play set between two funerals it's spirited and optimistic, a hopeful, buoyant piece which played to packed, appreciative houses just after the introduction of the government's notorious Section 28. It knocks barriers of culture and stereotype down and replaces them with humane reaction: Evaki comes to realise "there's a lot you don't expect grandmothers to do". It opens up possibilities for people limited by preconceptions of age, sexuality, race, what's expected of them. It parallels Evaki's findings and replays her grandmother's relationship with Maeve alongside the story of Evaki's friend, Sharon, and her fear of having AIDS or being pregnant after having complied with her boyfriend's expectations of *her*. But its theme is the same as *The Adoption Papers* – the need to discover or clarify an identity kept secret for reasons of societal constraint. As Maeve says "it's ridiculous still being scared at 58 of my mam finding out who I am."

The finding-out process is central to *The Adoption Papers*. It tells the story of a black child's adoption by white parents and her growth into adulthood. The story is told through three voices, the girl, her adoptive mother and her white 'birth mother'. It's a simple but important point that on the page each speaker's identity is highlighted by a different typeface: creating a sense of difference accompanied by a sense of sameness, these people share the same language, have related but different voices, will occasionally merge together. The poem sequence follows the process of adoption for both mothers (pointing out incidentally how much 'easier' it was to adopt a black child rather than a white for the adoptive parents), then follows the process of the grown child's attempts to trace her birth mother, trace the small details of where and from whom she began:

This morning a slim manila envelope arrives
postmarked Edinburgh: one piece of paper
I have now been able to look up your microfiche

(as this is all the records kept nowadays).
From your mother's letters, the following information:
Your mother was nineteen when she had you.
You weighed eight pounds four ounces.
She liked hockey. She worked in Aberdeen
as a waitress. She was five foot eight inches.

The poems examine what identity is, how it's made, how we make it, and explore the makings of the connections between people. But at its heart *The Adoption Papers* is about the important revelation of the complexity of identity, of a secret identity, so secret it's even secret from the self:

I don't know what diseases
come down my line;
when dentists and doctors ask
the old blood questions about family runnings
I tell them: I have no nose or mouth or eyes
to match, no spitting image or dead cert,
my face watches itself in the glass.

In an earlier poem, 'Kail and Callalou', she writes about how difficult it is even to begin to express the multiplicity of identity that makes up one individual, and how culture tends to reduce the self to stereotype:

Whit is an Afro-Scot anyway?
mibbe she can dance a reel and a salsa
remember Fannie Lou Hamer and Robert Burns
and still see Tam O' Shanter taken with Cutty Sark
– whit do you think of pair Meg's tail being pulled off like that?
mibbe they wear kilts and wraps
and know that Ymoja offered yams and fowl
and Corra could prophesize.

One of the important areas of difference her work foregrounds is sexual difference: Kay is one of the few Scottish writers to deal adequately with the subject of gay sexuality. In *Twice Over* Evaki is talking to her friend Tash about her disgust at finding out about her granny and her lover. "Come on Tash, Two women. Two old women. It's unnatural you've gotta think that." Kay has Tash reply: "I reckon natural's what you make of it ... My mum and dad staying together when they hate each other's guts, now *that* ain't natural, but people would say that it is." Poems in the second half of *The Adoption Papers* sensitively open up hidden lives. 'Close Shave' tells of a miner in love with his barber, and his confusion and fear about his feelings and what would happen if they surfaced too visibly. 'Pounding Rain' tells of two women, friends as girls, who meet later in life. The poem moves from memory into a direct discovered sensuousness.

Homosexuality is just part of what Kay writes about, but it's the part of her writing which, she says, would be difficult to bring to Scotland. "That's ... what's so good about living down here... I don't know if I could actually read lesbian poems there. I'm sure I will one day, but I don't know if I could at the moment." "You'd shut a few doors if you did", suggests her interviewer. And this is what Kay refuses to do in her work, to allow doors to be shut, boxes closed on people, identities to be tied down.

Her poem 'My Grandmother' seems to see this kind of closure as a stubborn Scottish tendency and examines the immense strength and cruelty of the identity that survives by having a closed mind. Her grandmother "is like a Scottish pine", her face like "ploughed land", "one of those women/ Burnt in her croft rather than moved off the land":

> She speaks Gaelic mostly, English only
> When she has to, then it's blasphemy
> My grandmother sits by the fire and swears
> There'll be no Darkie baby in this house.

"This irritates me a lot, that people can't contain both things... Being black and Scottish is always treated as a kind of anomaly, which I suppose it is." She aims directly in her work to transform "anomaly" into human.

> My family's all so squalid
> I'm trying to put it behind
> me – real typical working class
> Scottish: Da beats Ma drinks it off.
>
> ...I told ma ma years ago. She'd
> rather I murdered somebody than
> that. She wasn't joking either.
>
> ...See at Christmas I had
> on black stockings Santa would kill
> for and even Quentin Crisp would
> look drab beside my beautiful
> feather boa – bright fucking red.
>
> Ma ma didn't touch her turkey
> Finally she said What did I do
> I know what they call you, transvite.
> You look a bloody mess you do.
> She had a black eye, a navy dress.

There's a self-consciousness of the role of communicator built into the language she uses, it's never opaque, mainly the idiom of everyday speech whose inarticulateness she displays with an ear for the emotional weight behind language's banality. Kay says in the stage directions of her play, "the set should not be totally naturalistic". She has a corpse sit up suddenly in the first moments and go on to direct the proceedings. Nothing is ever totally naturalistic; the naturalism is often laced with the surreal, usually to do with people's dreams or fears. The birth mother in *The Adoption Papers*, after giving away her baby, buries the clothes in the garden and the 'crop' that grows is vivid and psychological:

> Later that same night
> she came in by the window,
> my baby Lazarus
> and suckled at my breast.

Her poems are energised by the dramatic voice. A sense of sympathy in her writing works dramatically, in that each poem carries with it the means of creating sympathy in its reader, who finds himself or herself acting the voice out. Voice and narrative are vital and linked in Kay's poetry: the first person singular, which she uses in every poem but one in her book, always has a story to tell so that you directly enter, become involved in, someone else's experience. Kay's work has a palpable design: reading her poetry you'll be forced to engage intimately with someone else. Many of her poems have single speakers, many set up dialogues within them, it's the search for and the assertion of shared dialogue that's at the basis of the voice construction of *The Adoption Papers*. In this, Kay has been deeply influenced by Liz Lochhead:

> Liz was my teenage hero
> OCH MEN and her stop and start rhythm
> I hadn't heard of Audre Lord then. ('Kail and Callalou')

This takes Kay a knowing step past Lochhead. One of the most important lessons learned from Lochhead, though, is the sense of performable poetry: "See me", she says in 'Kail and Callalou':

> See me. I can celebrate halloween and hogmony
> make a turnip lantern and dook for apples
> take a lump of coal and go first footing

and she goes on to denigrate the English in that pantomime-familiar manner of the identity-asserting Scot, the English having "nae sense of humour" and not believing in Nessie. But the importance here lies in the literalness of "see me" and "I can", as the "Celtic-Afro-Caribbean", the Afro-Scot, can, in *person* reading you this poem, reduce the stereotypes to just that, thin stereotype, and create visibly the state of being more than just a "Scot". Carol Rumens has called Kay's poetry 'performable' – "while its accessibility and groundedness in voice makes its ideal medium the public reading, it does not evaporate into triviality on the page." It's the "in person" sense of performance that's important – not just Kay herself, but the sense of a recognised link *and* difference between the reader or audience and the narrative of the person they're reading or hearing about.

Kay's poems are affecting and enjoyable. They build from simplicity into pertinence, often gripping and always involving. They play out the complexities of the connections between people, they honour difference and also call for unity, examining where the problematic reactions to difference start. They identify people's hunger for art – "There was no bread; he painted the sky ... she told a story ... she made a sculpture" ('Severe Gale 8') and they monitor with sympathy and humour those who live hidden or trapped lives, whose sense of themselves is not addressed by the mainstream of art. Her poems on AIDS sufferers, both those suffering from it and those who love them, celebrate ordinary people's exceptional capacity for courage. On the whole her poems work against isolation and towards acceptance and understanding of individuality: the promise of communication and connection is the promise of her work.

Kathleen Jamie

Kathleen Jamie was born in Renfrewshire in 1962 and brought up in Currie, Midlothian. She started writing in her teens, studied Philosophy at Edinburgh and now lives in Fife. She won a Gregory award at 19, one of the youngest poets ever to do so, with her first collection *Black Spiders* published in 1982, and has worked since at various writer-in-residence posts between extensive travelling. Travel is an important poetic impetus for Jamie: in her poem 'Clearances', to travel away from somewhere makes possible a poetic clearance and transformation of that place – the poem turns bare Scottish moorland, an infertile place, into somewhere it's possible to describe in exotic terms, where the moorland birds can take on the slightest of resemblances to Yeatsian Byzantine nightingales.

This is a more cerebral poetry than Kay's: Jamie's agenda is much less clearly defined, hasn't the immediate urge of moral communication of Kay's. *Black Spiders* is peopled with strange poems, at first deceptively simple and sensual then demanding more engagement of the mind, presenting their psychological territory or landscape below the given surface. The early poems deal mainly with the double edge of sexual attraction and sexual threat, the excitement of a culture clash as the genders come together. Several cite either withdrawal from or powerlessness in the clash, but the title poem explores it in unforgettable terms. In it, a couple are visiting a convent long after an atrocity there, the murder of its nuns by marauding Turks. The poem insists that attraction and threat exist at once, and both the horror and the attraction are in its final images:

She caught sight of him later, below, brushing salt
from the hair of his nipples. She wanted them
to tickle; black spiders on her lips.

– reflecting the co-existence of horror and attraction in the glut of violence as the nuns' lives are violently ended by "the Turks' swords" in a way that's somehow an answer to their prayers: "all their praying was done/ when they first saw the ships and the Turks'/ swords reflecting the sun." There's a certain amount of glee in the image of the eldest nun pealing the warning bell, waiting for the terrible consummation.

Formally, Jamie's early poetry is marked by her tendency to make the poetic line to push on past the just-given image:

her cane chair creaks to itself in the heat. She'll
be home before the sun lies smashed on the streets. ('Abir')

and you often find yourself pushed past the sensuousness of image into having to make sense of it in a larger context. Her use of rhyme is subtle, almost always internal, suggesting that a sense of completion or harmony is there somewhere but not simply found. Her language reverberates past its initial meaning. The people are vulnerable, all at the mercy of something larger than them that can violently and beautifully smash the sun. 'The Barometer' charts a futile war between human and nature, shows a family "throwing the barometer out", sitting stubbornly in a cold house refusing to light fires for warmth, hopelessly defying the winter.

One of the collection's finest poems, 'War Widow', is reprinted at the end of Jamie's second published work, *A Flame in Your Heart*, a collaboration with Andrew Greig which sets up a narrative of voices between a young Spitfire pilot, Len, and a World War II nurse, Katie, in the first year of the war. It was broadcast on radio under the title 'Rumours of Guns' in 1985 and published by Bloodaxe in 1986. Somehow, in the narrative context, 'War Widow' loses its power. Jamie has no problem with the narrative mode and it's all believable enough, but it limits her to a muted poetic reaction (not something that could have been foreseen from *Black Spiders*). Katie, as a character, is not exactly two-dimensional – she resents the war and the role it forces upon her, she as her own 'battle' to fight, her own 'show' as she faces possible pregnancy. Some of the poems are fine. But the set-piece nature of the work doesn't suit Jamie's interests in a poetic combination of the actual and the possible, in studying the movement of self through landscapes both real and abstract. Her notion of poetic persona involves a more solitary mental progress than *A Flame in Your Heart's* dramatic structure allows. "There are innumerable personae in my mind that I use," she says in interview, "like the character of Katie in *A Flame in Your Heart* ... but I can't hear dialogues. I can't hear two people talking together." (*Sleeping with Monsters*)

Jamie doesn't demand the direct response from the reader that Kay asks for, instead her poetry takes the form of meditation, overtly so in her first full-length collection *The Way We Live*, published by Bloodaxe in 1987. *The Way We Live* includes the outstanding poetry sequence 'Karakoram Highway', where a kind of meditation or "self-clearance" is set in motion. The sequence records the changes of both landscape and understanding on a trek across northern Pakistan and is prefaced by a merry journeying epigram from Whitman: "I tuck'd my trowser-ends in my boots and went and had a good time." "Stop thinking now," says the first line of the sequence, "and put on your shoes" – this is a journey to escape the ruts of thinking. In an earlier poem in the collection Jamie has described the continual "asking why" of thinking as an irritating mote, "just salt blown in the mind's eye," and here in 'Karakoram Highway' the self and senses are "about to be born again", coming "into the light", moving in to a new, and sensuous existence. Importantly, this existence will be dangerous:

> The river brawls beneath us, self-obsessed,
> narcissistic. Wheels turn, turn again, full weight.
> The bridge starts to undulate and we're hanging
> out of windows half-roads over the Indus,
> grinning at each other, impotent, enlightened.
> The world grew tight.
> It must have been about then we first saw the mountains.

A making impotent of the self is enlightening, she suggests. This is a direct progression from that fear and vulnerability lurking in the poems of *Black Spiders*: now the traveller comes face to face with something that's bigger than people, the unemotional natural. The challenge is whether we conquer this, allow it to conquer us, or learn to live with it, and it settles in her work into the metaphor of the climber or trekker faced with the massive black fact of a mountain. Mountains stand for something beyond humanity, a symbol of death, beauty, challenge and insurmountability. Humans are small, trivial and powerless below the mountains, "squatting on the steps of the K2 Motel ... tapping plastic spoons onto plastic plates". But there's the sheer delight and joy to be found in journeying, the "K2 going", "the shimmer of joy on the face of uncertainty" on the jeep-ride through the richness and the colour of being alive in this place:

> flashes
> on birds' wings, head shaking delight,
> beasts in the shade, greenery, embroidery,
> women in shawls with the same limbless sway

as a poplar. Grubby babies on roofs, goats,
yaks in a farmyard. Here and passed.
Tree-tips high against blue.
Berries fell to our laps – is this Eden? –
we ate them.

The knowledge or loss of innocence that travelling brings is the sense of powerlessness and delight held together. Being faced with the mountain changes you, makes you re-evaluate your perspective on being. "This is our world for a time", is something more profoundly known after the trip.

The thorny problems of desire surfacing in *Black Spiders* have been somewhat resolved by the poems in *The Way We Live* too, as if through the acceptance of vulnerability. 'Poem for a Departing Mountaineer' still concentrates on the painful sense of separation of people who desire each other, but 'Lepidoptery', a powerful poem where spirituality and sexuality meet up, shows the speaker hankering after the breathing and lusting sense of something "immortal" that she knows lies in desire, the "real angel" of it instead of the shadow, the pinned, dead specimen of a butterfly. Many poems in *The Way We Live* suggest Jamie's growing interest in exploring religion and in 'God Almighty the First Garden Made' she hints that Christianity is tamed and domesticated, its God a pottering ageing market-gardener waiting for his son to take over. One of the finest poems, 'Julian of Norwich', takes on the persona of the medieval anchorite, and rather than the nature of religion is concerned with love and passion, the shifts from love to resentment and back again. The poem examines at once the state of a cold knee-stiff prayer of desperation and a "joy, huge and helpless/ as the harvest moon in a summer sky." Religion has something to do with passion and passionate living in her poetry.

Jamie's next published was a book of travel-writing, *The Golden Peak: Travels in North Pakistan,* published by Virago last year and describing several visits she made to Baltistan. *The Golden Peak* is entertaining, informative, intoxicatingly readable, in a prose that sometimes has a curiously Victorian feel about it which suits the unpremeditated sense that arises out of it of Jamie as a pioneer. She details the strengths and strangeness of the country and analyses its religions; she examines the position of the Muslim women and families she meets or stays with, and compares it fascinatingly with her own position; she lays Scotland and Baltistan together, comparing cultures to understand cultures, and the main difference she finds is one of the strength of *idea* behind the country:

> though leaders come and go, the idea of Pakistan is still fresh and new. ...it is refreshing to be in a country which believes the future will be better than the past. Corruption is rife, governments are unstable and nepotistic, wealth is greedily held in private hands, but Pakistan is still an idea. ...When I come home I feel the West, in comparison, to be a place of slow but certain decline.

"Pakistan, everything possible!" – she shows the country to be a place that opens up possibilities, national and personal, and possibilities are scary, as scary as the facing of the mountain in 'Karakoram Highway': "sometimes, a glimpse of what we could be opens in our minds like the fearsome blue crevices I'd seen on glaciers." Again one of the main things learned on the journey is a sense of the frightening grandeur of what you could be; again a kind of "clearance" is needed to bring you near these possibilities, the honing down of the self to fundamentals, "a change of clothes; a shawl, a stick, a black notebook on a wicker table. My tin dish, comb, toothbrush, knife and torch", this is all you need to cross Pakistan.

Published by Bloodaxe, *The Autonomous Region: poems and photographs from Tibet* is Jamie's most recent work, with photographs by Sean Mayne Smith. It details the time in 1989 when Smith and Jamie travelled across Amdo and Tibet but were stopped at the border of Tibet's Autonomous Region by a military barrier and the happenings in Tiananmen Square. It examines the sense of a culture eroded and expanded by other cultures (a theme also in *The Golden Peak*). The poems weave past and present together in Jamie's weaving of her own journey and those of two historical characters, a nomad and a princess, whom she 'met' on her journey; the nomad Fa-hsien, a fourth century Buddhist monk, traveller and searcher for scripture, and the sixth century Princess Wen Cheng who travelled with her court bringing the new knowledge of Buddhism, beer, silk, glass and literacy to Tibet. The Princess also brought her 'sun-moon' mirror, and is remembered now, in a story that parallels those of Eve and Pandora, for dropping and breaking it – the broken mirror seen as suggestive of broken harmony and balance in the world.

Jamie calls the poems "my hopelessly inadequate response to the events of the time", and adds that "they celebrate the journey-makers, the seekers and disseminators of wisdom, those who would declare themselves an autonomous region." This questing, putting oneself into the unknown and unknowable dangerous place both actually and spiritually is central to these poems. The narratives Jamie imagines with Fa-hsien and Wen Cheng leave *A Flame in Your Heart* behind like a kind of trivia. With simplicity and great warmth Jamie creates the movements and dilemmas of the journeying mind across time in complex interplay with external reality. Her language of honed clarity constructs a metaphysical level always promised but never so convincingly delivered in the earlier poetry. There's even a stronger sense of imagery, a brilliant and simple vividness. Someone is described as being "horrified as flowers", and

> a lark's black flight
> leapt and leapt
> like a telegraph wire
> on a straight road.

Her historical characters travel in our own contemporary world. The princess lives effortlessly and likes to break things, comes with bottles, cigarettes, walkman and dictaphone like the western world discovering an untouched community. But she travels "a difficult, pre-cipitous and dangerous/ road, the side of a mountain/ being like a stone wall/ 10,000 feet in height," and Wen Cheng changes, develops her instincts as the narrative works up to a meeting between herself and the wise nomad:

> secretly he loved
> the way his lips cracked, loved

> to feel his head spin, loved
> to cough the dust and consider himself
> a journeying, a journeying.

The other meeting in the collection is between Scots dialect and Chinese landscape. Here Jamie uses Scots to bring the worlds together, suggest the locality of what happens in a language closer to the personal:

> she telt me
> they've killed 5,000 people in Beijing...
> This is a place your friens disappear:
> trust naebody. Luve a.
> The smearit wa's o a concrete room,
> a wumman sweepin. ('For Paola')

Smith's photographs are haunting and matched uncoyly to the poems. The poem quoted above is next to a photograph of a child standing by two old men and wearing military uniform, smiling, carrying a gun.

With Jamie we've got a poet who is limited by nothing, not a place, not a gender (though she explores both of these), not an ulterior motive or need. There is an exciting sense of freedom coupled with power in her work, these in a place which has only recently given them over to women, and Jamie highlights this by her travelling in places where women are less free and their powers are ones with which we are less familiar.

Jamie can layer the most simple-seeming language with meaning which resonates far beyond the surface, past metaphor to metaphysical; she is a poet of great clarity and depth. She sees poetry as a necessary and natural challenge which is met where the natural meets something beyond itself. Her poetry is robust, joyous and always brought down to earth, kept human at all costs, though the spiritual hovers tangibly in the background. *The Autonomous Region* is only the first peak of such work, the range we can look forward to is high, impressive; the journeying will be good.

But here's a good question: why do some writers 'make it', say, to Secker and Bloodaxe and others don't? Apart from the obvious reason of talent, and other pertinent reasons – current fashion, recent interest in writing from Glasgow, the north or regional writers, with double brownie points if they happen to be women. Who knows the vagaries of publishers' choices? Why haven't Bloodaxe picked up on the excellent Elizabeth Burns? Is she too preoccupied with gender yet not in as acceptable or marketable a way as Kay? Why hasn't someone like Secker picked up on Sian Hayton, is she too Celtic in her interests for mainstream tastes?

Janice Galloway hit a certain fashionability on publication. Here was a woman, at last, who could write fiction with a power that paralleled the Glasgow men. But looking at it now, Galloway's fiction seems peculiarly dated in a way, already it has a late-eighties- Scottish-dirty-realism tag on it. Even the postmodern experiment and form games in her work, things which suggested freedom of form at the time, now look stylistically *of* a time, like the membership badge of a club of an era that's passing. As a writer Galloway seems shackled to a lot of things in *Blood* and *The Trick* – to the expected gruff and bleak New Naturalism, to an expected formal experimentation, and to this as-yet-unsolved problem in her work of gender identity, the paradox of the woman writing fiercely and bleakly at once about how gender silences you, takes away your language.

Many of her stories suggest an area yet to be explored, a possible departure into the surreal or the psychological. It will be interesting to see where her work goes, whether she can take it past its sense of ensnarement and passivity. True, these notions of unsolved problem and paradox are in her work because they exist in reality, but although their relationship is complex and symbiotic, maybe she must yet tackle something she seems unwilling to trust, the transformational powers of fiction.

But already Galloway has found, articulated and answered a real need. She has created an important voice in our fiction, a questioning and fearful and outraged woman's voice. It's a voice that states a terrible dilemma of identity, and does so brilliantly, unignorably.

A L Kennedy's first novel was outstandingly skilful, a solid achievement, but somehow modest at the same time. I was left impressed but still with a sense of waiting for what's to come. As with Jamie, gender doesn't seem to be a barrier – she explores it and is not dictated to by it. There's a democratic basis to her work and this is its Scottishness, its preoccupation with the value of the ordinary. If she's like any other writer it's Gray in her feeling for this democracy coupled with the imaginative breath and control that surface in a story like 'The Role of Notable Silences'. Like Gray, and Jamie, she has the ability to put Scotland into this wider context whilst maintaining a sense of the personal importance and struggle of the individual. For a woman to write fiction with such authority, range and humour, and to be able to be so unconcerned about gender, is a real step forward. The margins have been pushed back.

It offends against what she so expressly does in her writing to say Jackie Kay's a type of any sort. Like Lochhead she is after all a prototype. Part of her success *must* come from the recognition of her originality. If there is a problem it's that sometimes it's hard to see which is most important, the poetry or its palpable design – and it does have one: it has a crucial agenda which none of the other writers deals with. Kay knows what to do about this – it's a high point of her skill. Palpable design is made very human, on the level of individual relating to individual.

For the most part she maintains the balance: poetry, with her, is morally connected to and only rarely subsumed under communication. Her work will last precisely because it's so approachable, purposefully populist. People like it and can appreciate what she does. It will last too because she is one of Scotland's genuine Whitman figures covering new territory. But it's a thematic exploration rather than one in form and I wonder if she can take the dual play of merging and difference of voice further than the surface expression of different typefaces and find a unique form for it. The seeds of this are there, the urge for it. I wonder what would happen, for instance, if she were to move away from the easeful dramatic into a more condensed poetic, something already beginning to emerge in her writing.

Alison Smith

Reviews

Women Studying Women

A Guid Cause, Leah Leneman, £11.95; *Bajanellas and Semilinas – Aberdeen University and the Education of Women 1860–1920*, Lindy Moore, £8.95; *Upstairs to Downstairs – Advice to Servant Girls and Weary Mothers*, ed James Drummond, £3.95; *Marriage and Property– Women and Marital Customs in History*, Elizabeth Craik, £6.95; *Katharine Atholl 1874–1960*, Sheila Hetherington, £6.95; *Strategic Women – How do they manage in Scotland?*, Elisabeth Gerver & Lesley Hart, £9.95, all AUP (distributed by Mercat Press); *A Woman's Claim of Right in Scotland*, the Woman's Claim of Right Group, Polygon, £7.95.

As 1993 is the 75th anniversary of universal suffrage it's an appropriate time to read Leah Leneman's exhilarating book on the women's suffrage movement in Scotland. The book is groundbreaking in demolishing the widely-held view that most suffrage activity took place in London. It documents the activities of Scottish societies working for women's suffrage who were not only numerous and wide-spread (there were branches in Orkney and Lerwick), but did not always lie down and take the party line from their leaders in London as has been previously suggested by historians of the Women's Social and Political Union (WSPU).

One of the most interesting things which comes to light is the amount of support by Scottish men for the women's struggle for the vote. In 1907 Tom Johnston of *Forward*, the Glaswegian Socialist weekly, allowed the suffrage campaign a voice in the paper and in the same year Graham Moffat with other male sympathisers formed The Glasgow Men's League for Women's Suffrage after his wife Maggie's release from Holloway. In 1913, after the funeral of Emily Wilding Davison there was such strong feeling amongst some men in favour of women's suffrage that a deputation of Scottish and northern men was organised to go to see the Prime Minister. More than 30 went including councillors, baillies, ex-provosts, JPs, ministers, barristers, solicitors and teachers. Asquith refused to receive the deputation when they presented themselves, but they addressed the crowd out-side Downing Street and sold pamphlets of the speeches they would have made to Asquith, which they had expediently had printed! After this rebuff the men returned to Scotland determined to form the Northern Men's Federation for Women's Suffrage.

However, throughout the period of the struggle it was women who did the bulk of campaigning. Much work was done during election campaigns since many prominent Liberal MPs like Winston Churchill had constituencies in Scotland. The local societies would co-operate in campaigning against Liberal candidates. The non-militant Suffrage societies concentrated on educating the public and organising sales of work, petitions and letters to newspapers while the militant Suffragette societies like the WSPU and Women's Freedom League (militant but non-violent) concentrated on more unwomanly activity such as census dodging, tax avoidance, marches, interruptions at political meetings, theatres, and church services.

The letters pages of contemporary newspapers were filled with appalled accounts by bystanders of the rough treatment of the women who spoke up in public. The brutality of the police, harshness of court sentencing and force feeding at Perth Prison escalated the militants' response. By 1912 violent militant activity started and headlines like 'SERVANTS AT PERTHSHIRE CASTLE NARROWLY ESCAPE AWFUL DEATH WHEN BUILDING IS FIRED BY SUFFRAGETTES' became common. Leneman lists seventy militant attempts or acts between March 1912 and July 1914. The tactics would not have brought the country to a standstill but they did cause considerable inconvenience. The non-violent Suffragists complained that each time another outrage occurred that they lost potential supporters.

Meanwhile in Aberdeen another supporter of Women's Rights got going in the 1890s as the Peter Lilley of Victorian Scotland. Lady Aberdeen was reviled by her peers for consorting with her servants. But what she was interested in was saving the virtue of Aberdeenshire farmgirls and servants. Despite a moral climate which modern Tories would no doubt applaud, many girls transgressed and became pregnant. When faced by the statistic that 4 out of 5 prostitutes in Aberdeen were former domestic servants she readily got to work and organised mass tea parties on crucial bank holidays to prevent temptation and started the Onward and Upward Association. The Association started with classes to keep the servants busy, then progressed to home study and producing a magazine. Extracts from the magazine are reproduced in James Drummond's *Upstairs to Downstairs – Advice to Servant Girls and Weary Mothers*. Much of it is very funny and the book would make an excellent 'stocking filler'. In "Comfort for Weary Mothers", Onward and Upward suggests *Blessed be Drudgery* by Dr Gannet BD as a helpful book. Under 'Healthy Ways Bring Happy Days':

> Be on guard against the physical and moral dangers of an over-heated home. … the hot climate of the tropics makes the inhabitants of these regions indolent, weak and enervated so that they are easily subdued by invaders from the temperate zones, who are strong and vigorous and so rule the world.

Despite the wealth of material here it is a disappointing book nevertheless. The introduction, sycophantic towards the present Lord and Lady Aberdeen, fails to bring out the really interesting points about imperialism and social control in the Victorian period which surfaces in the material. This would have made the book more than just a laugh at our 'funny' predecessors.

Paradoxically a staunch Anti-Suffragist, the Duchess of Atholl became the first female MP in Scotland. She was outspoken over appeasement, publishing an unexpurgated version of *Mein Kampf* to try to warn the British public of the dangers of Hitler. She worked tirelessly for the victims of the Spanish Civil War and visited Spain, where she met Hemingway who refused to broadcast an appeal on behalf of Spanish orphans on the grounds that he had his public to think of. With her contacts abroad she toured the beleaguered small nations just before the outbreak of the war. In 1938 she resigned her seat and fought a by-election as an independent candidate in order to draw attention to her stand against appeasement. She narrowly lost and soon after war broke out. Often misleadingly called 'the Red

Duchess', she did have a well developed sense of justice and fairness. *Katharine Atholl 1874-1960: Against the Tide* covers a complex period of politics in an interesting way with its subject coming out of a dirty period of British politics better than most.

Marriage and Property, edited by Elizabeth Craik, displays all the worst marks of academic writing, being long-winded and boring. The book contains essays on various different periods rather than a more focused look at a particular period and as has little in the way of quotes from primary sources (particularly rich in Leneman's book) to make it digestible. The essays eschew theory about marriage in a wider context: more debate and dissent might have made a more interesting read.

Bajanellas and Semilinas, Lindy Moore's study of the education of women at Aberdeen University from 1860–1920 avoids *Marriage & Property*'s faults and fills in gaps in our knowledge of the struggle for higher education for women. Once again Scotland comes out better than most. Higher education was made available to women in the Aberdeen area relatively painlessly, if rather slowly, compared to the riots and general unpleasantness in Edinburgh and Oxbridge. (Nan Shepherd was among the early graduates.) Many women students did better than the males, winning prestigious prizes and bursaries in spite of discrimination. Life as a woman student could be tough: often they were isolated in lodgings and *Alma Mater*, the Aberdeen student newspaper, sustained a condescending attitude towards women students which must have worn away at self-confidence. The second woman to graduate in medicine committed suicide. Like Leneman, Moore is excellent in covering the period with much material from primary sources.

Strategic Women by Elizabeth Gerver and Lesley Hart brings us to the contemporary scene. It is the result of in-depth interviews with 50 'strategic women' – women who have 'made it' in Scotland. Their research was prompted by noting that Scottish girls' exceptional academic achievement at school is reflected in exceptional *under*achievement in the workplace. Despite consistently getting higher academic qualifications than men, women hold between 0–5% of senior management positions in Scotland – alarming and depressing statistics which, in some areas, seem to be getting worse. Gerver & Hart identify historical patterns, social attitudes, employment practices and general lack of awareness of gender issues among the barriers to women succeeding in the workplace.

Politically speaking, with less than 4% of our MPs being women, Scotland hasn't moved on much since universal suffrage was granted. *A Woman's Claim of Right in Scotland – Women, Representation and Politics* came about from an awareness of imbalance in the Scottish Constitutional Convention, with only a 10% female membership. The book gives a good overview of the way the problem of under-representation of women has been tackled in other countries in Europe and the ways that women participate in politics and public life outside of formal parties. This section of the book, with histories of women in the church, media and arts and campaigning groups, is a useful filling-in of a contemporary and not-so-contemporary history of women which tends to get lost.   *Mary Gordon*

A Light on the Night

The Great Shadow House: Essays on the Metaphysical Tradition in Scottish Fiction, J B Pick, Polygon, £11.95; *Places of the Mind: The Life and Work of James Thomson ('BV')*, Tom Leonard, Jonathan Cape, £25

The essays on the metaphysical tradition in Scottish fiction which form J B Pick's book (the notion of fiction being extended to embrace the plays of Barrie and Bridie) are, as the author declares in the introduction, a work of scholarship; instead they are the observations of one very alert and intelligent mind deeply engaged with the dimensions of experience explored in the novels and dramas examined. J B Pick is, besides, himself a novelist who knows that "The accuracy and validity of a writer's perceptions are best tested by examining the clarity and exactness of the words used – a vision becomes real when it is realised." Fiction is of interest to him insofar as it attempts to express the truth, and it is in the light of the above criterion that the success or failure of his subjects is sympathetically but rigorously examined.

The book has two principal and inter-related themes: the sense, always strong in Scottish literature, of another world beyond or parallel to or behind this one, a world which is as real as our own physical world, and may perhaps be more real; and the distorting effects of the Calvinist world-view on Scottish perceptions of metaphysical reality. The first of these themes is approached by way of its deepest strata in Highland and Lowland literature, respectively the material collected in *Carmina Gadelica*, and the Ballads; and the second through Hogg, whom Pick shows engaging with Calvinism with a unique combination of inwardness and common-sense detachment, a balance which later writers, including even Stevenson, are repeatedly observed as failing to achieve.

Pick is a stringent but just critic, giving credit where it is due, and finding something good to say about most of his subjects, even the despised Kailyarders; but the bracing quality of his writing, and much of the book's value, lies in his exposure of the defects of some of the works – notably *The House with the Green Shutters* and *Gillespie* – which have acquired the status of sacred cows in their black reaction to the Kailyard. He acknowledges the power of Brown and Hay, but shows them to be hate-ridden and depressed in their negative inner stance, in which individual and cultural pathology interact to produce a doom-laden and imprisoning determinism.

Pick can sum up an author's inner attitude with a phrase and a flash of acid humour, cutting away unspoken assumptions with pointed and awkward questions. He is very good on Mac Colla, praising the force and exactness of his style and the power of his insights, but rightly pointing to the "inner bitterness" which makes him "one more example of Calvinism taking over its opponents."

The author is well known for his work on David Lindsay and Neil Gunn, to whom most space is here devoted. The essays on Lindsay provide an absorbing account of that writer's vision, "the most daring foray into an extreme metaphysical position that I have read anywhere in fiction"; a vision altogether clearer, tougher and more fully realised than that of his predecessor George MacDonald. Yet Lindsay continues to be shamefully neglected. Gunn's metaphysic is less systematic, less separable from its fictional expression; Pick's account of it is correspondingly more elusive and diffuse; but he finds in Gunn's novels the metaphysical balance which so many others strove after in vain. Pick writes throughout with great directness and economy, and goes straight to the point, and this is altogether, to borrow a favourite word of his own, a "tonic" book.

James Thomson had no truck with other worlds, but his concerns were for all that uncompromisingly metaphysical. His nihilism, quite unlike the brashly confident secularism of his one-time friend Charles Bradlaugh, was tortured and profoundly melancholic. Tom Leonard's biography, sixteen years in the making and scrupulously researched, documents with loving but clearsighted detachment the tragic life of this most eloquently pessimistic of poets, from his early years in Port Glasgow, through boyhood in an 'asylum' for needy Scottish boys in London, young manhood as an army schoolmaster, and years of ill-paid journalism for secularist periodicals in London, to his pitiful death as a homeless alcoholic at the age of 47.

'Documents' is the key word, for this is a biography which rejects 'causal models', presents the evidence instead of assessing character, exploring the sources and influences behind the work while making no attempt at evaluation. At first this approach is disconcerting for a reader accustomed to the type of biography which speculates freely and pads out the material with often dubious criticism; but as one reads on the method seems increasingly appropriate to its enigmatic subject, and in the end becomes intensely moving.

Tom Leonard leads us step by step through Thomson's masterpiece 'The City of Dreadful Night', quoting at length and providing prose summaries of the poem's argument between verses quoted. He devotes a chapter to a sequence of randomly-selected 'computer-generated' extracts from Thomson's diaries during the four or five years leading to his death, thus providing the reader with the unique flavour of the poet's daily life communicated through his own words. He gives us generous examples of Thomson's intensely-observed sketches of weather and natural beauty. He quotes verbatim and without comment the opinions of contemporaries. The biographer is himself entirely invisible until the final chapter entitled 'Postscripts', to which all speculation – notably on the identity of the lost love whose early death has been thought to have confirmed Thomson's predisposition to melancholia – is relegated.

The account of Thomson's last days is presented entirely through contemporary sources. The effect is eerie and deeply involving, but there are drawbacks. We never learn (even in a note) the identity of the T E Clarke who describes the events of the day on which, after a prolonged drinking bout, Thomson collapsed at the home of the poet Philip Bourke Marston with the bowel haemorrhage which killed him a few days later, or discover why Clarke (never before mentioned) went there to meet Thomson 'by appointment'; and it would have been interesting to have known whether the William Sharp also present on that occasion was the Scottish 'Celtic Twilight' writer who called himself 'Fiona Macleod'. There are occasional inaccuracies: correcting W M Rossetti's estimate of Thomson's age at the time of their first meeting, Leonard curiously says that he was 29 at a date when he would actually have been 38.

These details do not detract from the stature of Leonard's compelling tribute to a great and unfortunate writer. Thomson's later photographs have a look of gentle, wistful, almost puzzled sadness. It seems likely that the deepest source of his depression was the death of his little sister, from measles contracted from him, when she was three and he was five. By such obscure and forgotten events, no doubt, are human lives and their products shaped.

John Herdman

Mythic Times

Hidden Daughters, Sian Hayton, Polygon, £7.95; *Alice in Shadowtime*, Iona McGregor, Polygon, £7.95; *Child of Fire*, Eileen Townsend, HarperCollins, £15.99; *The Other Woman*, Eileen Townsend, Grafton, £4.99; *An Apple from a Tree*, Margaret Elphinstone, The Women's Press, £6.95

I approached this collection of novels with considerable trepidation, because these writers seemed so very different to each other. But as I read I realised they share several common interests and concerns, among which romance (in all the connotations of the word) and the realms of myth and folklore predominate. Years spent working on women's and teenage magazines have taught me many things, not least that Romance is big business. From teenage girls worrying about first kisses to married middle-aged women bored with their lot, it's what many want to read.

In her novel *Hidden Daughters*, Sian Hayton skilfully constructs a whole new world in which Celtic fantasy and Dark Age history (to quote the dust jacket) merge. The effect is both impressive and slightly bewildering, perhaps because this novel is the second part of a trilogy, and offers few clues to help the reader find a point of reference in the world it creates. I'm fairly sure that reading the first part of the trilogy (which I didn't) would make this novel more easily accessible.

That said, it's worth persevering, for the reward is an adventure of mythic proportions, set in a magical world full of "spae-wives" and "waelcyrgies", "battle-fetter" and "elf-shot". Beings with superhuman powers, like Barve, live alongside ordinary mortals. Barve and her sisters are daughters of the great giant Usbatheden. Cast adrift in the mortal world without her father's protection, they have to come to terms with the knowledge that, one day, they will die.

The Celtic religion Barve follows is contrasted with the pious Christianity of Hw, the monk who becomes her travelling companion. At first, Hw feels threatened by Barve's independence and wisdom, but as the novel progresses, and he is forced to spend a great deal of time with Barve, his views alter. When Barve is sentenced to death, he tells her, "All I know is that one as wise as you should be saved for the good you can do." What she is has ceased to matter.

The creed Barve follows is not dissimilar to Hw's, and in many ways it's more humane. Certainly, it's more in touch with the realities of existence and less mysterious than the doctrine of the Christian Church. Hw perceives Barve's strengths as evil, but the Christian monks in general feel threatened by a woman with intelligence and initiative. It's far easier for them to shriek 'harlot' at her than to consider another system of belief.

There is a lot of theological discussion between Barve and Hw in this novel, and I felt that after a while it became tedious, distracting the attention from the plot. However, that's only a minor complaint, as this novel is well worth a read. The ending, when it is reached, doesn't disappoint, either. Barve has the strength to escape but doesn't, sacrificing herself in order to bring some stability to the land she is leaving. There could perhaps be parallels drawn with the Crucifixion – but no doubt Hw would condemn that as blasphemous!

I was brought back down to earth after Hayton's soaring adventure by *Alice in Shadowtime*, a murder mystery with a Victorian setting. McLevy, the Edinburgh detective who investigates the crime, is little more than a name with a dog; he has almost no character at all, and the author makes few attempts to get inside her 'creation'. In fact, nearly all the characters are either flat or slightly unsavoury, which leaves the reader without any point of focus in the story. The effect of this is to cancel out any sense of justice you might expect to feel at the end of the novel, when the murderer's identity is revealed. Instead of a feeling of satisfaction at the tying up of all the loose ends, all I experienced was a sense of relief that it was all over.

The main reason is this: to my mind there's no satisfaction in reading a mystery when the means of solving it are deliberately withheld from the reader. Whenever McLevy uncovers a piece of evidence, the reader is not told what it is. For example: "Fifteen minutes later he discovered not a cartridge case but something much more significant."

The ending of the novel includes the unveiling of the murderer in a set piece reminiscent of a TV detective story. The motives themselves are flimsy; the murders have been carried out by someone with a personality defect the author has given us no evidence of. It's almost as if McGregor was unable to come up with a plot of sufficient complexity to keep the reader guessing even when presented with the evidence. Many crime writers use red herrings, which is acceptable, but cheating the reader, as McGregor does, is not. In this sense, the story is more fairytale than mystery.

Where McGregor conceals facts, Eileen Townsend manipulates them. Her novels, too, have historical settings, chosen in an attempt to give her stories an otherworldly, bygone-era charm. "Childhood was pulling out of that station along with her friend's train", Townsend writes in *Child of Fire*, setting the tone for a hefty novel that's packed with romantic hyperbole and fanciful imaginings. Townsend takes her readers to 1930s Yorkshire, whose inhabitants are members of a "proud race", descended from the Druids and Vikings. The local laird and his son Amos are keen Nazis – Amos is a member of the Yorkshire equivalent of the Ku Klux Klan and dabbles with a spot of devil-worshipping, so we're left in no doubt that Amos is the villain.

The way in which good and evil are presented in this novel is at best naïve – at worst dangerously deceptive. In Hayton's novel, Barve and Hw could not be defined morally as black or white, but Townsend sets Amos, her villain, against Horst, her peace-loving German hero. Evil is presented as a weakness and a susceptibility to propaganda. The Nazis, Horst declares, "all believe the way to the New Dawn, as they call it, is through the Powers of Darkness." While not wishing to suggest that any good can be found in Hitler's doctrine, such a crude and sensationalist contortion of history does, I believe, belittle and undermine its seriousness. *Child of Fire* is misleading historically, realistically and romantically.

The Other Woman fares no better under scrutiny. Here, the author attempts to make the setting somehow "magical" through Gaelic folklore abounds. Unfortunately, because the descriptions again rely heavily upon clichéd romantic images, the effect is lost. No matter how often the narrative describes the mystical qualities of the Isle of Skye, it fails to present us with any proof.

I know Eileen Townsend must have many fans who find great pleasure in reading her novels, but I have to say that I find their underlying implications rather disturbing. Mhairi Cloud, the heroine of *The Other Woman*, is a native of Skye who becomes the darling of the New York theatre during Victoria's reign, but who never forgets her Scottish roots. She tells Ralph, the Scottish laird she falls in love with, about the Highland Clearances: "they were cast out to perish, or flee the land that they loved – a land that had been theirs since time immemorial." The dialogue is ridiculous; the sentiments little better. If Townsend is to be believed, Skye is populated by mothers telling their bairns "beloved tales" from the Ossian legends, and though the people are poor, "in their soul they had a treasure greater than any king's ransom." It's all very well for a writer to use her imagination, but when related to real events surely it should be contained within reasonable parameters?

There's a faint chance that the novel could have carried all of this if only Mhairi Cloud had been a strong central character. Unfortunately she's little more than a name and a series of physical descriptions. We're told she's 'two people', but at no point does the narrative bear this out. Perhaps her adopted name is more apt than the author intended?

Character is not a problem for Margaret Elphinstone; her collection of short stories, *An Apple from a Tree* is one of the best books I've read this year. Her stories blend folklore and myth with the real world in a way that is both intricate and effortless. Common themes recur again and again: gardens and water; fertility; two worlds existing in parallel; mysticism and ancient mythology. They're given twists and permutations as the stories explore and stretch the boundaries between myth and reality. Sarah in 'Green Man' goes walking between Dumfries and Stranraer and encounters a man who is, literally, green, and who shows her how to love, and how to find herself as an artist. He belongs to an ancient world which seemingly exists alongside our own. He's part of the very fabric of existence, outside society, and the 'real' world, while at the same time integral to everything.

Boundaries are more blurred in 'An Apple from a Tree', the story that shares its title with the book. A woman in the Botanic Gardens catches a falling apple, takes a bite, and is catapulted into another world, where a woman stands beneath an apple tree. Somehow the apple has penetrated the curtain between the two levels, and it's the means through which the two women can explore them. Each depends on the other, and their actions have direct consequences for them both. They also have a choice – as Nosila, the second woman says, "She's free to do what she likes. Who's got the right to stop her?" It's a crucial theme that runs throughout this collection, not least in 'Conditions of Employment.'

I first read this funny, clever story in *Chapman*, and it didn't disappoint on second reading. It's a light-hearted, irreverent blend of myth and mundanity with a more serious message at its core – a woman can do *anything* if she puts her mind to it. Miranda applies at the local Job Centre for the position of Well Guardian and sets to work in a refreshing, unorthodox style. She finds she can make things happen, in contrast to the Watcher of the Sleepers, a rather dozy individual who can't do anything without asking advice.

In the end Miranda achieves all she's ever wanted. As Oddny, the real Guardian of the Well realises, "There are two sides to everything." She could have been talking about any of these wonderful stories. I only wish I had time to mention more.   *Angela Finlayson*

Heads above the parapet

Coming Out With It, Angela McSeveney; *Heroes*, Chris Hurford, both Polygon, £6.95; *Recovery*, Chris Woods, Enitharmon, £6.95; *Coming Home the Long Way Round The Mountain*, Rosalind Brackenbury, Taxus Press, £5.95; *The New Poetry*, ed Michael Hulse, David Kennedy & David Morley, Bloodaxe Books, £7.95

Coming Out With It is Angela McSeveney's first collection, although her work is already familiar to many. Her poems are characterised by a freshness and openness which although often childlike in their simplicity of style are adult in their content. In 'Sunbathing', for example, she tells us, as she dozes, how the sun "pressed a warm belly flat against/ mine" until, opening her eyes: "...gazed at china plate blue./ Oriental style, one branch of blossom grew from a/ corner./ Sunshine held my face between his warm hands."

Her observation is sharp and evocative. Her description of the simple act of sunbathing takes on a sensual and exotic appeal; almost as if McSeveney, in her own private world, into which we have been invited, takes on the role of the only woman ever to have been caressed by the warm touch of the sun.

This sense of intimacy occurs throughout much of McSeveney's writing, focused on the experiences of adolescence, human relationships and work. She opens herself up for scrutiny, not in a harsh self-critical mode but just for observation, to be seen and understood just as she is; as she exists as a woman. In 'The Lump', McSeveney reveals how at fifteen she "felt a hard knot of tissue" in her breast. The benign lump is removed; when the stitches come out she states, "I felt ashamed/ that the first man to see me/ had only been doing his job." It is McSeveney's candour and ability to catch such a feeling in stasis that enables the reader to empathise and take part in her poetry.

A clarity of perception and often ingratiate wit typifies this collection – a collection which is an invitation to enter into her personal world of feeling and experience that is as welcoming and comforting as the smell of home-baked bread.

By contrast, Chris Hurford's first collection *Heroes*, has been described as being written with "brio". There is an engaging liveliness and vivacity to the poems, yet overall the impression is often of tenderness and a painful sense of despair. This arises when he comes up against an inability to find justifiable meaning and significance not only in the sphere of relationships between men and women, but also in the wider political forum. For example, in 'The Querist' he sets before us a scene that is both "domestic and debauched". His lover, naked after sex, mends her skirt and then proceeds to "remove at last that stubborn thorn,/ buried deep in my palm". Hurford sees the needle as a "trembling querist... "

Its tiny bloodied point
felt deeper, searching for an answer.
My dull pulse thudded its monotone:
'There's none. There's none.'

There is something terribly sad in the repetition of the last line here. This is obviously an intimate act – the woman piercing and entering the male flesh with a needle takes on sexual undertones coupled with a sense of maternal care in retrieving a splinter that has caused pain for over a year. Hurford acknowledges that this act, in all its minutiae, ought to be symbolic of something, but what?

In a manner Hurford questions the meaning of the sense of his own poetry – recognising that the *raison d'être* of some poetry is to focus on a single small event and use that as a pointer for understanding a greater and larger reality. Because Hurford can find no comfort or meaning in the gesture (which to others might suggest tenderness, caring and even a certain humility) his life takes on a mode of dissatisfaction, devoid of warmth and love.

Some of the work takes on a lighter tone, partly due to his idiomatic and sometimes romping style. In fact through this collection Hurford proves himself to be a young, erudite poet capable of diverse image and scope – an interesting poet to look out for.

Not quite so interesting or unusual is the poetry of Chris Woods. *Recovery* is competent, the language is precise and well-honed to its range of subject matter, which vary from his domestic and personal life to that of his other life as a working medical doctor. His poems are characterised by their considered compassion and intelligent observation but tend to smack of an over-careful bedside manner that can become tiresome and lacking in originality. This is a shame as there is much that is enjoyable at an individual level but as a whole the collection lacks direction and is held back by its tameness and seeming addiction to the safe and the run-of-the-mill.

What Wood lacks in his poems can be found in plenitude in the scope and lyrical ingenuity of Rosalind Brackenbury's *Coming Home The Long Way Round The Mountain*. The main theme of this work is the idea of a journey, not just the obvious journey into one's self but also that of a physical journey embracing Scotland, Australia, Morocco and America. Her choice of imagery carefully matches the landscapes she finds herself in; signifying her wonder in things both familiar and new. In 'Azaleas' she studies "soaked flowers" that are "cindered to softness" like "bonfires of desire" the result of one of Scotland's "remarkable downpours". In 'Leaving Sydney' colours are evoked through the language of flowers – "cyclamen, hibiscus, rose" – that colour and stain the landscape. The "native/ frangipani" throws "flowers in my path" indicative to her of a "warmth of air" matched by "warmth of blood" that allows "nakedness to be an ease". Here, Brackenbury experiences a languorousness of being, different to the "sharp winter pleasures" ('Northern Light') of love beside the fireside, but still an aspect of herself released and discovered

through a different setting.

Many more aspects of her self are explored as Brackenbury travels through imagination, memory and landscape. This is a varied collection held together by its strength of imagery ("the valleys of paradise are full of women's laughter") and a power of insight that is spellbinding in its depth and colour.

The New Poetry is a work on a much larger and ambitious scale – promoting itself as the first anthology to feature British and Irish poets of the 1980s and '90s. The lengthy introduction spells out clearly its aims and objectives, these chiefly being that "poetry and politics are inseparable" and that no subject is taboo for poetry which has now established itself as a medium for a "public voice". By and large these assertions are justified. Over fifty poets are included, coming from a wide and diverse background of culture and experience.

The Scottish contingent is strong – the anthology cannot be accused of tokenism – containing a healthy and varied batch of Scottish poets such as Robert Crawford, WN Herbert, Tom Leonard, Kathleen Jamie and Liz Lochhead. This choice alone backs up the editors' convictions that "alternatives to the real or imagined English centre vigorously informs the current resilience of Scottish writing." I dare say that Tom Leonard's entry from 'Unrelated Incidents' will baffle but intrigue readers unfamiliar with anything but standard English language and form:

its the lang-	thi langwij
wij a thi	a thi
guhtr thaht hi	intillect hi
said its thi	said thi lang-
langwij a	wij a thi intill-
thi guhtr	ects Ingish

Along with the Scottish voice there is also a feminist and a black voice to be heard, reflecting the changing nature and acknowledgement of such a diverse British society. This is hopefully indicative of a changing awareness towards poetry as a viable form of protest – be it against nationalistic stereotypes, sexism or just to convey a familiar truth through a different or humorous new slant. And as long as poetry is enabling us to see our world and society through as many varied eyes (and tongues) as possible then long live anthologies such as this one! *Sara Evans*

Theatre Round-Up

A German student recently told me how disappointed she was at the paucity of productions by Scottish theatre companies in the Edinburgh Festival and Fringe. Her perfectly reasonable assumption had been that the world's largest arts festival was bound to boast a substantial quantity of home-grown work. By contrast, my perspective is that the 1993 Festival was a relatively healthy year for Scottish representation. The difference is, I suppose, that I'm used to the idea that to perform in Edinburgh in August involves a bigger risk than at any other time of the year. It takes special circumstances (an invite from the Festival, the Assembly Rooms or the Traverse) to ensure the participation of the likes of the Tron, 7:84 and Wildcat or the regional reps.

Nonetheless, there are several companies which have come to regard the Fringe as a focal point of their year, as regular an event as the spring tour and the Christmas show. The Traverse is the obvious one, but audiences are getting used to seeing Clyde Unity, Fifth Estate, Borderline and Communicado every summer, not to mention the long list of amateur companies. But the significant factor about 1993 was that Festival Director Brian McMaster went against recent practice by taking on board several Scottish companies in a programme that was far from lacking in international vision. What was gratifying to see was that the Scottish contingent, while not always successful, held its own in a formidable arena populated by giants of the avant-garde like Robert Wilson and Robert Lepage.

The most accomplished Scottish contribution was also, as is often the case, the most ambitious. TAG Theatre Company set about adapting not just one, but all three instalments of Lewis Grassic Gibbon's *A Scots Quair* trilogy for the stage. By the end of the company's tour, which stretched into November, the show had notched up 102 performances and had been seen by 78,450 people. This was well deserved. Director Tony Graham, working closely with choreographer Andy Howitt on a script by Alasdair Cording, found a true theatrical voice for Gibbon's tales of early-century Aberdeenshire life. Structurally, the plays might not have shaken off the sprawling

form of the novels, but on a moment-to-moment basis there was no sense of the kind of leaden reverence to hallowed literature that makes for deadly theatre.

Instead, what TAG created was a vigorous, impressionistic melange of music, movement and words, drawing us in through swift cross-fades from scene to scene, charming us with a song, beguiling us with delicate theatrical economy. As with the books, the first instalment, *Sunset Song*, worked the best. It has a narrative drive and a balance between the individual and the broader community which is not equalled in *Cloud Howe* or *Grey Granite*. But even if the latter two never captured the sublime beauty of the first, all three were characterised by the inventive and well-integrated choreography and music and, crucially, the modest, understated performance of Pauline Knowles in the central role as Chris Guthrie. For me, one of the most satisfying aspects about it was to see the London critics, who had been snootily sceptical in private at the start of the Festival, change their colours quite dramatically once they saw the shows.

Brian McMaster likes to gamble and the least likely contribution to his programme was a revival of a typical Scottish Variety Show from the 1950s. Put together by Jimmy Logan, the twice nightly *Fabulous Fifties* drew on original performers (Jack Milroy and Mary Lee adding zest to a routine that can hardly have been hilarious first time round) as well as current acts from the summer cruise circuit. So we had Tiller Girls, young Glasgow jugglers Flipside, comedy from Logan, Johnny Beattie, Anne Fields, *et al*, plus an assortment of singers and novelty acts. As an entertainment it was a mixture of the delightful and the excruciating, certainly for anyone not old enough to watch with nostalgia, but it distinguished itself in the love and attention to period detail with which it was put together. And symbolically it was an important gesture by the Festival to recognise a form of popular entertainment that the élitist establishment normally sneers at.

Perhaps better to sneer than to ignore altogether which is what tends to happen with the oral tradition of storytelling (which in Scotland has a better claim than most to being a genuinely indigenous art form). Again,

McMaster made a significant gesture by programming a nightly series of yarn-spinners who drew on myths ancient and modern to beguile sell-out houses with the pure power of imagination. A couple of months later, Donald Smith at Edinburgh's Netherbow mounted another of his annual International Storytelling Festivals, helping to put on the cultural map this largely unsung craft that is beginning to win deserved recognition.

The one remaining Scottish contribution to the EIF was Philip Prowse's production for the Citizens' Theatre of *The Soldiers* by little-known 18th century playwright Jakob Lenz. Typically stylish, the production seemed to confuse Lenz's concerns – the abuse of power and exploitation of women – by making the transitions from scene to scene (and in Lenz there are a lot of them) perhaps a little too seamless and by grafting on a heavy-handed allusion to the Nazi war crimes that postdate the play by some 150 years.

By focusing on the Scottish contribution to the International Festival, I don't mean to negate its many other treasures. In terms of novelty, scope and quality, this was a Festival that easily eclipsed the Fringe. Love them or loathe them, there was no denying the provocative and visionary achievement of the work of Peter Sellars in his spartan Gulf War update of *The Persians*, of Robert Wilson in his visually stunning *Dr Faustus Lights the Lights*, of Peter Stein in his epic, large-scale *Julius Caesar* and of Robert Lepage in his breathtakingly filmic *Bluebeard's Castle* and *Erwartung*. There were of course many delights on the Fringe, but that essential Hot Ticket, the show that could turn normally civil people into salivating animals, remained elusive.

Nonetheless I was mightily impressed with Clyde Unity Theatre's *Accustomed to Her Face*, a play which confirms that John Binnie's playwriting and directing skills have developed immeasurably from the early cute, but home-made work of this politically radical Glasgow-based company. What Binnie achieved here was a piece that dealt with the still-sensitive idea of lesbian love in a joyful, positive way, that neither made an issue of the subject nor patronised the audience, that used hard-edged humour where a less accomplished writer would moralise, that turned a

simple, uncomplicated story into a hilarious and touching performance. A friend up from London commented that she had never seen such a sophisticated piece of theatre designed for community venues (the show toured after the Festival and will be revived in the New Year) and it strikes me that Binnie is now reaping the rewards of years of touring, learning his craft and learning from his audiences.

The rest of the Fringe was the usual rag-bag of hits and misses, so I'll quickly name-check the other Scottish contributors that I managed to catch up with. Borderline came up with a Scots adaptation of Hasek's *The Guid Sodjer Schweik* starring Andy Cameron; it lacked progression but struck an amiable groove early on and stayed that way. The same company also acted as producer for *The Audition*, a one-man show by novelist AL Kennedy starring Mike Hayward; sadly an uncharismatic performance brought little life to what I suspect to be a rather colourless script. At the Assembly Rooms, Glasgow's Arches Theatre Company gave a very funny performance of *Accidental Death of an Anarchist*, starring Craig Ferguson; Andy Arnold's production glided across Dario Fo's play with a skipping pace and just the right amount of ad-libbing, self-referential remarks and topical up-dates.

I enjoyed Communicado's *The Legend of St Julian*, a near-wordless adaptation of a Flaubert short story, even if it was more an exercise in inventive stage-craft than an emotionally involving performance. Benchtours' staging of *The Death of Don Quixote* failed to create a persuasive central double-act and consequently missed out on much comedy, although audiences were appreciative. And seeing The Grassmarket Project's *Risk* (one of three shows the company performed on the Fringe) did not substantially change my opinion that real actors with a real play can tell you a lot more about real life than real people can.

I regretted missing Cat A's *Dirt Enters at the Heart* and Anthony Neilson's controversial *Penetrator*, but lost no sleep over missing Fifth Estate's production of Donald Campbell's *The Ould Fella*. And Invergordon's Zoom Theatre, the adult wing of the Clown Jewels, produced in *Exhibit A,* an insubstantial piece of hi-tech nonsense, one of the few shows I actually regretted seeing. *Mark Fisher*

Pamphleteer

So high is the standard of *A Mindin'*, selected from the second Michael Bruce Poetry Competition, (c/o MBMT, Kinnesswood, Kinross) that one can only hope that the trustees will continue on into the future. The title poem, by Pat Smith, is in a fine, natural Scots – a well-chosen winner, though I can hear the girning about the orthography. There are some familiar names among the less well-known in John Glenday's compilation, linked by a sense of well-judged understatement, or simple peacefulness. Invidious to quote, so I won't. Another, very different portmanteau is Edwin Morgan's *Glasgow Poets Past and Present*, the lecture he delivered on being invested with an honorary Doctorate at the University of Waikato. (£2.95, Scottish Studies Association, EngDept, U of Waikato, PB3105, Hamilton, NZ) In giving a thorough and entertaining overview of the subject in such a short space, Morgan manages a characteristic tour-de-force which would serve as a useful primer in important strands in Scottish poetry generally, particularly the social and political background.

Crowded a little forbiddingly into 44 pages, *Back o' Bennachie* (£3.95, Hammerfield Publishing, Aberdeen) is the latest collection of poetry and short prose in Doric and English from the prolific pen of Sheena Blackhall:

> I am a Doric stereotype
> That thing ye'll niver meet
> I whyles chant Buddhist mantras
> An read René Magritte.

('I am a Doric Stereotype'). If, as a collection, it daunders a bit, the quality of the writing, no less than its vigour and humour sometimes as bitter as biting, grabs attention and holds it all the same.

"Politics in poetry/ is not permissible unless/ it maintains the ancient practice of pleasing the prince" runs 'Excerpt from Section XVII of *The Magical Well*' in TS Law's *The Clearances* (Fingerpost Publications, Blackford Lodge, Blackford, Perthshire PH4 1QP, £4.95). There's passion here in plenty, angry, political passion to bring a scowl to the face of any prince. The Excerpt is part of a long poem in a garrulous English that dominates this otherwise mostly Scots collection, in an elegant parallel with its theme. Otherwise the highlight is the uproariously abusive 'The Great Sutherland Clearance'.

Whiles amang the Scots, from a series of Scottish Plays from Brown, Son & Ferguson of Glasgow, which I see are all comedies, comes *The Puddok an the Princess* by David Purves. The story of the Frog Prince is a familiar one, which makes it a good vehicle for the Scots, sin the clekkin's gey weel-farrant. More for playing than reading – as the play's extensive success on the stage attests – tho a fiver seems a bit steep.

I was put off, browsing Hamish Brown's *The Bothy Brew and Other Stories* (Luath Press, £5.95) on spotting the line "A wife fractionally as nagging could be divorced on the grounds of cruelty", in a story about corncrakes, if only because it suggests that no great insights into humankind will be found elsewhere among the pages. Nevertheless, the collection has a nice fireside quality to it – stories better heard than read, perhaps, though artfully made and absorbing in a non-demanding kind of way. In any case, *offputting* is a title like *Sold as Seen: It's not that bad – it's verse* (GD Brown, Bookbound, £1). Boom boom, as Basil Brush might say. Opening reluctantly, 'Traverse', near the beginning, runs "You ask how I go about writing/ First my pen to the page is applied/ Then when I've thought what I'm going to write/ I move my pen from side to side." Surely people don't *really* find this amusing, do they? *The Madhouse of Love* (Tetrahedron, 30 Birch Crescent, Blairgowrie, PH10 6TS, £2.75), by contrast, neither really novel nor autobiography, is Peter G Mackie's account, written when 17, of a teenager in a psychiatric institution who falls in love with a fellow-patient and finally manages to discharge himself. It is a remarkable accomplishment, one that successfully defies the urge, brought on by the book's dismal presentation, to put it down.

Jaspre Bark's *Bark Bites* (Poetry Now, Unit 2-3 Wulfric Square, North Bretton, Peterborough PE3 8RF, £9.99 including cassette) puts me in mind of John Betjeman for its sometimes vicious evocations of middle-class life and its sense of scornful indifference to the livers of such lives. Occasionally the wit can be as sharp, as in 'Deprivation', which takes as its text Larkin's remark that "Deprivation is to me what daffodils were to Wordsworth" and ends:

For oft when on the page I scrawl
My dour diatribes, I think
Books are a load of crap, but mine
Were hardly worth the printer's ink.
Then my heart with deprivation fills,
Words withering like dead daffodils.

The rhymes and rhythm are familiar too, if artless beside those of the late Poet Laureate, because Bark is a performance poet. In the end, though, the simplicity and sometimes crudely violent imagery begins to pall. Of *Linear A*, a literary review edited by Johan de Wit (£2.50 from the author, Flat 1/Sylvia Court, 81 Putney Hill, London SW15 3NX) I'll quote a characteristic passage, from a review of Hazel Smith's *Abstractly Represented*:

Liminary moments are illuminating the subvocal ordering of the personal sound system. When catapaulted into the fabric of grains and graces spiritual rebirth and materialistic progress go hand in hand.

and leave you to decide whether it's your thing or not. I'll slip Ian Grimble's Neil M Gunn Memorial Lecture of September 1991 in here (Peglet Press, Orchard House, 50 Arthur St, Ampthill, Beds MK45 2QQ). *Caveat Emptor*: because of the circumstances, Dr Grimble's text is not one that dwells on Gunn's shortcomings as a novelist, though he acknowledges that criticisms have been made. Like Edwin Morgan's *Glasgow Poets*, nevertheless, Grimble does a fine job of summarising concerns and directions in Gunn's fiction making the text a useful primer.

The fashion for minimalist poetry, a sprinkling of words on a page, sometimes dribbling down a word here, two or three there, creates a variety of impressions, usually founded in uncommunicativeness of one kind or another. Sometimes it's an anger that leaves the writer almost speechless, sometimes it's emotional withdrawal; occasionally, even, it's serene profundity. In Kath Beattie's *Tangihana and other Korero* (£5.99, Peter Youngson Publications, St Andrew's Manse, Glamis Road, Kirriemuir DD8 5BN), the author tends to the angry in 'Kath's Impact Report', a poem about incest, and skilfully communicates uncommunicativeness in 'Each Others Names', about

parents not using each other's christian names. Otherwise I find myself torn between enjoying the imagery, so well captured from her native New Zealand, and getting irritated at the unrelenting waterfall of words in this attractive, well-illustrated book. In Rupert M Loydell's *Between Dark Dreams* (Acumen, £4.95), the prevailing sense is of emotional withdrawal. He is painfully honest in revealing his equivocal feelings as his father dies in a hospice, but distressingly reluctant to vent what is plainly a tumult of emotion.

Also from Acumen, same price, John Gurney's *An Average Revenge* is an interesting collection of poetry inspired by "repeated visits to places closely connected with poets". An impressive range of literary history is covered in skilfully-wielded language, though the insights are sometimes a little portentous.

Encouraging Shakespeare is an attractive first collection from Robert Hull (Peterloo, £6.95), characterised by gentle but mordant humour, as in 'The Case For Burning Books', which conjures vividly rooms stuffed with useless books and the psychological necessity for clearing some space; or 'New Reading Glasses', which ends:

...I want the kerbful
of Dandelions

to be a choir of saffron again,
the phone book

to have a million
numbers all the same.

Harry Clifton's *At the Grave of Silone: An Abruzzo Sequence* (Honest Ulsterman Publications), too, is an all-too-brief collection of lyrics rich with resonance and colour, finding the well-travelled author's stay in the Abruzzo mountains inspiring reflections on what changes and what does not change from location to location. The title of Sudeep Sen's *Kali in Ottava Rima* (Paramount, London, £3.95) sets the alarm bells off all over again, but this is an altogether compelling collection. Generous and loquacious, virile and full of pungent imagery, ambitious to a degree that few attempt these days, Sen has the ability to place human emotions within the cosmic scale without belittling them. The scholarship is deep but not obscure, and the fusion of Indian and Western is uncritical and joyous.

Peter Cudmore

Catalogue

A tribute to Virago seems a good way to begin. This is their 20th birthday and still the books churn out. Virago's great quality lies in their cosmopolitan spirit: Margaret Atwood's *Poems* and *Conversations* sit alongside editions of Jessie Kesson's *Glitter of Mica* (an undervalued novel) and *Where the Apple Ripens*. The *Virago Book of Birth Poetry* (ed Charlotte Otten) trawled wide, including even poems by Hugh MacDiarmid and Seamus Heaney in a selection that includes Dutch, Chilean, Russian and Argentinian poets. Sad to note, though, not a single Scottish woman. Why, I wonder?

Ellen Galford's brilliantly witty *The Dyke & the of Dybbuk* was one of the volumes brought out to celebrate the birthday. It forays into the underworld of European Jewry in a most engaging way. Her *Moll Cutpurse,* now republished by Virago, first burst upon the world through Stramullion (see Elizabeth Burns article). Among anthology editions, Janet Sternberg's compilation *The Writer and Her Work* will be a useful reference point for years to come. *Infinite Riches* (ed Lynn Knight), a selection of short stories, features only 'Until Such Times' by Jessie Kesson from the vast range of Scottish stories by women. Pity too that they didn't acknowledge the first publication of that story in *Chapman* in 1984. The volume is really a showcase for the main authors in the Virago Modern Classics Series, which is in part the explanation, but it proves that there's a way to go yet.

Belatedly mentioned here is Polygon's *Meantime, Looking Forward to the Milennium,* which included several new voices like Magi Gibson and Helen Lamb. There are a few years to go yet to the Millenium and time to do another volume like this! And, talking of trawling widely, the annual *New Writing (2)* published jointly by Minerva and the British Council offers a respectable selection, but also features the relatively new, a welcome cultural spread across the UK with women quite well represented. The book is dedicated to George MacBeth and Angela Carter.

An angry storm in a tea-cup was aroused by John MacLeod's *No Great Mischief if You Fall* (Mainstream). MacLeod makes a living out of largely unnecessary controversy and expressing contradictory opinions. This book is a compilation of his opinionated, self-centred ramblings about 'The Highland Experience'. Dropping a misty tear for the good old days past, MacLeod pulls himself up by the jockstrap and trumpets realism: Gaelic is dead, and if you deny this you must be one of the incestuous Gaelic mafia, among whom, I note, he numbers Iain Crichton Smith, a great critic of the negative influence of the Church; but MacLeod's assertion that this gentle, humorous man is so incensed by seeing a man of the cloth that he can barely resist the impulse to cross the road and punch his nose is too ridiculous to bear thinking about. MacLeod's account of his meeting with Sorley MacLean is as much about himself as about MacLean. MacLeod dings facts to suit the colour of his spite, most of the time. I've never been able to understand why his florid, overheated prose is given valuable column inches. There are better books to read...

Such as *The Way Back* by Enrico Palandri. Published by Serpent's Tail and translated by Stuart Hood, this is a most sensitive study of an individual's journeying, about how the journeys one must make in life are not always about going away, travelling. It's about self-discovery through travelling to your own roots. Telling parallels are drawn between Scotland and Italy as the psychiatrist hero, Davide, finds much to emphathise with in the background of Julia, his Scottish wife. *The Way Back* combines purity of emotion with lightness of touch. The outsider/insider theme is also explored in Natascha Wodin's *Once I Lived,* plainly but effectively translated by Iain Galbraith, in which the protagonist explores the conflicts between her Russian background and her adopted German homeland, coming to perceive both with remarkable clarity. Serpent's Tail are to be congratulated for such finely produced books.

I wish I says the same of the National Poetry Foundation's five volumes of poetry by women which come next to hand, but the production and design are deadly dull, and much of the work mediocre at best. Of *Sex...* by Liz Yule, *No Telegrams,* Fay Green, *Few Other Sounds* by Joan Booker, Judith Wright's *Broken Glass* and Margaret Toms' *Clay's*

Bright Soul, there's little inspiring to be found. Liz Yule can handle conventional form, but most of her rhymes are tired and obvious, Joan Booker's verse is clear, exudes good nature, but mainly anecdotal, similarly Fay Green's. Judith Wright's poetry shows a stronger, more individual voice, but by far the best work comes from Margaret Toms who has a range and a density of thought and emotion mostly lacking in the others.

A more arresting presentation comes from Sinclair Stevenson for their poetry series. Particularly welcome is *News from the Brighton Front* by Nicki Jackowska, always a bright and original voice, and Roy Fuller's moving volume *Last Poems,* in which the poet openly faces his impending death. Secker and Warburg too keep expanding their poetry coverage, last year producing John Burnside's provoking first collection *Feast Days.* Burnside's poetry combines simplicity of diction with clarity of thought, although I was less impressed by his prose paragraphs than by his easily flowing poems.

Taranis Books produce some most unusual volumes, prominent among which is *The Necessary Goat,* Alison Prince's collection of essays on formative thinking. The title of the key essay makes a strong case for the need for the creative principle in education, and society in general. Prince has at heart the genuine integration of the individual and makes strong protest against those features of modern society which lead to the fragmentation of the individual and the diminishing of his or her worth. This is a fine, stimulating collection, although the production could be much improved at little extra cost. Lion Publishing on the other hand have given a very smart presentation to *Coroskirr,* Jenny Robertson's latest novel, a compelling, limpid story for teenagers set on the West Coast of Scotland. The novel skilfully combines modern reality for young people today with older, more legendary resonances.

The burgeoning interest abroad in Scottish literature has been further boosted by the enormous and impressive *Études Écossaises,* essentially the papers from an international conference held at the University of Grenoble. It contains scholarly but enlightening essays on Scott, Hume, Gunn, Dunbar, Scottish identity and history etc by a range of contributors from Tom Nairn to Valentina Poggi of Bologna. Edited by the enterprising Carla Sassi, Supernova Press in Italy has published *Poeti Della Scozia Contemporanea,* an anthology containing the work of Norman MacCaig, Sorley MacLean, Tom Scott, Hamish Henderson, Edwin Morgan, Douglas Dunn, Liz Lochhead and Valerie Gillies. These most welcome volumes can only stumulate yet further interest in Scotland and Scottish studies abroad.

Now for the stocking-fillers. Two sides of Glasgow are presented in *Keeping Glasgow in Stitches,* edited by Liz Arthur (Mainstream), the nostalgic and the realistic vision represented emblematically by the two 'Where is the Glasgow' songs by Adam McNaughtan and Jim McLean in a very thumbable volume. A harder, more uncompromising stance is taken by *A Real Glasgow Archipelago* by Jack Withers (Argyll Publishing). Its commentary and analysis take no prisoners; Wither's targets are rarely missed, and his work is complemented by illustrations by Ian McCulloch and introduction from Alasdair Gray. A wee thing for Edinburghers is *The Edinburgh Literary Guide* by Andrew Lownie (Canongate) with some rather coy illustrations from Richard Demarco, no less. Also from Canongate comes the compelling *Russian Gypsy Tales* collected by Yefim Druts and Alexei Gessler and translated by James Riordan. The very thing for a slack moment. Quite the most beautiful book in this large pile is the tiny volume, *33 Poems by* Miklós Radnóti. Thomas Land's translations from the Hungarian were one of the highlights of *Chapman* 68. This compact edition from Maecenas is irresistible.

And on a serious note, two books to savour and digest. If you feel bamboozled by the complexities of the Orkney child abuse case, then close reading of Robert Black's *Orkney: A Place of Safety* might be more likely to provide you with a sane view of this distressing and complex matter. Alistair Simpson's *Maison Therapy* (New Horizons) is a handy DIY book for those thinking of moving to France; finally, Tom Lowenstein's *Ancient Land: Sacred Whale* (Bloomsbury), is a stimulating and superbly written celebration of the life and culture of the Tikigaq Eskimo Indians. A book to savour and keep.

Notes on Contributors

Sheena Blackhall: short-story writer, poet, illustrator & single parent, currently studying for Hons. Psychology with the OU. 11th book *Braeheid on ither Doric Tales* due out shortly.

Pat Buik, London Scot, freelance journalis: has a children's play published by Macmillan, and numerous poems in magazines.

Elizabeth Burns worked for Stramullion for several years, was a member of Pomegranate writing group. Her first collection, *Orphelia and other Poems*, is published by Polygon.

Margaret Fulton Cook: Glasgow poet, former editor of West Coast Magazine, shortly to launch *Coastlines*. Collection of poetry forthcoming from *Chapman* next year.

Mairi-Ann Cullen was educated at Edinburgh and Oxford Universities and now works as an educational researcher. She is particularly interested in Scottish medieval literature and in Scottish women's poetry.

Maud Devine: Born Glasgow 1948. Poems in various magazines, also *Original Prints, New Writing Scotland, Behind the Lines, New Makars*.

Margaret Elphinstone writes novels and short stories. Her next novel, *Islanders,* is forthcoming from Polygon in 1994. As well as writing she teaches English Studies at Strathclyde University. She has two daughters.

Irene Evans: Born in Glasgow, 1943. Now lives and works in Muthill, Perthshire. Other poems have appeared in *Lines Review, West Coast Magazine, Cencrastus* and Scotia Bar 1st of May Anthology.

Angela Finlayson: Born in Edinburgh, now living in Kinross. Occasional *Chapman* volunteer and full-time magazine sub-editor.

Anne Frater: currently doing PhD in Glasgow on women gaelic poets.

Janice Galloway: Writer and media personality, currently among the presenters of Radio Scotland's *The Usual Suspects.*

Magi Gibson is Writer in Residence with Renfrew District. Her first collection of poetry *Kicking back* (Taranis) includes an up-to-date version of 'Deadheading the Rose'.

Helen Gilbert lived in Canada for many years and has travelled widely elsewhere. She currently teaches literature and drama at Monash University, Melbourne, Australia. The Husking wont the 1991 Australia Day Short story Competition.

Mary Gordon regrets being born to late to be a suffragette. Her job at *Chapman* has no scope for arson.

Ann Gwilt: American citizen, resident in Edinburgh. Musician, writer of poetry.

Jane Harris is Writer in Residence at HMP Durham. Her work appears in a variety of magazines and anthologies.

John Herdman: novelist, short story writer and critic who lives in Perth. His most recent book is *Imelda and Other stories* (Polygon).

Kathleen Jamie's latest book is *The Autonomous Region* (Bloodaxe 1993) She is working on a new collection of poems, likely to be called *The Queen of Sheba.*

AL Kennedy: Born Dundee 1965. Author of *Night Geometry and the Garscadden Trains* & *Looking for the Possible Dance.* New collection *Now That You're Back* from Jonathan Cape in Feb '94; working on a second novel.

Eva Fleg Lambert: "Born in Germany, educated USA, Skye resident since 1971 where I write, tend sheep & spin & dye their fleece."

Mary McIntosh: Ex-weaver, retired teacher living in Kirriemuir. With colleagues published children's anthology in Scots, *Caa Doon The Mune.*

Janet McKenzie: Born Glasgow, lives and teaches in Perthshire. Frequently published in magazines unknown to the SAC. Pleased to be moving up-brow to *Chapman.*

Naomi Mitchison: the *Grande Dame* of Scottish letters, nearing her 100th year and still going strong!

Agnes Owens: Began writing after joining a writer's group in Alexandria, now a successful novelist and short story writer.

Janet Paisley is a full-time writer from Falkirk. Collections, poetry and short stories, include *Images* (Moray House), *Pegasus in Flight, Biting through Skins* (Rookbook), *Wild Fire* (Taranis Books).

Tessa Ransford is director of the Scottish Poetry Library and editor of *Lines Review.* Her most recent book is the long poem sequence, *Seven Valleys.* Forthcoming is *Medusa Dozen and Other Poems.*

Val Warner: Four books, two pamphlets published; short stories in magazines and anthologies. Was creative Writing Fellow at Dundee University 1979–81.